GW00685234

The Essential T.C. Lethbridge

The works of T.C. Lethbridge published by Routledge
& Kegan Paul:

*Gogmagog: The Buried Gods* (1957; reprinted 1975)
*Ghost and Ghoul* (1961)
*Witches: Investigating an Ancient Religion* (1962)
*Ghost and Divining Rod* (1963; 2nd impression 1967)
*E.S.P.: Beyond Time and Distance* (1965; 2nd impression 1966)
*A Step in the Dark* (1967)
*The Monkey's Tail: A Study in Evolution and Parapsychology* (1969)
*The Legend of the Sons of God* (1972)
*The Power of the Pendulum* (1976)

# The Essential
# T.C. Lethbridge

Edited by Tom Graves and Janet Hoult

Foreword by Colin Wilson

Routledge & Kegan Paul
London, Boston and Henley

This arrangement
first published in 1980
by Routledge & Kegan Paul Ltd
39 Store Street,
London WC1E 7DD,
Broadway House,
Newtown Road,
Henley-on-Thames,
Oxon RG9 1EN and
9 Park Street,
Boston, Mass. 02108, USA

Set in 11pt Plantin by
Wordsmith Graphics
Street, Somerset
and printed in Great Britain by
Redwood Burn Ltd
Trowbridge & Esher

ISBN 0 7100 0396 X

# Contents

# Foreword

The late Tom Lethbridge had two qualities that made him a good historian: a lively imagination and a consuming curiosity. And after he left Cambridge in disgust — I shall tell that story in a moment — and retired to Devon, they helped to make him one of the most brilliant and stimulating parapsychologists of modern times.

You can see both the curiosity and the imagination at work in a typical passage from his book about the Scots, *The Painted Men.* He is talking about the ruins of a Roman fort near Melrose: 'Why was the skeleton of a female dwarf found in a well beneath those of nine horses? Why were several valuable parade helmets flung into other wells, with swords, spears and bits of armour?' Lethbridge reasons it out, like Sherlock Holmes. The female dwarf — a servant? — and the horses were thrown down the well to poison the water and make the fort useless to the enemy. But the horses and the dwarf would not have been dead unless the enemy — the Britons — had not forced an entrance first. If the Britons had held the place, then there would also be Roman corpses down the wells. So what happened is clear: the Britons burst in, there was violent hand-to-hand fighting, and the Britons were driven out again. The Romans cleared up the mess, poisoned the main well with dead horses, tossed parade helmets and other equipment down other wells, then abandoned the fort.

Lethbridge goes on to complain that archaeologists never use their imagination; they only want to know what date something took place, or where the artifacts originated:

There is room for both points of view, but I regret to say I like the more dramatic version. When I find a dead man with a sword cut in his head, or something of the kind, I like to try to follow up the mystery of how he came by his death-blow. Entirely by chance I have stumbled on quite a lot of them: old women eaten in cannibal feasts; men with skulls cleft in war; old women beheaded to prevent their ghosts walking; prisoners executed by the sword; men with their faces hacked to pieces by exultant enemies and so on. These were all living persons like ourselves. The solution of the mystery of their ends is quite as important as the dating of some particular shape of pot. Tiny scraps of evidence may enable you to see more vivid pictures of past ages than can be obtained from months of study of the more material relics of antiquity. The arthritic femur of a headless old woman told me why her head had been cut off and laid at her feet. She was bad-tempered from the pain; nobody wanted her ghost to haunt them. You lay a ghost by cutting off the corpse's head.

It takes a peculiar type of imagination to realise that 'these were all living persons like ourselves', not just old bones. Lethbridge possessed it, and it explains why he produced such fascinating results when he turned his attention to 'ghosts and ghouls' and other such strange matters.

Lethbridge, who was born in 1901, came from a west-country family. In his unpublished autobiography, *The Ivory Tower,* he remarks that family records date back to the twelfth century, and that the Lethbridges are mostly landed people — soldiers, explorers, members of Parliament and churchmen. His own branch of the family possessed that independence of character and natural eccentricity that were so notable in himself; he tells how his grandfather came up to London from the country, and was arrested for leaning out of his bedroom window and shooting a cock that kept him awake.

Tom was destined for the army; but he was only 17 when the First World War ended, and someone persuaded his mother that since there would never be another war, it was pointless to send him to Sandhurst. University seemed the next best choice. His family were traditionally Oxford men, but Tom knew no Greek, so had to go to Cambridge. There he was thoroughly bored by the lectures, but spent much time reading books on archaeology, and making drawings of ancient brooches in the museum. He made the acquaintance of the curator, Louis Clarke; and when Tom left Cambridge, after taking his degree, Clarke invited him to come back and work for him as a volunteer 'digger'. Since Tom had a private income, this seemed as good an idea as any; so he became an archaeologist. In the autobiography his life sounds idyllic: digging up Anglo-Saxon remains all day in quiet country churchyards, and sipping port in the evenings with eccentric characters like Sir William Ridgeway, Sir Cyril Fox, James Wordie and Louis Clarke. The story of those Cambridge years is told in *The Ivory Tower*, that entirely delightful autobiography which will, I trust, see print in the not-too-distant future. In due course, Tom became the Keeper of Anglo-Saxon Antiquities at the Archaeology Museum; he remained in Cambridge until 1957, except for a brief period in 1944 when he and Mina — his second wife — tried to become cattle farmers on an island off the west coast of Scotland.

After the war, he found Cambridge increasingly unpleasant and dreary. Most of his old friends were dead. He disliked what he called 'academic trade unionism'. But it was the Gogmagog affair that finally decided him to leave. Tom had become acquainted with that extraordinary lady, Margaret Murray, who believed that witches were actually practitioners of an ancient pre-Christian religion of fertility worship. When he heard of a legend of a giant figure cut into the turf of Wandlebury Camp (an Iron Age fort near Cambridge) he decided to try and find it. He did this by driving an iron bar into the turf of the hillside and noting which of the holes went deeper than the others. He was working on the assumption that the 'giant' had been carved into the chalk of the hillside, like the famous Cerne Abbas giant with his erect penis, and therefore the turf that covered the outline would be deeper than the surrounding turf. In due course, Lethbridge located the giant figure of a woman on horseback, with a sword-waving warrior on one side of her and the sun god on the other. There could be no doubt that the woman, obviously a goddess, was the central figure; the symbol of the moon behind her suggested that this was the moon and earth goddess Matrona, the Celtic equivalent of Diana, goddess of the witches. Lethbridge wrote a book all about it — *Gogmagog, the Buried Gods* — in which he argued strongly in favour of Margaret Murray's theories. It made him thoroughly unpopular at Cambridge. The days when Margaret Murray was sufficiently respectable to be regarded as the leading authority on witches were long past. Lethbridge's critics said that his giant figures were nonexistent — the result of his own wishful thinking. It was the last straw; Tom was already sick of Cambridge, and decided it was time to leave for good.

Which explains how, in 1957, the Lethbridges came to move into Hole House, near Branscombe, in Devon, and how Tom began the most remarkable and fruitful period of his crowded life.

I should explain that Lethbridge had never taken much interest in the 'supernatural'. As an archaeologist and historian, he regarded it as irrelevant. But this is not to say that he was a sceptic. During the course of his life, he had had a number of odd experiences. At the age of 18 he had been walking in the woods near Wokingham with his mother when they both experienced 'a horrible feeling of gloom and depression, which crept over us like a blanket of fog over the surface of the sea.' They hurried out of the wood, convinced that something ghastly had happened there. A few days later, a man's body was found close to the spot where they had been standing; he had committed suicide. Lethbridge later became convinced that the man's own misery and fear had somehow 'imprinted' themselves on the surroundings. When at Cambridge, Tom had seen a ghost, although he was not aware of it at the time. Leaving a friend's rooms, he saw a man in hunting kit, who stood as if waiting for him to leave. The next day he asked his friend the identity of his visitor; the friend looked at him blankly and said nobody had entered the room.

Two years later, in the Chorister's School, he and a friend confronted an 'icy presence' at the bottom of the stairs; it was known to the masters as 'the ghoul'. They tried walking into it, and it retreated up the stairs. They walked on, and it stayed ahead of them. At the top of the stairs they began to feel alarmed in case it should materialise, so they linked arms and took the last step. The 'ghoul' reappeared behind them...

So Lethbridge had some slight practical acquaintance with the 'supernatural' when he came to Hole House. He also knew that he could 'dowse'. He had tried it years before on Lundy Island, when searching for volcanic dykes. As a test, he had allowed himself to be blindfolded, then led along by a friend; he held a divining rod in his hands, and it accurately located every one of the volcanic dykes.

Still, he might well have spent the remainder of his life pottering around Iron Age sites, and writing more books like *Merlin's Island* and *The Painted Men*. Fate intervened, in the form of an extraordinary neighbour who seemed to be a practising witch. She told them casually that she possessed the power of 'astral projection' — leaving her physical body — and readers of this book will find evidence in the first chapter to suggest she may have been telling the truth. She also renewed Tom's interest in dowsing — not, this time, with a forked stick, but with a pendulum.

And here Tom's innate curiosity led him to make an interesting discovery. Instead of using the 'short pendulum' that most dowsers seem to prefer — any fairly heavy object on the end of six inches of string — he decided to try making a far longer pendulum, varying its length by winding it round a pencil. He soon made a discovery that filled him with excitement. The pendulum seemed to react to various substances *at different lengths*. For example, if he wanted it to react to copper, he had to make the length precisely $30\frac{1}{2}$ inches — in which case, the wooden bob would stop swinging back and forth, and go into a circular motion above the copper. Held above sand, it rotated at 14 inches. Iron was 32 inches, lead 22, mercury $12\frac{1}{2}$. He used the pendulum for detecting lead-glazed pottery in the courtyard of Hole House. The pendulum even detected truffles in the nearby wood.

The next discovery was even more exciting. The pendulum would react not only to objects, *but to ideas*. If he thought about the moon, the pendulum reacted at 30 inches. It reacted to the points of the compass — or the thought of them — at 10 inches, 20 inches, 30 inches and 40 inches. And if he wanted to distinguish between the moon and silver, both at 30 inches, he merely had to count the *number* of times it rotated; each object — or idea — had its own individual number.

The next decade of Lethbridge's life was quite literally a detective story. He conducted a long series of experiments into the pendulum and its reactions. He discovered, for example, that it could distinguish between sling stones that had been used in battle and the same stones gathered from a beach, as well as between stones that had been thrown by Mina and stones that he had thrown himself. And the clues kept coalescing to indicate new lines of thought. If anger could impress itself on a sling stone, then surely it explained how a suicide's misery could impress itself on the place where he died? In which case, his reaction to the place where the man committed suicide was a *dowser's* reaction. If he and his mother had suspended a pendulum in the woods near Wokingham, it should have gone into violent rotation at 40 inches, the rate for death.

What had happened, basically, was that Lethbridge had rediscovered something that had first been noticed more than a century earlier by an American professor, Joseph Rodes Buchanan. Bishop Polk — later a Civil War general — told Buchanan that he could detect brass in the dark simply by touching it; it produced an odd taste in his mouth. Buchanan tested him and found he was telling the truth. So clearly, Polk possessed some curious 'sense' that the rest of us lack. Buchanan discovered that some of his students were even more sensitive, and could name various chemicals even when they were wrapped in heavy brown paper packages. But it was his next discovery that intrigued him most — that these 'sensitives' could also hold a letter, and describe the sort of person who had written it, and whether the writer was happy or sad at the time. The writer's personality and mood had apparently imprinted itself on the letter. Buchanan's brother-in-law, William Denton, was a professor of geology, and he tested his students with geological specimens wrapped in thick paper. They received clear *pictures* of times in the remote past, convincing Denton that this new faculty — which he called psychometry — was a kind of telescope through which man could contemplate the history of the earth.

For a few years, 'psychometry' attracted wide attention in America; then scientific scepticism triumphed, and it was consigned to the rubbish bin of 'occult' superstitions. Lethbridge, whose reading was limited, had most certainly never heard of either Buchanan or Denton. He had simply stumbled upon their discovery from a completely different angle.

But as he realised himself, he had stumbled upon something far more important than a half-forgotten faculty. (After all, dowsing has been known for thousands of years.) What it really amounted to was that he had discovered a *new dimension of reality*. As a scientific archaeologist, he had always assumed that the world is made up of solid matter, and that the task of the mind is to try to understand its laws. The behaviour of his pendulum told him quite plainly that it is not as simple as this. The pendulum is, as he discovered, as accurate as a voltmeter. But it is not connected *directly* to the effects it is trying to measure. These have somehow to pass through the intermediary of the human brain. Here, as it happens, I can speak with personal experience. I first discovered that I could use a dowsing rod at the standing stones called the Merry Maidens, near Penzance. What amazed me was not so much that the rod twisted violently in my hands as I approached the stones, but that I felt *nothing:* no prickling of the hair, no tingling in the hands. It reacted just like any other scientific instrument that I might have been testing. Some unknown part of my brain — almost certainly the right cerebral hemisphere — was 'picking up' some curious force in the stones, and causing some involuntary contraction of my muscles that twisted the rod in my hands.

*This* is what fascinated Lethbridge. Not only, it seems, is nature full of curious 'tape recordings', some dating back millions of years, but our brains possess the electronic equipment to *play them back*. It is enough to make a good scientist feel faint and queasy. How can we hope to keep the mind and nature — or the 'objective facts' and our interpretation of them — in separate compartments if there are aspects of nature that can only be observed by some unknown part of the mind?

As the years went by, Lethbridge became increasingly fascinated by this problem. He said that the sensation reminded him of a time in Iceland when the ice suddenly gave way under his feet, and he found himself in freezing water. Yet the freezing water does not seem to have alarmed him unduly. He had the courage — and imagination — to recognise that his old scientific view was distorted and incomplete. The mind does not *study* nature; it is intimately involved with it, and cannot escape this involvement, except when engaged in the crudest kind of measurement. Nature is somehow *alive,* as Goethe realised — not only trees and flowers, but rocks, water and minerals. In fact, as ancient man seems to have realised, the earth itself is a living body, not a mere cooling fragment of the sun.

And so Lethbridge moved from his early experiences of 'ghosts and ghouls' to the study of dowsing, and from dowsing to the force of evolution. He became convinced that the physical world in which we live — and to which the pendulum responds between 1 and 40 inches — is only one level of reality, and that other levels — other 'dimensions' — coexist with our own; they can even be detected by the pendulum. His interest in the problem of time led him — like J. W. Dunne — to study 'precognitive dreams'. Reports of flying saucers led him to look into the subject of Unidentified Flying Objects, and their possible relation to the forces of the earth — he came to suspect that monuments like Stonehenge could be 'beacons' for guiding UFOs. Yet he never lost his sense of humour, or that good-natured pragmatism that makes his early books on archaeology so delightful.

Between 1961, and his death in 1971, Lethbridge wrote ten books, all of them fairly short (about 150 pages). In these he described in detail the progress of his investigations. These books, I believe, form one of the most fascinating records of 'paranormal research' of the twentieth century; I have read and re-read every one of them. In the present volume, Tom Graves — himself a dowser of remarkable ability — and Janet Hoult have attempted to extract the central story of Lethbridge's development from these volumes, allowing him to describe for himself the progress of his discoveries, from ghosts and ghouls to precognitive dreams. The result, I believe, justifies my description of Lethbridge as a kind of Sherlock Holmes. Let us hope it also has the effect of provoking younger investigators to follow in his footsteps. It would be stupid to allow his discoveries to suffer the same fate as those of Denton and Buchanan.

Colin Wilson

# Editors' Preface

To edit the later work of Tom Lethbridge has not been easy. It spans a long period of continuous research, the last fifteen years of his life, and consists, in its printed form, of over a thousand pages in nine books: from *Gogmagog*, published in 1957, through *Ghost and Ghoul, Witches, Ghost and Divining Rod, ESP: Beyond Time and Distance, A Step in the Dark* and *The Monkey's Tale*, to *The Legend of the Sons of God* and *The Power of the Pendulum*, finally published in 1976, five years after his death. It covers a vast range of themes and areas of research, far beyond any mere category like 'parapsychology', and each of these themes appears in almost every book. And his wandering from theme to theme, and anecdote to anecdote, is not as casual as it seems: his anecdotes and digressions were selected with deceptive care, and his loose rambling style conceals a concise and meticulous planning of the presentation of his ideas. It is difficult to edit this without destroying the sense, the style or the continuity, or all of them — and it is these that are the essence of Tom Lethbridge's writing.

What we have done is to select three of the major themes of his work, and develop these with his own digressions and interconnections to his other themes. These major themes are stated by Lethbridge himself at the end of *Ghost and Ghoul*: that ghosts are pictures produced by human minds, rather than the spirits of the departed; that there is something entirely wrong with our conception of time; and that magic, in the traditional sense, is the application of resonance, the interconnection of all things. These themes lie behind the work on ghosts and energy fields in *Ghost and Ghoul*; dowsing in *Ghost and Divining Rod* and *A Step in the Dark*; perception in *ESP*; dreams and precognition in *The Power of the Pendulum*; and the questioning of the theory of chance evolution in *The Monkey's Tail*. These form the bulk of the first eight chapters of this abridgement, and are presented in what seems to us to be the most logical sequence: from ghosts and field theory, through the uses of dowsing and psychometry, to a theory of a 'master plan' beyond evolution and physical death.

The work on archaeology and the old gods, as developed in *Gogmagog* and *Witches*, does not connect directly with this sequence, although it is essential to the unity of his work; but Lethbridge refers to it often in his other books, and we have included and expanded these references wherever practicable. We have been forced to leave out much of the detail of his research on the old beliefs and on the stone circles and standing stones, but this is inevitable in an abridgement of this nature. But the development of these ideas, connected back to the sequence we have developed here, culminated in the work presented in *The Legend of the Sons of God*, which we have used as a theme for the last two chapters of this edition. It covers the same area that was made notorious and disreputable by von Däniken and his followers; but Lethbridge, as he himself explains, covered it independently of von Däniken and, unlike the latter, presents several credible alternative explanations of this difficult material.

Most of our abridgement work has consisted of selecting the most suitable example from the many that Lethbridge gives to back up each of his ideas and theories, and also limiting the digressions that he makes throughout his work. Many of the examples, such as that of the Ladram Bay ghoul, are repeated in revised forms in different books: so we have selected the version which seems to us to be most complete and relevant in the context of the sequence we have developed. But beyond essential 'linking' we have not done, and have not needed to do, any re-writing: to have done so would have destroyed what we wished above all to retain — the unity in his style, his thought and his work.

Tom Graves and Janet Hoult
Somerset

# Preface

For a number of years I have been working on the confused and difficult subject of the ancient gods in Britain. In the course of this work it occurred to me to wonder why there had been any beliefs in gods at all. One is told that the forces of nature are so impressive that primitive mankind was compelled to believe in the existence of Beings greater than himself and that these powers of nature became his gods. The natural in fact evoked a supposed supernatural. Somehow this did not seem to me to be a probable answer. It seems much more reasonable to suppose that the occurrences outside the ordinary run of affairs were responsible for the surmise that invisible and sometimes visible spirits existed and that the greater of these became the gods. The ghost and poltergeist have always been known. What was thunder and lightning but a poltergeist on a greater scale?

This book is the result of an entirely personal investigation into these unusual occurrences, as it seems that I am more prone to bump into unusual experiences than the majority of my friends and acquaintances. I have also taught myself to dowse, and using this means of divination I have been able to look still further at some of the strange, unexplained things we see and feel about us. It is no longer taboo to admit this, fortunately, for of recent years this kind of study has become respectable and it has been shown that many of the phenomena are capable of scientific proof. ESP (Extra-Sensory Perception) is being studied in laboratories on both sides of the Atlantic and the stigma of being interested in such things has gone the way of that which once rested on the chemist, or the astronomer. It is the man who does not believe in such things who is now a touch old-fashioned, and not the believer who is regarded as superstitious.

I have enjoyed one great advantage over many of my contemporaries. It has never been necessary for me to stick closely to one line of study and thus work it to death. There has always been time enough to gain at least a passing acquaintance with subjects other than archaeology, with which for many years I have been mostly concerned. Although I studied Natural Sciences at Cambridge, which resulted in ten years of almost total lack of interest in natural history, it then became again for me quite as interesting to watch a peregrine falcon stoop at a passing pigeon, or a hermit crab emerge from its borrowed shell in a rock pool, as to recover some unusual and long-forgotten piece of information from the earth. Although this may well have led to my becoming a 'jack of all trades and master of none', it has nevertheless provided me with a great store of experience, with some of which I at times bore my friends.

There is one further point which I must emphasise before coming to the occurrences themselves. It is this: many of the ideas which I have expressed are tentative. They are theories, which may work, or may not work. When I see flaws in them, I shall have no hesitation in changing them myself. The last thing I want to do is foist dogma on my readers. Dogma is the curse of learning and very often the ruin of religion also. When you hear someone say, 'Such and such a thing must be right because so-and-so says it is', you can be pretty safe in thinking that there is considerable doubt about the matter. We all of us really know very little indeed. Scientific thought is in the melting-pot and nobody can really forecast what will come out of the brew. But anything which can stimulate others to think things out for themselves must be of some value. There is an old Gaelic proverb which says, 'Two heads are better than one, even if they are sheep's heads'. The more heads that can be got to take an interest in this subject, the larger is the chance that something important will be discovered.

I have been attempting to bring the paranormal, supernatural, or whatever you like to call it, into some relation with the world of science and I have done this quite informally. The results have surprised me. Although I have been able to divine water and do other simple things of that kind for many years, it never occurred to me that with a little practice I should be able to go to a given piece of turf, say the composition of many of the objects which lie in the soil beneath it, then dig it up and show what they all are. In fact using this method of dowsing, quite unexpectedly and with no intention of doing so, we seem to have stumbled upon a new argument in favour of the survival of human mind after bodily death.

There are no mediums, or sensitives as they are now called, in this part of the story. It is simply the result of experimenting with a little ball on a length of thread and the subsequent employment of a pencil, a pair of compasses and a ruler to plot the tabulated results on paper. The inferences I have drawn from this may not be correct; but anyone who can work the pendulum, and this includes the bulk of humanity, can obtain the same results and work out the inferences for themselves.

When we — that is my wife and I — began the investigation several years ago we were by no means certain that there was any real subject to study. We might merely have been prying into an aspect of psychology, but it did not take long for us to find that there was a practical side to the whole matter and that this could be studied like any other scientific subject.

To keep our minds clear of outside suggestions we have read very little about the results obtained by others in working with a pendulum. The results described in this book are entirely produced by our own work, and so if there is error in them it has not come from reading other people's theories. This is more important than it may seem; for it is quite clear that some selective influence from the mind is at work when you use the instrument. In fact it seems to me that the pendulum only supplies a means of communication in code between one part of one's mind on Earth and another part not bound up with the human body. It helps anyone who can use it to be in a sense a medium. But there is a great advantage in using the pendulum, for its code can be measured and written down. There is no quibbling or mumbo-jumbo and the messages it gives can often be tested by digging up, or finding in some other way, objects completely concealed from the five senses.

Here I will pass the various problems on to the reader with the caution that to get any convincing results from this study he, or she, must work at it for themselves.

Much of what I have to say will seem incredible to those who believe in the apparent completeness of modern study. But there is absolutely nothing to prevent the most normal persons from obtaining the same results as we have done. The only real obstruction appears to be mental laziness. The proof of the pudding must always be in the eating and not in the theories of the author of the cookery book. The dogmas of Victorian science will no longer fit. Many of the better scientists know this. We have to cope with something far beyond the limited approach of exact measurements in three dimensions. It may take a revolution in thought to do this but it has to come.

Throughout these investigations my wife has been of the greatest help to me. We act as a team and she has the gift of an incisive mind and can see straight through to the root of a problem, which would often take another person weeks of concentrated effort to solve. Many pen friends have written confirming some of our observations, but she alone, with her shrewd judgement, is a real partner in the work and deserves my greatest thanks, both for this and for the hours of labour she gives to typing out the scarcely legible and much corrected manuscript. I am not surprised that the pendulum's 'rate' for femininity is the same as that for gold.

T.C.L.

# Chapter 1

You often hear people remark, 'If I saw a ghost, I think I should die of fright.' This is not the case at all. On several occasions I have clearly seen figures of people who were not really there, in the ordinary sense, at all. In none of these occasions did I appreciate till later that there was anything strange in what I had seen.

> As I was going up the stair
>> I met a man who was not there.
> He was not there again today,
>> Oh, how I wish he'd go away.

(I do not know where it comes from, but I like it!)

One of the first incidents happened near to our home in Devon. Our water at Hole is pumped by a ram, and on this particular Sunday morning the ram stopped. The house stands at about 300 feet and the ram is nearly 150 feet lower down the steep side of the combe and some 300 yards away. Directly below us, at about the 150-foot level, is Hole Mill, which belongs to Mrs N, who has considerable and unusual faculties of extra-sensory perception.

Our ram having stopped pumping, it was necessary to start it again. My wife and I, accompanied by her black cat, which follows like a dog, but makes more noise about it, complaining all the time, walked down the hill away from the direction of Hole Mill and started the ram again. The morning was so unusually lovely that we sat on the concrete roof of the ram's

1

house and admired the quiet view. The cat, according to custom, sat looking in the opposite direction, ignoring us. A small river, with no name today, but probably once called the Bran, ran below us, having passed Hole Mill, which was almost out of sight in the next field. At 11.15 a.m. my wife said she must put the Sunday joint in the oven. I said I would wait another quarter of an hour to see that the ram did not stop again. She said she would come to meet me on my way back and that I was to remember everything of interest I happened to see and report it to her. She then departed up the hill accompanied by the cat, which was complaining loudly as usual.

As it happened, I did not sit out my full fifteen minutes. For some five minutes I sat in the sun, seeing nothing more remarkable than a wheeling buzzard. I was beside a large sycamore tree and directly above the Mill, which was about fifty feet below me and about sixty yards away. I was thus looking on to the Mill roof and well above the tops of its chimneys.

While I was bending down, I heard a motor-bicycle start up, followed by the furious barking of dogs. I stood up and looked down, to see the paper-man riding off on his bicycle followed by Mrs N's four large dogs in full cry. It was clear enough to see the papers in a box on the back of the bicycle. As I watched, I saw Mrs N emerge from behind the left end of the Mill, calling off the dogs. She was dressed in a bright blue sweater and had on dark blue tartan trousers and some kind of scarf over her head. She looked up from near the corner of the house, saw me and waved. I waved back. At this moment a second figure appeared behind Mrs N and perhaps a yard from her. She stood apparently looking up at me. Mrs N went back behind the corner of the Mill and the other woman apparently did so too. I did not know the other woman by sight. She looked about sixty-five to seventy years old, was taller than Mrs N and rather slight. Her face appeared to be rather dark, or tanned, and she had a pointed chin. She was dressed in a dark tweed coat and skirt and had something which looked like a light grey cardigan, or spencer, beneath her coat. Her skirt was long. She had a flat-crowned and wide-brimmed round hat on her head. The hat was black and had a wreath of white flowers round the bottom of the crown. She was, in fact, dressed as my aunts

2

might have been dressed any day in spring before the Kaiser's war. She did not look the sort of person who was likely to be staying at Hole Mill today. Neither did she look the type of person you would expect to find at the Mill during its active days. Beyond that, I thought nothing of the incident (Figure 1).

I walked up the lane and met my wife coming down it from Hole. We were actually screened from the Mill by a bend in the hedge. We leaned over a gate in the sun and admired my tenant's calves. I had to repeat everything I had seen and my wife remarked on the improbable character of Mrs N's apparent guest. Then the dogs started to bark once more and my wife said, 'Here they come. Now we shall see who she is.' We waited, leaning over the gate. Soon the dogs arrived, leaping up at us in friendly welcome. As we were beating them off, round the bend in the hedge came Mrs N alone. 'Oh!' said my wife in a disappointed tone. 'We were expecting to see two of you.' 'How is that?' asked Mrs N. 'I have only seen Tom [me] and the paper-man all the morning.' I explained what I had seen and she remarked, 'So you are seeing my ghosts now, are you?' We then remembered that, a few weeks previously, she had reported having seen the figure of an unknown man standing very near the spot where I had been when I saw the other woman.

Figure 1. General impression given by figure seen at Hole Mill on 22 February 1959. All clothes black, or dark grey, except spencer and blouse.

Although my description tallied to some extent with that of a friend of hers who was no longer alive, we could not be certain of the identification. Whoever the figure was, it was evident that not only had Mrs N not seen her, but she must have almost passed through her when going back behind the Mill. The incident seems impossible to explain in terms of everyday events.

When I examined this experience, there was a close similarity to an occurrence in a friend's rooms at Trinity College in Cambridge in 1922, when I saw a figure of a man in hunting kit. There was the same overall greyness and lack of colour about the figure then. Although perfectly sharp, it was perhaps a little thin, as one would say of a photograph. In both cases, no one would have suspected that it was not the figure of a living person. The figure at Hole was full-size compared to Mrs N, and so was the figure at Cambridge.

My wife remembered the date the following year, and we decided to try to see whether anything happened on the anniversary. The true solar time anniversary fell on a Monday at about 5.30 p.m. But as we had no idea what kind of time was important, we decided to try first on the nearest Sunday at 11.30 a.m. The Sunday might be the important thing. The morning might be important. We just did not know. We therefore went at the correct clock time on the nearest Sunday, which was actually 21 February and not the 22nd. We did not tell Mrs N of our intention, but went at 11.20 a.m. and stood beside the sycamore tree. The day was again fine and fairly warm, but not so hot as on the previous occasion. Mrs N could be observed bending down and working like a fury in her garden by the stream. The paper-man had already done his round. We stood silently by the sycamore tree, unobserved by Mrs N, and saw nothing. We did, however, both experience a kind of electrical tingling in the atmosphere, which by experiment could be confined within a few paces of the tree itself and which felt strongest over the drain, which ran out beside it. We also found that this tingling could be felt all the way up the drain, which ran as a rivulet beside the roadway, for some fifteen yards. It was entirely absent from the other side of the lane and ended at the point at which the rivulet vanished into a bank. It seems that this tingling has some connection with the passage of running water. Mrs N tells us that she has been spoken to, and distinctly heard the words 'Good morning' spoken, while no one was visible, when in the proximity of this

4

rivulet. One of her dogs heard it too and rushed down barking to the mill, as if it expected to find someone there, and re-appeared looking puzzled. As well as the tingling feeling near the tree, we appeared to experience a certain muzziness of vision about everything. This could, of course, be accounted for in various ways, but we both noticed it.

At 11.30 a.m. on the following day, the correct solar anniversary, but the wrong solar hour, I was unfortunately absent at the dentist. At 5.30 p.m., which was the exact anniversary within a few minutes, it was raining hard. We shall have to wait therefore, before we can continue the experiment with anniversaries. We have, however, tried on other occasions and have established that the tingling feeling is usually to be observed on that particular spot and that other people feel it too. Some remark on the general friendliness of the atmosphere at that place. If we are fortunate by continual experiment, we may be able to learn something from this spot; but in any case it seems possible to make a few observations from what has been learnt already.

Now it seems evident that if these ghosts are produced by something external to my own mind, then some force is necessary to project them. I do not think that they can be the result of thoughts from any level of my mind, as some ghosts are thought to be by people who investigate them, for several reasons. The first is that the figures on both occasions fitted into their surroundings. They were perfectly clear and moved naturally within the features of the places where they were seen. There was no blurring. If you produce one photograph on the same plate as a second, it is most hard to avoid over-lapping the two images. The second reason is that I can imagine no possible explanation why my mind should have thought up these two figures and put them into the surroundings in which I saw them. There are certainly recorded cases of ghosts being apparently produced in this way and seen by their author; but I am certain that this is not the case with my two ghosts.

The whole production, in each case, was exactly comparable to a television scene. There was the same curious lack of atmosphere and same general grey drabness. The figures were just pictures. I do not know whether I saw them with my eyes or whether they appeared in the mind direct. But, in whatever

5

manner they were presented, I feel pretty sure that they were not spirits. They were pictures projected by somebody other than myself and I was nothing more than the receiving set. Who projected them and how it was done cannot be determined from the evidence available. One does not know, for instance, whether they are projected at a set time on special occasions and would be visible at those times to anybody on the correct wave-length. There are, however, some slight clues. There often seems to be some kind of pressure built up, possibly by the running water, at the point from which the second ghost was seen. The pressure appears to be comparable to an electro-magnetic force.

Now it can be shown, both by dowsing and with scientific instruments, that fields of static electricity exist in just the same kinds of places as those in which we have experienced our ghosts and ghouls. These have been studied by scientists. They consist of what are known as ionised particles, but it is not necessary to remember that term now. All we need to notice is that these static fields are to be found in connection with such things as waterfalls, springs and streams, or woods and trees, deserts and moorlands and mountains. This is extremely important to anyone who is interested in mythology. For these are just the places which were peopled with nymphs and spirits by the peoples of the ancient world and by simple modern ones. These nymphs and spirits must be the result of observation by people at what is known, somewhat contemptuously, as a primitive level of culture. Such people are far more observant than the bulk of the population today. Their observation includes far finer degrees of appreciation than that of a man who spends his working hours with electronic gear and his evenings watching television or reading the reports of his colleagues. The primitive people really observe, and they evidently notice things at certain places which are quite outside the range of observation of the bulk of civilised man. The things which I believe they notice are, amongst others of course, the static fields at these particular places. They also observe the movements of beast and bird and the signs which indicate these movements.

If we look for a moment at the conclusions of the ancients about such places, we find that they believed that there were nymphs, supranormal persons, to be found in association with waterfalls, springs and streams, whom they called 'naiads' (nïads). They had nymphs who frequented trees and woods and named them 'dryads'. There were others associated with mountains and deserts styled oreads; and there were sea-nymphs named nereids. I propose to use these names now to designate electro-magnetic fields found in such places. This will avoid the constant use of the term 'field of force'. Most people will know the names already and in any case they are far more attractive than such terms used in physics as ohm and dine, watt and erg. A dryad-field then becomes our term for a field of force connected with trees and a naiad-field one around a spring or streamlet. An oread-field is some such field in the mountains or deserts. And a nereid-field is a field of the sea. I do not think this will complicate our investigation, for I hope some traces of classical study still cling to our educational system, poor though it now appears to be. We must, however, introduce a few more terms. The most important concerns the human field of force. I shall call this the 'psyche-field'. The word psyche is in constant use by psychologists to describe what I believe to be the same thing. I think their psyche is our electro-magnetic field, a field which is known to exist by scientists and which we can easily detect with a divining-rod. It extends beyond the person for at least a foot. There is also the field of the earth itself, which is often forgotten. I suppose we must term this 'Ge', which everyone should know, for it is the *ge* in geography and geology. The *o*'s are only put in to make the words sound a little less ugly. *Ge* is the Greek for the earth.

Let us look at these fields as a kind of electric haze and not be too concerned with what that haze really is. The conception of matter consisting of innumerable holes kept in temporary co-operation by electrical fields is quite impossible for the ordinary man to grasp and certainly far more incomprehensible than ghosts. These fields can be located by electrical devices; or, and this is much more important, by man's own bodily equipment, the psyche-field. Some skilled dowsers habitually find water without any aids at all. They find it by impulses which they receive through their fingers. I have myself felt a kind of electrical tingling in connection with running water. Since man, or rather his psyche-field, can be shown to be a field of force, this electrical tingling must clearly represent a flow of electrical current between the psyche-field and the static field, the naiad, dryad or whatever it is. The dowser locates the invisible static field by the flow of current between him and it. So our magic in this case is nothing more than the well-known phenomenon of physics that current will flow from one field to another.

At least two fields are involved in this incident. There is my psyche-field, which was in contact with the naiad-field of the streamlet and another psyche-field, which produced the picture. Since no one really knows what their own body looks like when seen by other people, the second psyche-field must have been that of someone who had once stood very near the point where I was standing and had been so impressed by seeing the figure standing down below him, that he imparted some of that impression to the naiad-field of the streamlet. The naiad-field only acted as a conductor and leaked the original impression back to me. I may be completely wrong in my reasoning; but it seems to me that the original situation must have been something like this: somebody standing near the point where I stood, looked down at Hole Mill and saw this woman looking up at him. For some reason this impressed such a strong emotion in his psyche-field that a picture of her was impressed in the electro-magnetic field of the streamlet. My psyche-field being in a far less accelerated state, and consequently at a lower potential, the charge leaked back again and I saw in my mind the original picture which had caused the emotion.

However, I think that the original impulse was a double one, for Mrs N, who owned the Mill in 1959, told us that a week or two before I saw my ghost, she had seen another. This was the figure of a man in a tall hat, who was standing near the point where I stood. She had seen this on a misty day. Other people remark on the pleasant atmosphere of the spot. It seems then that the emotion which impressed these two ghosts on this one naiad-field was a pleasant one. The two people had been delighted to see each other. Each impressed the picture of the other on the one field of force. Whether the impulses have now been expended by the incidents experienced by Mrs N and myself, I do not know; but the naiad-field is still there. People experience a tingling sensation when near the streamlet. I expect the ghosts can still be picked up. All this is an astonishing and, at first sight, improbable conclusion. But it is in no way more remarkable than television. It is in fact very much the same thing. This seems to suggest a line of thought. Are ghosts 'television' pictures carried by the force of resonance from a projecting machine in one mind to a receiving machine in another? If this is so, then the probability is that if you see a ghost when in company with another person, then that other person may be the unconscious projector. This is certainly not always the case and it does not take into account the manner of the projection. This we may perhaps take to be the same as psychokinesis, which can throw plates and stones about when it occurs in the form of a poltergeist.

Years of research by teams of workers will be necessary before the laws governing these occurrences can be worked out. We can, however, make a few suggestions. First, that there is nothing that anyone need be afraid of in the sight of a ghost. The great bulk of these are no more than mental pictures produced by living people. It is even on record that some have been deliberately produced. The method of projection is probably the natural equivalent of mechanical television, just as telepathy is the natural equivalent of ordinary broadcasting. The machines used for it are human minds and the power is provided by the force known as resonance, which appears to be akin to electro-magnetism. This same force is harnessed by water-diviners and those who practise a form of healing at a distance, which is known as 'The Box'.

Of course, people vary very much in the trust which they place in the statements of others. Some believe every word they see in print and doubt all that is told them by word of mouth; others have the reverse attitude. One finds that the majority of naturalists will only credit the statements of other people when they happen to agree with what they have themselves observed; while trained scientists will scarcely believe anything which they cannot weigh or measure.

But not all these pictures of emotion held in the fields of force are pleasant, or just eerie. In fact some are very unpleasant, and for these I prefer to use the word 'ghoul'.

Whether a true ghoul has ever been recorded in Britain, I am unable to say. The term is applied to a revolting form of demon,

9

found in Asia, which feeds on corpses. I am using the word ghoul, however, to describe a feeling of oppression and horror which is often accompanied by the sensation of intense cold. I have met the ghoul on several occasions. It is not a premonition, and it is not a ghost, which is a visible thing. Neither has it the properties of a poltergeist. As far as I am aware, it is never seen, but I may be wrong in this, for many ghost stories appear to combine the ghoul and the ghost. All that I can say is that I have never experienced the two together.

On 27 January 1962, at about three o'clock in the afternoon to be precise, we met with one ghoul. My wife wanted some seaweed to manure an asparagus bed and we heard that there was plenty to be found at Ladram Bay, about two miles south-westward of Sidmouth. It is easy to get close to the beach in a car, which was the reason for our choice of the place, for a sack of wet seaweed is heavy. The day was very warm and muggy.

Ladram Bay is a blunt-ended horse-shoe cut in the red sand-stone. It is surrounded by cliffs which I suppose are about 75 feet high in places. There are two red stacks of rock, covered with seagulls, standing at either end of the bay, which is 500 yards from horn to horn. The only approach is near the north-east end where a cleft in the sandstone rock is wide enough for a single cart-track and one line of fishing boats to be hauled up bow to stern. At the seaward end of the track there is a capstan on a concrete ramp down to the shingle. As I stepped on to the beach, I passed into a kind of blanket, or fog, of depression and, I think, fear. Still, we had come to get seaweed and I took no notice of this unexpected happening. We walked south-eastward along the shingle, stuffing rotten and rather smelly seaweed into the sack.

Presently my wife wandered off to look at the south-west corner of the bay. I had forgotten the ghoul and was busy with the seaweed. After about ten minutes I heard crunching on the pebbles and looked up to see her hurrying back with an armful of weed. 'I can't stand this place any longer,' she said. 'It's horrible. There's something frightful here. Let's go home.' And so we did. There was just enough seaweed to cover the asparagus bed.

That evening my wife had to ring up her mother, a process of somewhat long duration. In the course of the conversation, the visit to Ladram Bay was mentioned. My mother-in-law remarked that she had once been to the bay, on Christmas Day five years earlier, and had been struck by the curious feeling of depression there. I then remembered that she had told us about it soon afterwards.

But to show that we are not unusual in experiencing these things, although perhaps more ready to note their occurrence, my wife's brother happened to come to lunch next day. The Ladram affair was mentioned and caused him no surprise, for both he and his wife had met the same kind of ghoul one evening in a field near Avebury. Something then clicked in my mind. I remembered how field-telephones were prone to short-circuits in warm, damp weather. 'What was the weather like?' I asked him. 'Very warm and muggy,' he replied.

These incidents started a train of thought, which I shall presently try to discuss. But I have not yet finished with Ladram Bay.

The success of the seaweed gathering of course suggested a need for more. Although I have no affection for these ghouls, curiosity was too strong for me to refuse. The following Saturday, 3 February, we set out again for Ladram, with two sacks this time. The idea of water was now firmly in my head. The weather was as warm as before and it was drizzling. As soon as we reached the track down to the beach, it was clear that a small streamlet ran down beside it and lost itself in the pebbles. The same bank of depression greeted me at the same place as before and it was right above the point where the streamlet was running beneath the shingle.

We walked through the bank of depression, which did not appear to extend far beyond the streamlet, and walked to the opposite end of the beach. Here my wife pointed out the spot where she had thought of sitting on a rock before the ghoul had driven her away. Here the feeling was at its worst. It was so strong as to make me feel almost giddy. The nearest I can get to a description is that it felt not unlike one feels with a high temperature and when full of drugs. After the death of Mrs N at Hole Mill, in August 1960, an unpleasant field similar to that at Ladram Bay could be felt around the house. It had definite limits over which you could step at a single stride.

I looked about. The red cliff, quite close at hand, was perhaps

11

50 feet high, with a line of fencing posts on a broken wire hanging forlornly down it. We were standing in the area between two streamlets, which fell as tiny waterfalls down the face of the cliff. They too, of course, vanished into the pebbles at the bottom. It was hard to take in more than this. The whole condition made one's mind confused. We hastily filled our sacks with seaweed, half-expecting something to appear over our shoulders, and humped them to the car. Then we examined the cliff-top.

It is a curious place. The red cliffs and stacks of rock in the sea give an unusual appearance. There is an air of unreality about it, not unlike that of stage scenery. My wife wandered off to look at another bit of cliff, while I tried to find a place to make a sketch to include the unusual points. She was back very soon. 'It's just as horrid there,' she said pointing to a spot about 75 yards from the lane to the beach. 'Come and see.' I went to look and found that it was so. Then she told me that when standing at this point, something put into her mind: 'Wouldn't you like to jump over?' 'I didn't want to of course,' she added. We were surely picking up the thoughts of someone who had either jumped over the cliff, wanted to do so, or even perhaps, since time does not seem to follow its normal course in these things, may even be going to think of jumping off in the future.

I originally wrote about this ghoul in 1962, after our experiences, and at that time several people had already experienced this ghastly phenomenon. In 1964 an empty car was found on Peak Hill above Sidmouth. The owner was a respected citizen, not of Sidmouth, but of a town some miles away. A search was made. Nothing was found of Mr X until some of his gear was found at Ladram Bay. He had evidently walked along the cliffs from Peak Hill to Ladram Bay looking for a suitable place to jump off, and had eventually found it. His body was later picked up near Portland Bill. Has the ghoul gone? I don't think so. We went to investigate.

This example gives a very good idea of what a ghoul is. It is the result of a terrible mental strain projected into another dimension. It can lodge in the naiad-field of a stream, or the dryad-field of a tree and probably also into rocks. And there it becomes timeless. The Ladram Bay ghoul was there at least nine years before the event happened. It may still be there in a thousand years.

All this of course sounds quite nonsensical to those who have not experienced things like these. However, some observers can read the figures on a thermometer without putting on their glasses, while others cannot do so. Because you do not happen to be able to read a thermometer with the naked eye, it does not follow that there are no figures on it to read. You do not even doubt people who say they can see them. All it means is that your eyesight is somewhat defective. At Ladram Bay at least five people on different occasions have observed something which many others have not observed. Does that mean that there was nothing to observe, or only that the other people were so engrossed in other matters that they noticed nothing and that they were just unobservant? A vast number of people are quite incredibly blind to things they are not expecting to see; while others are talking so much that they notice nothing at all.

It can be shown by scientific methods that these static fields do exist at the places where these experiences occur. The thoughts collected at these points must come from the electrical fields of persons who are not at these places when others experience these thoughts. It therefore appears to be clear that thoughts can be transferred from human minds to the static electrical fields which can be generated and observed at these particular places. Since it is known to science that each person is surrounded by an electrical field, it appears obvious that thoughts are transferred from one field to another in accordance with the laws of electricity. The current flows from the high potential to the lower.

But since other people can pick up thoughts from the static fields, it is evident that the electrical laws must still hold good and the current flow back from the static field to that of the person who has the experience. At the time this happens the person who has this experience must have a field at a lower potential to the static one. The mean potential of the human field must be of very nearly the same potential as the static one; but something can raise or lower this human potential. The condition which causes the rise in the human field appears to be intense emotion, whether of pleasure or of the reverse. This is as far as we can get for the moment but it is something which

13

seems to have hardly impinged on modern thought at all. Our philosophers do not seem to have considered that a human field, crammed full of thoughts, must be quite distinct from a human brain, which only appears to be capable of dealing with impressions from the five bodily senses. One must surely assume that the psyche-field, as I am calling it for convenience, is attached to the real mind of the person to whom it belongs. It is of course linked to the brain; but it also appears to be capable of being linked to static fields quite external to that brain. Or at any rate it is capable of passing thoughts to them by something resembling the induction of electricity and also of receiving them back again from such a field. This induction is apparently the same as what is known to workers in radionics as 'resonance'.

There may well be many grades of ghoul, ranging from a slight feeling of discomfort to full-blooded horror. In fact this is evidently the case. What we have not yet appreciated is the capability of the human transmitting and receiving set. I am not denying the existence of personalities surviving bodily death. I am simply suggesting that many of the unpleasant phenomena which worry and frighten mankind and are known as supernatural are in reality the result of unconscious transmitting by people still in this life. They may, or may not, be assisted, or even displaced, by transmissions through their machines by entities on another plane. If one knew this, and realised what was happening, it should be quite easy to 'jam' the transmission and not to suffer any discomfort at all. On none of the occasions so far described had I any inkling of the possible cause, nor any idea of how it might be interrupted. I was still under the domination of traditional superstition in spite of years of training in scientific thought. But this scientific thought did not even recognise the existence of the phenomena, which were and are so obvious to a multitude of observers. It was completely useless as a guide to behaviour in such circumstances. I have had to become my own guinea-pig and do my thinking from my own observations of what happens to this guinea-pig.

I experienced a combination of ghost, ghoul and poltergeist some years ago, when I went on a trip with my friend W.S.B. W.S.B. and myself both have an interest in islands. His interest

14

is largely in spiders, for the study of which he long ago gained a world-wide reputation. Mine is chiefly archaeological, but birds and sometimes insects and plants play a part in it. In the latter part of June 1929, we decided to examine some of the islands off the south-west coast of Ireland.

At Valencia we chartered a motor-launch to take us out to the Skelligs. These islands lie out in the Western Ocean, perhaps six miles from the Kerry coast. On 24 June, which was a beautiful day with very little wind, we set out. The long Atlantic swell was comfortable and the views magnificent. We passed the Lower Skellig, covered thick with nesting gannets, gleaming white in the sun, and made for the landing place on Skellig Michael, a name which is pronounced something like Vickel.

There is no beach on Skellig Michael. You jump from the boat on to a ledge of rock. This has been the only landing-place for at least twelve hundred years, for a flight of stone slab steps leads up from nearby to a monastery on the top, which was known to be there in the eighth century. The top of the island itself consists of two small peaks, separated by a little grassy alp on the coll between. This is perhaps the size of a tennis court and is known as Christ's Saddle. The monastery is deserted now. It was built before the days of the Roman Catholic Church in Ireland. It consists of six beehive huts, built of dry stone, and a ruined chapel. A low dry-stone wall was the only protection the monks had on a dark night from falling over the edge of the cliff.

I went up to look at the monastery, which I had long wished to see, while W.S.B. set to work to collect 'pill box fodder' in the shape of spiders. It did not take long to examine the monastery. The beehive cells were perfect, except that a former covering of turves had long since blown away. There were a few rough crosses of no particular interest except their great antiquity. I wandered away and came on to a great slab of stone, thrown across a cleft in the rock and overhanging the cliff. This, I thought, must have served the same purpose as the pole of a latrine. Some way down the cliff and below this slab of rock was a slight ledge, and this was covered with a luxuriant crop of stinging nettles. It was perhaps a hundred feet below me and six hundred from the sea. On many occasions

I have located old rubbish dumps, on exposed coastal sites, by the nettles growing on them. The temptation was great. Rubbish shot from the monastery had lodged on that ledge and there might be something interesting in it. I had done a great deal of cliff climbing in the last twelve years and could see that it was perfectly feasible to climb down to the ledge. I always carried an old sheath knife in case I wanted to dig a small hole to examine something.

The actual climb down was in shadow for the first fifty feet or so. Then one had to traverse sideways and downwards to the left into the sunlight. I did not find it difficult. and was not bothered by the height above the sea, nor by the idea of falling into it. But when I was about half-way down and preparing to traverse into the sunlight, I had a remarkable sensation. Somebody, I felt, was wanting to push me off the cliff. 'Nonsense,' I thought, and went on with the business. But ten to fifteen feet further on, the feeling got so strong that I stopped to think about it. 'This is absurd,' I thought. 'It is a lovely day. I am not giddy, or liverish, or anything. There is nothing to prevent my completing the climb.' All the time I was thinking, the unpleasant sensation was increasing. In the end cowardice won. I was faced with something I did not understand and could not shake off. I climbed carefully back with the same feeling clinging to me all the time. On the way I picked a metal disc out of a cranny, but it proved to be a modern label off a bale of wool. Feeling very ashamed of myself, I sat in the sun on top of the cliff and thought the matter over.

The only possible explanation I could think of at the time was that the place itself had the wish and the power to discourage a heretic from finding out its secrets. I did not really believe this, for supposing such a power could exist, I did not feel that it would regard me in that light. Heretic, in the strict Roman Catholic sense, I might be, but I have always had considerable sympathy with the old Celtic Church, which had founded the monastery on the island. The Celtic Church seemed to me to have had the right ideas.

With no real solutions in my head, I walked down the short distance to Christ's Saddle, and stood looking out over the sea to the north-west. The grass was nibbled short by animals and the ground was nearly flat. Something made me think of turning round and I was about to do so, when without a sound and with no apparent feeling, I was suddenly flung flat on my face on the grass. There was no gust of wind, no person, no animal, nothing. I was not in the least hurt, but it was an unpleasant surprise.

Thinking it was time to leave an unhealthy locality, I walked to the top of the stone steps and saw, about twenty-five feet below me, W.S.B. climbing up. 'Oh, there you are,' he shouted. 'I have just been having a bet with the lighthouse keepers that you at any rate would not mind spending a night on the island.' Up to that moment, I had not known that there was a lighthouse on the island. However, although I felt rather mean at letting W.S.B. down, I said I would rather go back to dinner in the hotel and we returned to the boat. It was weak of me, I know, but some things seem rather too much of a good thing.

At dinner, I told W.S.B. something of what had happened, which he naturally received with a grin of disbelief. I did not blame him. He then said we must go down to see old so-and-so, whose name I had forgotten, who had been up at Cambridge at the same time that we were and was now running the Transatlantic Telegraph to America.

When he had greeted us, he said, 'You were out on the Skelligs today, weren't you? — everyone in the west always knows what other people are doing — see anything of the ghost?' W.S.B. did not give me away. 'What ghost?' we both asked. The story he told was briefly this: during the previous winter a ship had been lost off the Skelligs. When it was all over, the lighthouse keepers had gone in to their meal and sat down at the table, then the door opened and several pairs of seaboots were heard to tramp through it and vanish into the sleeping quarters. Since that time, till we went out that day, doors had been continually flung open. There were frightful screams and cries resounding throughout the building and other happenings which were not described. Two lighthouse keepers had gone off their heads and had been removed.

The story was comparable to the famous hauntings at Frodis Water in Iceland as told in the Eyrbyggjar Saga. Here is the relevant part of the saga-man's grim description of the worst haunting of all the many in Iceland, as Morris and Magnusson translated it:

17

But in the winter a little before Yule, goodman
Thorod went out to Ness after his stock-fish. There
were six of them together in a ten-oarer, and they were
out there night-long.

The morning that Thorod and his men went out
westaway from Ness, they were all lost under Enni; the
ship and the fish drave ashore there under Enni, but
the corpses were not found. Then when this news was
known at Frodiswater, Kiartan and Thurid bade their
neighbours to the Arvale, and their Yule ale was taken
and used for the Arvale. But the first evening whenas
men were at the feast, and were come to their seats,
in came goodman Thorod and his fellows into the hall,
all of them dripping wet.

This was by no means the end of the story, which became
worse as time went on. I have only quoted the part which so
closely resembles the affair on the Skelligs. We should call the
Arvale feast a wake today. People did not believe in the extinc-
tion of their friends at death and a drinking party was held so
that they should not feel lost and lonely before they became
accustomed to life in the next world. A wake is held for the
entertainment of the dead man as much as for his friends.

My story of the Skelligs has a sequel. A few years after the
Hitler war, I had to give a talk on the BBC about ancient
voyages to America. A few days later, I had a letter from the
owner of the Skelligs, asking me if I had ever thought of visiting
them, as he thought they would interest me. In reply, I told him
the story, much as I have written it here. Not long afterwards, I
heard from him again. He told me he had discussed my story
with three priests and they had produced a theory as follows:
the Skelligs, they thought, had been a pagan sanctuary before
the Christian monks took it for their monastery. The monks had
left and the demoniacal powers of darkness were loose once
more. These powers had wished to get rid of me on account of
my value to the powers of light. Flattering though this theory is
I very much doubt whether it is the correct answer. But I
believe the priests to have been right in one particular. When
Pope Gregory circulated his celebrated instructions in the
eighth century, he said that pagan customs, which were too

deep-rooted to be easily abolished, were to be turned round into Christian ones. In this way, several pagan gods and goddesses became Christian saints. One of these was Lugh, whose name is the Celtic form of Lux, or Lucifer. He was Light, or the Sun. Now Lugh was, by a curious twisting of beliefs, turned into St. Michael, who was also believed to have thrown Lucifer, or Lugh, out of Heaven. It is probable then that St. Michael's name has become attached to the larger Skellig for the very reason that it was once a sanctuary of Lugh.

The happenings on the Skelligs, however, really come under the heading of poltergeist. Much has been written about this subject, for a poltergeist is a real trouble. In past ages it was a malevolent demon. They are still found today all over the world and have been studied with considerable care. A poltergeist is an invisible force, either without a mind behind it, or a mind so small that its actions appear to be completely irrational. Poltergeists throw material objects about, move considerable weights, produce apports from somewhere else, make noises and even start fires.

The results collected by many observers show that most cases of poltergeist are found in association with some living person who is not quite normal and is often on the verge of becoming adult. This much has been realised for a long time; but many still think that the mind of the individual concerned is linked with that of some sub-human personality. The force used to handle the objects which are thrown about and so on, has only recently been demonstrated scientifically to exist by Professor J.B. Rhine, of Duke University, North Carolina, in his experiments with dice. It is known as psychokinesis. But psychokinesis is only a form of a much more widespread force which is known from de la Warr's experiments as resonance. The most ordinary example of resonance, with which many people are familiar, is water-divining. Resonance appears to be akin to electro-magnetics, but is not able to work without the linkage of a human mechanism to it. It may be that resonance is human or living electro-magnetism. At any rate I have taught myself to be quite efficient at water-divining and have also been able to show that it is possible to study fields of force with nothing more elaborate than a hazel fork in my hand. The study of all this is in its infancy and the dead weight of scepticism, from those who were educated before the force was recognised, has to be eliminated before the real origin of a poltergeist is known. It seems clear, however, that it will probably be unnecessary to call in any discarnate spirits to account for the phenomena. These will follow the natural laws of resonance, whatever they may prove to be. Professor Rhine has, however, clearly demonstrated that the mind has an extra-muscular power of doing things. He has also shown by practical experiment that telepathy, which is a kind of wireless communication between two minds, can also be demonstrated to exist. Its existence was well known to thousands before the experiments were made; but it now becomes a respectable subject for professional scientists to study.

Poltergeist phenomena appear to involve both telepathy and pyschokinesis. Objects are moved, and noises are made, by the power of the mind alone. The generally held theory, however, is that a second and more primitive mind is also involved, which gives the orders to the semi-adult, or neurotic, mind of what we may call the operator.

If we take the case of the Skelligs, we can easily see that the shock of the loss of the vessel off the island and the horror felt at the drowning of the crew may have had a damaging effect on the mind of the onlookers. There seems no reason for doubting that the disaster to the boat from Frodis Water and the plague which followed it had the same effect on one of the inmates of that Icelandic Hall. For what it is worth, I think that the poltergeist effects arose from that damaged mind in each case and there is no need for calling in a second and sub-human one. We know experimentally that one sane mind can affect the fall of dice in the manner it requires; Heaven alone knows, as yet, what can be done by the subconscious of a deranged one.

It may not be a great achievement to prove that something exists when all the world knows that it does. But Professor Rhine did something with his dice experiments which must eventually alter the whole complexion of scientific thought. Before long the study of telepathy and psychokinesis will have become commonplace. The work of a few courageous people is breaking through the Victorian crust of science and the taint of superstition is going from the research workers on the so-called supernatural. Innumerable people have seen ghosts; but only a few brave ones have had the courage to study them. If ghosts do not exist, how is it that people see them? The fact is there. It is the explanation of why and what and how that people want to know.

These ghosts may be memory pictures created at some level of the observers' minds. They may be imaginary pictures produced in the same way. They may be entities in their own right. They may be creatures of this world, or of another, or both. These are the points which require study. The question is not whether people see ghosts or not. There is ample evidence that they do so. The records of the Society for Psychical Research are crammed with reports of the seeing, hearing and feeling of ghosts. But what is it that they experience? I am not competent to make any dogmatic reply to these questions. All that I am doing in this book is to present reports of incidents which have come under my own observation and examine them. Where possible I shall treat them as if I were investigating ordinary concrete human mysteries, as little detective exercises so to speak. At the end I shall try to speculate as to what it all means. Those who think my observation was at fault and are convinced that no such things occur, are welcome to their opinions; but they are missing something as surely as if they were colour blind or tone deaf.

I have on several occasions worked with sensitives who were practising psychometry, 'picking up' in their minds images caught like our ghosts in the field of force of some inanimate object like an arrow-head or trinket of some kind or other. Inanimate objects each have their own field of force: a sheet of corrugated iron, for example, is shown by the dowser's rod to have a field of force covering a considerably larger area than itself. It would require much more delicate instruments to determine the field round a letter, or anything of that sort, but the fields are there.

What I suggest happens in the action of psychometry is that tiny fields surrounding the objects act as conductors between the two psyche-fields of the sensitive and the inquirer and that, as in telepathy at long ranges, the current passes back and forth through the Ge-field of the earth. The thoughts are not in the object, but in the psyche-field of the inquirer. But we now come up against a new difficulty, which is best illustrated by turning

21

back again to the subject of ghosts. There is something quite wrong with our conception of time.

We came from Cambridge to live down here at Branscombe in the autumn of 1957. We had not been here for many months when the daughter of the former owner of the place came to see it again. She had not lived here for about thirty-five years. In course of conversation, she remarked to my mother-in-law that she hoped we did not mind living in a house with a ghost. My mother-in-law replied that she was sure we would not mind at all, but what was the ghost like? The women told her that she had never seen it herself, but that her mother had often seen it about forty years ago. It was a little old woman with white hair and a red coat. Others have told us the same thing. A little old woman in a red coat was quite commonly seen here about forty years and more ago.

Now we have never seen this ghost, neither has anyone who has stayed with us, and we have never heard of it being seen since the years between the two wars. Of course it is the sort of house which would be expected to have ghosts in it, for much of it is of the sixteenth century and some earlier still. When the lights are not on, the Tudor hall is dark and anyone might expect something to boo out of a corner at them.

Some time before the visit of the ghost-seeing woman's daughter, we got to know Mrs N, who has been mentioned already in connection with the ghost at Hole Mill. She was evidently lonely and took to dropping in of a winter's evening for tea and a chat. Frequently the first intimation we had that she was in the house was for one or other of us to come into the hall in the dusk and find a little figure, half-seen in the corner, taking off a pair of seaboots and putting on some slippers. To anyone not used to it, the sight was quite enough to make them jump. In cold weather she invariably wore a long cherry-red coat. She had no hat, had a shock of curly, white hair and usually carried a large 'otter-hunter's' thumb-stick. The coincidence is remarkable and I have no doubt that Mrs N was the ghost. More than that, it seems probable that, since you do not know what you look like in given circumstances, Mrs N did not project her own picture forty years out of its correct time. Either my wife or I must have done it.

This is by no means a unique case. There are other very well-

22

attested cases of ghosts of people appearing to others before they actually arrive in the flesh. They have then been greeted with such words as: 'Why, you are the ghost who has been coming here for years.' Our Red Lady is, however, the one furthest ahead of her time who has come to my notice. She is spoken of by many people in the village; but since the idea of time playing tricks is not widely acknowledged, I do not think that anyone else has drawn the conclusion that I have. Perhaps I should add that Mrs N was an adept of the art of magic and had studied it intensely for seven years before she came to live at Hole Mill. She is now dead.

Now these jumps in time are characteristic of many forms of the so-called para- or supra-normal. They occur in psychometry, just as much as when a gypsy tells fortunes. They are of course anathema to scientists, whose experiments require a rigid attention to a normal time-scale. They would get out of the Red Lady difficulty by saying that there must have been two ladies in red coats and neither of them was a ghost. Well, they can believe that if they wish. But their answer is dogma and not science. The business of science is to find things out and not to play at being ostriches.

We had another very remarkable experience with Mrs N, which most people in ordinary circumstances would dismiss as utter nonsense. It did not involve the unverified experience of one person. Three were concerned in it, Mrs N, my wife and myself. All were, in their separate ways, trained observers. Mrs N, besides her magical activities, was an expert at interpreting X-ray pictures. On one occasion, while I was busy on a bit of stone-walling outside the house, Mrs N passed by and stopped to talk with me, thereby causing some anxiety lest my cement should dry hard before I could use it. Her conversations were frequently of long duration, but generally of interest. On this occasion, she had been irritated by someone and told me she proposed to put on some preventive magic to stop them bothering her again. Of course I asked her how she proposed to do it. She told me the method was quite simple, you visualised a pentagram, or pentacle, that is a five-pointed star, constructing this clockwise in your head. You visualised this figure in such a place that it would obstruct the path of the person you wished to prevent from coming to see you. She assured me that she had done it before with complete success and had watched the persons she wished to obstruct walk up to the invisible penta-gram, change their minds about their intention and walk away again. I did not really believe this of course. One does not believe such things easily. However, I was interested.

That night, after my conversation on magic with Mrs N, I did not go to sleep as soon as my wife. Being in a lazy, comfort-able, somnolent mood, I amused myself for a few minutes con-structing imaginary protective pentagrams round our bed. There was no idea in my head except to see if I could draw them correctly. I soon got the trick of it and went to sleep.

A fortnight later my wife woke in the night with the uncom-fortable feeling that there was someone else in the room other than me. She could not see the supposed person; but she did see a faint glow of light near the foot of the bed in the angle between the south and west walls. This faded out and we were apparently left alone.

The succeeding evening Mrs N dropped in for tea. In the course of conversation, she suddenly remarked, 'I hope you won't mind, but I came into your house last night to see if you were all right, and I couldn't get near the bed in your room because of the triangles of fire all round it. Has someone been putting protection on you?' she asked. I told her of my experi-ment. She was told that we did not mind; but would she please not do it again, as she had been felt doing it and it was uncom-fortable.

Now it was quite impossible for Mrs N to get into the house in the ordinary way without burgling it. Not only were all the outside doors locked, but the doors giving on to the foot of our stairway, the only approach to our bedroom, were also locked. If Mrs N came in at all, she did it in thought. But if this is the case, how did my wife feel that she was there and see the light and how did Mrs N's thought know that I had been putting pentagrams round the beds and see them as triangles of fire? This fantastic situation is similar to the fairy stories of rival magicians fencing with invisible weapons. In this case, how-ever, it happens to be true. That is, it is true as far as the account of any observed impressions subsequently remembered can be true.

Can this be fitted into the ideas we have been thinking out

already? To begin with, there is no difficulty about static fields. Springs arise in the banks and hillside close to the house and some of them join to form the streamlet which I have mentioned already in connection with the ghost at Hole Mill. Mrs N's psyche-field could have been linked therefore to our fields by means of the naiad-field, which we know extends down to her former house. We have seen how it appears to be possible for thoughts to be conveyed by means of these fields. In theory then Mrs N, if she had learnt how to do it, could have transferred her psyche-field to our house and back again. In the process, she made contact with my wife's psyche-field and also, although I did not wake up, apparently with mine. Mine had already accidentally put pentagrams in the way of Mrs N's psyche-field and these appeared to that field as real objects. In other words psyche-fields, consisting of bundles of thoughts held together by electricity, find other bundles of thoughts as real to them as our bodies find tables and chairs in ordinary earth life. But these tables and chairs, being matter, also appear to scientists nowadays as nothing more than collections of holes held together by electrical fields.

Whether I have got this right or not, it does appear that even such an apparently impossible story, as I have just told, does not seem to be in the least impossible if the first steps in the theory are correct. One begins to see how magic could work and that, although its real working belongs to the psyche-fields and sixth senses, since these are closely linked with the material bodies of their owners, magic could react on these bodies. If this is the case there is no difference between magic and miracle. All are concerned with unexplored electro-magnetic conditions and, since nobody really knows what electricity is, they are probably just a facet of life itself.

Perhaps this is similar to or the same as what is known as a 'double'. All Buddhists and Hindus believe they have a double. The same story is told by those who study these matters in the West. People are said to be able to leave one body resting or asleep and travel where they will with the other. We have some evidence that this is correct. Anyway, if you see such a double, it is not a ghost. I have once seen what I take to have been a double, but it was not human. The story is worth telling. On Friday 28 October 1966 I was rung up by a woman I did not know, who asked if she might drive down from the home counties and consult me about some matter or other. I agreed to the suggestion, and rather to my surprise an interview was fixed for 11 a.m. on the following Monday. On Saturday my wife's old cat was found to have a broken tooth and poisoned mouth. An appointment was made with the vet at Axminster for 11.30 a.m. also on that Monday morning.

At about five minutes to eleven on the Monday morning my wife started out in the car up the hill at the back of Hole with the cat in his travelling basket. It is about twelve miles that way to Axminster. On the top of the hill she met another car in the lane, bringing the visitor to see me. It arrived here almost exactly at eleven o'clock.

I greeted the visitor, who was being driven by her sister, and brought them both into the hall. This is a real Tudor hall with a Henry VIII doorway, but it is not open to the roof, as someone has put a second floor above it. I put the woman who wanted to see me in the corner of the sofa nearest to the fire, and her sister near her. I myself sat, not in the chair under the window, but in the other so that she would not get the light in her eyes when talking to me.

We had just begun to talk, and the time must have been about seven minutes past eleven, when she said 'Is this the cat you write about in your books?' I looked up and saw what was unmistakably my wife's cat standing with all four feet on the fire stool and apparently smelling the visitor's hand, which was almost touching his nose. 'Yes', I said, 'that is our cat, but he's getting very old now.' In point of fact he was over eighteen. Then I thought no more about the cat, and was involved in a conversation I had to think about. I never saw him go, although I have a feeling he did jump down off the fire stool and walk away to the corner where his drinking bowl was kept. I did not think again about the incident for over a week. It seemed perfectly normal at the time. Presently the visitors left, and afterwards my wife returned having left the cat with the vet to have the tooth out under an anaesthetic. She told me that she had had to sing to it all the way to Axminster to stop it yowling. It was half Siamese.

The cat never got over the anaesthetic and poisoning and in ten days it was dead. We were very distressed for it was a very wise animal and skilled at making its wishes known by telepathy. Still it had had a wonderful life, and like Nimrod was 'a mighty hunter before the Lord', although I rather drew the line when it brought in live adders.

After the cat's death I suddenly remembered the incident with the visitor and realised that it was an impossibility in a three-dimensional world. All the time the cat was standing on the fire stool, it had also been in a basket on the road to Axminster. It was a twelve-mile journey and my wife was only just in time for the appointment with the vet at 11.30 a.m.

I wrote and checked up with the visitor, who confirmed that the conversation had taken place, but said that neither she nor her sister had seen the cat. How the conversation could have taken place unless she had seen it, I do not know!

I cannot explain this happening in terms of ghosts. Neither, since the conversation was confirmed, do I think it was possible for me to have imagined it. The only explanation seems to be that cats do have doubles, and that he had projected his double to his home in preference to being shut up in a basket. If this is the correct answer, then the cat is still alive on another plane. Curiously enough, this explanation has been accepted without hesitation by some Roman Catholic priests. I do not think that in the East it would cause any comment at all. They know that this kind of thing is quite natural.

Actually the cat had a psi potential of 45, as measured by the dowsing pendulum, which would be very high for a human. It had been observed to exercise a kind of radar to learn about happenings 450 yards away on the other side of a stone wall 2ft thick, and it knew where any of its friends were when they were quite out of sight. I think it had really performed this trick with the double on many occasions, for it was frequently found on the far side of shut doors where it seemed impossible for it to have appeared. In fact, for years it was spoken of as a key-hole cat!

These things may all sound very strange and new, but they have been known about since mankind began, and have usually been labelled as some form of magic. Magic can be 'white' or 'black'; that is it can be used for either good or bad purposes. Yet it is all magic. There is no distinction between magic healing, prayer, or blessing, and destructive magic, such as cursing, ill-wishing or actual magic killing. The difference is only in the mind of the practitioner. Christ's disciples learnt how to work the most potent white magic and then killed Ananias and Sapphira with it. This was black magic. If anything goes wrong with the operation of black magic, it returns on the head of the magician. It is a well-known trick of sorcerers to make some gift to the person they wish to harm; a link for resonance is established either by gift or confiscation and the sorcerers could, in theory, use it for black magic. Of course it could be used for white magic also, and this is what is now done, using a mechanical projector for the resonance, by those who heal with the 'Box'. Until resonance is studied in much greater detail, it is uncertain how this works, but it seems clear that a link, comparable to some extent with the copper wire in electricity, or the pipe in running water, is in fact established. The object is a link between two minds and not in itself a container of force, beneficent or malevolent.

This seems to me to be clear after some investigation of the faculty known as psychometry. In this 'art' an object is handed to a sensitive by a person who wishes to learn something about it. The practitioner holds the object and from it appears to read descriptions of past events, or rather to see pictures of past events and those of people, alive or dead, formerly connected with the thing. It must be evident to anybody who gives the matter thought, that, if such a form of memory were indeed attached to objects, then, properly interpreted, it could be of very great value in the study of archaeology. De la Warr infers, from his experiments with resonance, that it should be possible to establish facts about extinct animals by using their fossil bones as links. This is perhaps less difficult than with objects that have never been part of a living organism; but the distinction may not be great, for all cells appear to resonate. According to this theory, by mechanical application we should be able to see a 'Carboniferous' swamp by the agency of a lump of coal.

Not being tied to any particular school of thought, I felt at perfect liberty to see what I could learn about the subject of psychometry. I was warned by friends in the world of science that it might be very damaging to my reputation, but, having no interest in my reputation, I took no notice. A sailor who fears to chance his arm is not much use at sea. I was only making the investigation for my own enlightenment and did not feel bound by any particular rules of investigation. Actually I have tested quite a number of sensitives, both professional and amateur. All produced answers of a kind, but those of the professionals were sometimes quite footling. In no case were the practitioners of the slightest use when presented with an object without my being present at the same time. The faculty appears, like the seeing of ghosts, or the feeling of ghouls, to require the conjunction of two or more minds to make it work.

One of my amateur sensitives, E, was extremely good at psychometry. I do not think she had ever tried to do it before, but she was very interested in the whole subject and most co-operative. The first object I gave her to hold was a snuff-box made out of the timbers of the *Royal George,* sunk in 1787. I handed her the lidless box and awaited results with interest and scepticism. I do not believe for a moment she could have known what the object was, and even if the lid had been on it, she would not have had the slightest clue as to what the name meant. She was very lacking in historical information. E took the box in her hand and fondled it for a moment. Then she suddenly went green and apeared about to be violently sick. 'It is frightful,' she gasped, 'the movement is terrible.' I took the thing away from her and asked her to come out into the air. After a short time she recovered and wanted to hold the box again. I thought it very courageous. No one likes to feel seasick.

She took the box once more and this time went into a vivid description of a gun's crew grouped around a gun run up to an open port. She appeared to see the whole scene. Being well versed of pictures of such situations, and being very doubtful about psychometry in general, I thought that she might be getting it all from my own mind. But now I am not so sure. I have on several occasions been seasick for days on end, but it has never seemed to me to be particularly terrible and in any case I should not have had a mental association between a sunken line-of-battle ship and seasickness. I might have had one with the gun's crew and gun, and in fact that is how I interpreted the incident, as something from a picture.

But I began to think that E's reactions to the snuff-box were the real thing and that she was getting memories from some long-dead sailor forced into the field of a part of the ship. Of course I do not know the answer; but if this second interpretation is right, it opens up a most astonishing line of research. You will never get neat historical information by this means, but you may get vivid emotional scenes, which could alter your whole appreciation of a given age. One of the points, which seemed to make the greatest impression on E when holding ancient objects, was the stink of the dwellings. One does not think of this when excavating old sites, but the smell of modern Eskimo houses was more than I could bear and I never went inside one. People in antiquity, except the Greeks and the Romans in the western world, seldom washed. Although the Celts invented soap, they washed their hair with urine.

However, one must be careful, for it is all too easy for the sensitive to pick up merely what is in the mind of the observer rather than from the object itself. On one occasion, one of the children was taken ill. I went upstairs to the nursery to see him at bedtime and, as usual, was made to invent and tell him a story. I told him one, which I placed in the days of the first Elizabeth. There was not much story, but it ended up in a duel between two men in slashed doublets, ruffs and so on, in a panelled hall. I had to draw it on paper. Before I had gone upstairs, I had left the sensitive a piece of a glass vase, which had come out of an Anglo-Saxon grave of somewhere about AD 500. The vase had been what is known to archaeologists as a 'claw glass goblet' or 'beaker'.

When I returned to the drawing-room, where E was still holding the fragment of Anglo-Saxon glass, she launched at once into a description of two Elizabethans fighting a duel in a panelled room. There was a looking glass, with a glass frame, hanging on the wall and the fragment she was holding came from it. The Elizabethan duel had come straight out of my head, while the glass looking-glass was a Venetian one hanging in the drawing-room itself. There had been no looking-glass in the story I had told to the sick child. The whole thing had been built up, like a dream is built up, at some unconscious level in my own mind. Once again we must be cautious, and not deny that psychometry has any value at all. But it seems to me that, when cases are quoted of the wonderful revelations obtained by psychometry about incidents in the lives of people who are now dead, we must remember that both telepathic foresight and hindsight have been proved by experiment to exist.

Let us look again at what is scientifically known and then see whether we can tear a small hole in the screen which separates us from knowledge. From Rhine's experiments it has been shown that the mind can influence the movement of matter. The mind can also see through apparently impenetrable matter and learn what is behind it. It can remember, if that is the right word, thoughts about incidents which have happened in past time, and also those which are to happen in the future. All these faculties have been demonstrated by scientific tests carried out over a long period of years. If we add to this list the use of Abram's Box and the discoveries yielded by De la Warr's experiments, these show that one mind, coupled with a mechanical instrument, can influence the cells of the body of another person at an unlimited distance away, solely through the link of a spot of blood, hair or even spittle. Here are all the ingredients of magic. Magic then includes, if it does not entirely consist of, the use of the force of resonance, which, in its turn, includes dowsing or water-divining.

# Chapter 2

No one ever taught me water divining. I taught myself more than thirty years ago and have done a certain amount of experimenting, both with the rod and with its cousin, the pendulum. Divining is now more widely known as dowsing, which is a term with a wider range, but not a very attractive one. The subject as a whole has been christened 'radiaesthesia', in itself a somewhat confusing term. The old name of divination is as good as any. It is, of course, a kind of magic. But it is obvious to anyone who can dowse that this is a subject which properly belongs to physics. The twig reacts to what appear to be electromagnetic fields of force. You can put down a sheet of corrugated iron on your lawn and plot out the field of force with a hazel twig in just the same way that you can plot the field of force round a bar magnet with iron filings. If this is not science, what is? You can repeat the performance with the sheet of iron day after day if you can be bothered to do so. I have found graves and ditches cut in the chalk rock in Cambridgeshire which were invisible on the surface, and also various metal objects which had been deliberately concealed. So, as far as I am concerned, dowsing is a scientific method of finding things. Those who try to find out how it works are pursuing a serious scientific study. It is those who deny that it can exist who are being dogmatic and superstitious. There is nothing to be afraid of. Measurements can be made and this is vital to orthodoxy.

A dowser has more instruments than one at his command. There are of course such variants of the hazel twig as the watch spring; but the chief alternative is the pendulum. This very

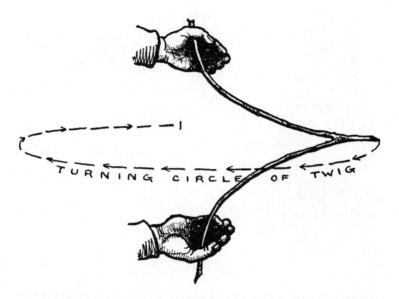

Figure 2. Diagram to show method of holding the divining-rod, and the manner in which it rotates towards the dowser.

unexpected, and at first sight most improbable, device probably originated in a well-known primitive method of determining the sex of an unborn child. It is in fact still in use by Japanese experts who are called in to determine the sex of chickens in eggs. A wedding ring is suspended and swung over the stomach of the pregnant woman. If it retains its backwards and forwards motion the child, if I remember right, should be a boy. If, however, the pendulum motion changes to a circular swing, the child will be a girl. I have seen this operation performed with great hilarity in the Museum of Archaeology and Ethnology at Cambridge. The subjects for the sexer's art varied from a spider to a human skull. As no one present admitted being capable of distinguishing a female spider from a male, the test was considered inconclusive. With the skull, however, there were several persons present who believed themselves to be expert judges and the test was considered a success. It was an obvious male skull and the pendulum said so.

Since the dowser's pendulum is not so widely known as the divining-rod, I will attempt to describe it and also its method

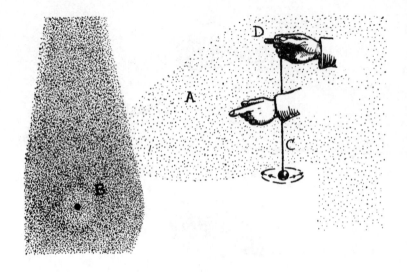

Figure 4. Diagram to illustrate various fields of force, plotted with the hazel twig.
A An old apple tree, 2 feet thick.
B Young apple, 4 inches.
C A walnut, 1 foot.
D A sheet of corrugated iron, 5 feet 6 inches long.
E The psyche field round a woman.
The 'fields' of the trees cover them completely, but are wider round the trunk.

of employment. Many dowsers use a pendulum for various purposes, but few do so in the same manner as we do. I got the idea many years ago from a pamphlet by some French brigadier whose name I have forgotten. He claimed to have been able to find enemy mines in the sea by swinging a pendulum with the correct length of thread on it, and pointing with his other index finger. He obtained the correct length of thread by tuning in over a sample object on the floor and lengthening the pendulum cord until it gyrated. Presumably he found the mines by tuning in over a piece of iron to obtain what is known as the 'rate' for iron.

The pendulum itself is a small ball of wood, or some similar substance, suspended from a length of thread. The ball may be an inch or rather more in diameter, but it must not be too heavy to hold easily. The length of thread, perhaps two yards of it, is wound round a short wooden rod of about the thickness of a pencil. The ball hangs free, on the thread, from the rod. The rod with the thread wound on it is held between the thumb and forefinger of the dowser's right hand, with the finger so placed that, when he rotates the rod to unwind the thread, the finger will act as a brake, or stop. He must be able to control the length of the thread between the ball and his finger exactly.

When the dowser wishes to look for a particular substance, he places a sample of this material on the ground at his feet, having first decided that the spot he has chosen is free from nails or other foreign bodies. Then he slowly unwinds the thread by rotating the rod between his finger and thumb. At the same time he keeps the ball swinging on its length of thread in a backwards and forwards motion. When the ball has slowly descended, perhaps eighteen inches, the pendulum motion will change into a circular swing. At this point the unwinding of the thread is instantly checked. The length of thread for this particular ball will now be a constant for that type of material. This 'rate' can be shown to be different for different substances, but always a constant for each with the same operator.

Now that the dowser has established the rate for what he wishes to find, he proceeds to search for it. With his left hand and standing upright at a fixed spot, he uses his forefinger as a pointer and moves it, with his arm extended, in all directions towards the surface of the ground. He does not move from his stance or crawl about: he just points. The ball meanwhile is set swinging on its pendulum motion. As the finger moves, it may happen that the substance which the dowser is looking for will come in line with it. If this happens, the pendulum motion of the ball changes into a circular swing. The dowser has found what he was looking for and his left forefinger indicates where it lies concealed. Improbable though it may seem, this apparently strange operation does work. The dowser is using a primitive scientific instrument; one might describe it almost as a kind of radar, and this description may well be correct.

Years ago I experimented with this kind of pendulum and was able to locate silver coins hidden without my knowledge under one of a series of caps or books placed on a tiled floor.

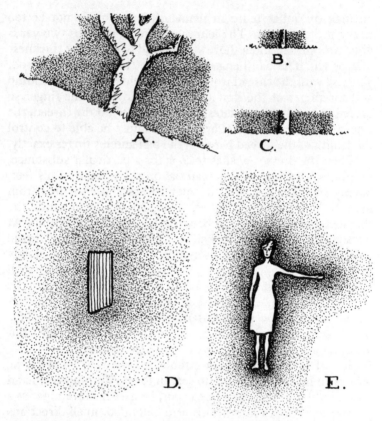

Figure 3. Diagram to show method of dowsing with a pendulum.

A  The dowser's personal psyche-field extended by the projection of his left forefinger.

B  The static field of the object sought. When A meets B, the pendulum (C) will change its motion from a the simple oscillation indicated by the arrows to a circular swing shown in broken line.

D  The rod on which the length of the pendulum's cord is controlled between the right thumb and forefinger.

There is reason for thinking that the fields about small objects are conical, or biconical, extending upwards for about 50 feet.

Except on a windless day, a more complicated instrument is needed out of doors, because the ball blows about in the wind. A heavier ball would be inconvenient to hold from the fingers.

Of course I do not believe in any of these things without convincing evidence. I was brought up and trained as a scientist

36

and still retain an attitude towards them which is, I hope, more scientific than one of blank incredulity. If then I find that a hazel twig turns over in my hands with such force that it breaks when I attempt to prevent it doing so, I look round for explanations other than the one that it does this as a supernatural indication of the presence of water. In practice I have found it will do this with other things than water and have come to the conclusion that the problem is one of electro-magnetic forces, about which I know all too little.

It occurred to me that the courtyard of Hole house was an admirable place in which to carry out some simple experiments. One side of it is apparently of fourteenth-century date and two of the others certainly of mid-sixteenth century. Surely objects must have been lost in it from time to time. Coins were the obvious things to have been dropped. I had already recovered specimens of the reigns of Edward I, III and IV from a rubbish tip nearby. So I tuned in my new pendulum in the stone-flagged hall, where it should have been unaffected by outside influences. I put a silver salver on the flags and obtained a length of twenty-two inches as the right length for the registration of silver. Then I went into the court and slowly began to survey it with the pendulum swinging and my left finger pointing. Before long I had located two spots and fixed them with cross-bearings. I then swung the pendulum directly above them. Each gave the reaction for silver by changing the oscillation into a circular swing. If there was anything in this pendulum dowsing therefore, these two points hid silver objects below the surface of the grass. It would be enough to satisfy me that the thing worked.

I went off and got my spade and digging tools and sunk a hole at the first place located. I took off the turf over a hole two feet square and tested the pit as I sunk it at every three inches. Right under the turf was a large piece of seventeenth-century pottery. Six inches lower down I found a piece of Rhineland *stoneware* of the same century and put it on one side, where it accidentally became covered with spoil. Then I tested again. The pendulum did not take up the circular swing as it had done before. Theoretically I must have dug out a piece of silver and it must be in the spoil heap. I tried the pendulum over the spoil heap and it went into its circular swing. I carefully went through

37

the spoil with my trowel — it was too sticky to put through the sieve. I found nothing. I did not think I could have missed a small coin; but I tried again and moved the heap backwards and forwards several times. I went deeper into the hole and found nothing but a few bones and chips of slate. Feeling that the pendulum was a fraud and that I was wasting time and energy, I started to fill the hole back and, in doing so, paused at intervals to test the heap. Always the pendulum went into its circular swing. The object was still in it, but I could not see it. At last little was left. I tried the filled-in pit with no result. I was just finishing the filling-in when I uncovered the piece of stoneware pottery. Something made me try the pendulum over it. To my great surprise it at once went into a violent circular movement. I had found the object, which was utterly unlike what I had expected. I muttered to myself terms which, in spite of the modern trend in literature, I hesitate to put in this book, filled the hole in tidily, and went indoors to think it over.

I am no chemist and, as far as I knew, stoneware was glazed by throwing salt into the kilns. It was not, I thought, 'lead glaze'. Of course old lead contains a quantity of silver. However, I tried the pendulum over a lump of lead. It gave the same reaction as for silver. Then, having found large quantities of stoneware in the rubbish dump previously, I tried samples of that (Figure 6). Always the pendulum reacted as for silver. I tried local medieval glazed pottery. There was no reaction. I tried modern pottery. There was none. In fact, although I made many attempts, no pottery but the imported German stoneware of the sixteenth to eighteenth centuries had any positive reaction.

I returned to the second spot in the courtyard and swung the pendulum again. Yes, the object was still there. Although I still hoped it might be a silver coin, I felt pretty certain that it would be a potsherd. I dug a hole fifteen inches square and repeated the performance I had gone through in the first hole. Six inches deep the reaction in the hole ceased and the pendulum showed that the object had been transferred to the spoil heap. But, although I had dug with great care, I had seen nothing. I worked through the spoil heap methodically. There was no potsherd. Then I found the object. It looked just like a small flint nodule, but it was much too heavy. It was a small rod of

Figure 5. The corner of the court at Hole where the experiments were done with the pendulum. Everything was found beneath the grass in the angle between the two windows. No walls are straight at Hole, and no windows put in level.

old lead 1½ inches long and ½ inch thick. I should imagine that it was a bit cut off to be used for fixing the bars of Tudor windows into their stone sockets. In any case it was certain to have contained a small quantity of silver.

Figure 6. A, B and C objects found beneath the turf with the pendulum at Hole.
A Fragment of German stoneware (complete pot of same ware, D, shown for general interest).
B Lump of lead.
C Brass tag from a lace.
All probably of sixteenth- to eighteenth- century date.

After this I changed over to copper. Tuning in over a tinned copper pot, I found that while the length of cord for silver or lead on this pendulum was 22 inches, for copper, brass or tin it was 30·5 inches. I went into the court and repeated the previous operation. Within two or three minutes a reaction for copper was shown by the pendulum. I fixed the spot by cross-bearings and tried the thing directly above it. Having fixed it as closely as possible, I put in a peg. The same process as before was carried out. The object remained in the hole, 15 inches by 12 inches, until I actually saw it in the ground 9 inches below the surface. It was a tiny copper, or brass, tube just over an inch long, which had been on the end of a lace, probably from a woman's dress.

I must say I found the whole performance quite ridiculous. It was too easy. The pendulum was absurdly accurate. The field of force round each object may be small, for it can be pin-pointed underground within six inches; but the human field must be widely extensible, for I had located the three objects at a distance of two or three yards. You had only to take the pendulum to the place you wanted to search, adjust the length of the cord for the metal you wished to find, swing the ball and point with the left hand. When the back and forth motion changed to a circular swing, you had located your quarry and apparently, if you kept your instrument going at intervals, you were bound to find the object. It could not dodge away like a submarine from an asdic. Once you had it in your focus, you had it. But, and this is the point which is vital to the under-standing of all these unusual phenomena, only a human field can make the thing work. The human field can only be elim-inated by making use of elaborate electrical equipment.

Naturally I did not end my tests at this point. The next two were on the 'silver' rating. From the first contact I obtained another piece of stoneware, and from the second another lump of lead.

Then, although I had little hope of finding anything, except perhaps a fragment of ornamental china, I tried gold. To my incredulity there was a reaction quite soon. I dug it up as before, having pin-pointed it within six inches, or less. After all the difficulties which had happened on other occasions, I finally located the object from which the reaction was obtained. It seems scarcely credible, but this object was the larva or cater-pillar of a carnivorous beetle. Although it is a long time since I took any interest in beetles, I am pretty certain it would have turned into one of the *Geodephaga*, probably *Harpalus*.

This was again quite as surprising as finding that German stoneware gave the same reaction as silver. My first thought was that there is gold in minute traces in the blood. But then I remembered the traditional method of finding the sex of unborn children and chickens with a wedding ring. Could I have stumbled on the 'rate' for femininity? I think this is the answer. My wife at once sent the pendulum into a circular swing when I tried the instrument over her. Our cat looked up sourly at it when I swung it over him and it retained its back and forth oscillation. My wife tried it over me with the same result. In fact it seems reasonable to assume that the rate for femininity is the same as that for gold. One imagines that it is not exactly the same, but more accurate instruments than a pendulum are needed. We can proceed as if it were the same.

We can soon, in fact, produce a little table of rates for one pendulum, operated by one man (Table 1).

Table 1

| Length of cord | Responding to this rate |
| --- | --- |
| 22 in. | Silver, lead, German stoneware |
| 26·5 in. | Water |
| 29 in. | Gold, femininity |
| 30·5 in. | Copper, brass, etc. |
| 32 in. | Iron |

When my wife operates the same pendulum, sometimes the rates appear to be less, namely 20 inches for silver and 27 inches for gold. In fact the length of the cord may vary from person to person. It is clear also that the rates which we appear to have established bear no relation to those given in the International Table of Atomic Weights, which are shown in Table 2.

Table 2

| Lead 207·1 | Gold 197·2 |
| --- | --- |
| Silver 107·88 | Copper 63·57 |
| Iron 55·85 | |

It is not difficult to add other rates to our table. Wood and vegetable growth rates at 20 and stone or concrete at 13. All this looks very much as if we can establish a reliable table of rates for all substances. It does not, however, tell us what is happening. The rates may vary from person to person, although in the same order and not from pendulum to pendulum. It seems highly probable that our rates are those of resonance between one field and another, whatever resonance may mean.

With a little more experimenting our table now reads as in Table 3.

Table 3

| Length of cord | Responding to this rate |
| --- | --- |
| 13 in. | Slate and concrete |
| 14 in. | Glass |
| 20 in. | Vegetable growth, bread, potatoes |
| 22 in. | Silver, lead, German stoneware |
| 26·5 in. | Running water |
| 29 in. | Gold, femininity |
| 30·5 in. | Copper and brass |
| 32 in. | Iron |

Of course there is nothing very accurate about all this. I am just exploring something I do not know anything about. No one could have guessed that the ball would tell this story. It has found things for us hidden from sight beneath the turf and it has told us something which we know from other evidence must be correct. After a short and elementary series of experiments, which would horrify a serious student by the casual manner in which they were conducted, I produced Table 4.

Table 4

| Length of cord | Responding to this rate |
| --- | --- |
| 7 in. | Sulphur |
| 10 in. | Graphite |
| 12 in. | Carbon |
| 13 in. | Slate, concrete |
| 14–15·5 in. | Glass, medieval glaze, Chinese and modern porcelain, quartzite, flint |
| 20 in. | All animals (men, women, cats, etc.), plants, wood, rubber, coal, paper, bread, potatoes |
| 22 in. | Silver, lead, salt, sixteenth century German stoneware |
| 23·5 in. | Vegetable oil, amber |
| 24 in. | Male principle, diamond |

Table 4 contd.

| Length of cord | Responding to this rate |
| --- | --- |
| 25·5 in. | Alcohol (wines and spirits) |
| 26·5 in. | Running water |
| 29 in. | Female principle, gold |
| 30·5 in. | Copper, brass and perhaps tin |
| 32 in. | Iron |

Finding the rate for salt explained the puzzle of the German stoneware, because salt was thrown into the kilns to glaze it. It is probable that silver, lead and sodium all have approximately the same rate. Salt is sodium chloride.

From this I proceeded to try simple analysis. I do not for a moment suppose that this is very accurate; but I do know that it conforms to the scientific theory that experiments can be repeated. The first object I tried was a silver snuff-box full of snuff. It was more or less airtight. This gave me what I regard as a positive reaction, namely a circular swing. I found this at 20 inches and 22 inches with a negative oscillation in between. I had thus obtained the right reaction for vegetable material (snuff, tobacco) and for silver.

The second object was a stoppered bottle of Australian Burgundy, without its lead cap. Here I obtained positive reactions at 14, 20, 25·5, and 32 inches. From our table we can see that these should indicate glass, vegetable material, alcohol and iron. As I make my wife drink this stuff for her health because of its supposed iron content, I thought this fair enough.

The third object was a little model of the barque *Passat* in an old Irish whiskey bottle. I had made, and put the model in the bottle, in that ship in 1934, undergoing considerable indignities at the time from a number of Finnish apprentices who breathed down my neck and swore it would not go in. Here the pendulum gave rates of 14, 20, 22 and 23·5 inches. These are glass, wood from the cork and model ship, oil from paint and putty and the lead, an oxide, from either paint, putty, or both.

These three experiments were enough to show me that I was

44

on the right lines. They were experiments of a simple nature and can be repeated again and again. If anyone should complain that I knew what was in the counters and influenced the swing of the pendulum wittingly or unwittingly, the answer is that I could not possibly have known what I might find beneath the turf in the courtyard. This objection is quite without value. However, to make sure, there was an obvious test which could be applied. This was to analyse a given area of the courtyard, beneath undisturbed turf, and then dig it up to see whether the pendulum was telling the truth.

Therefore I went out into the court again, marked out an arbitrary square 18 inches by 18 inches and proceeded to analyse it. There were strong reactions at 13, 14, 15½ and 32 inches and weak ones at 22, 29 and 30·5 inches. According to the table already worked out, I ought to find slate or concrete; glass; glazed pottery or china and iron. I ought to be able to locate also traces of silver, lead or German stoneware; copper, brass or perhaps tin; and either gold or something female. There was an unexpected quantity of broken slate (13) beneath the turf; at the strongest point of reaction to glass (14) was the stopper of a large bottle, there were also two fragments of window glass; there were five small fragments of china, two of medieval glazed pottery and two of seventeenth-century glaze (15½); and then a three-inch wire nail (32), a small 'bloom' of iron, a small nail and a flake of rust. Thus all the strong reactions were abundantly represented in this small hole. The silver or lead reactor was a tiny screwed-up ball of silver paper (lead, 22); the gold or female (29) a small and very lively earthworm (so worms, although hermaphrodite, sometimes give the female reaction). But the faint copper, brass or tin reaction caused a lot of trouble. I ran it to earth in the end as a very heavy two-inch lump of flint. This is clearly coated with an ore, but not copper; I suspect that it is tin — ordinary flint reacts to a 14-inch rate. In any case the specimen still reacts to the 30·5-inch rate.

Although I deliberately avoided the 20-inch rate, because the ground was covered with grass, I had found everything that the pendulum had indicated and this process could be repeated as long as turf remained undisturbed in the court. I feel completely justified in my contention that we are dealing with a scientific subject. The human apparatus, with a very simple indicator, can locate hidden things and decide what they are made of. I expect this has frequently been demonstrated and conveniently ignored by those who cannot see how it could work; but I have deliberately refrained from reading about the subject before making these recent experiments, because I like to see things for myself and to form my own judgement on the observations.

Another point remained to be investigated. Would the pendulum react to objects beyond really solid obstructions? Well, it will pick out silver objects invisible on the far side of a stone wall two feet thick. In other words, these fields surrounding objects pass through solid materials. We begin to see how ghosts can pass through walls. If ghosts are thought images contained in static fields, then the material obstruction of a wall would have no hindering effect on their passage. Neither has a wall any obstructing effect on television pictures. What we now think of as 'waves' pass through the enormous gaps in matter, through empty space, without hindrance. The waves of our fields evidently do the same.

Now I was not investigating the dowser's art as a possible means of attaining wealth by finding hidden treasure. An ordinary mine-detector would be better for the purpose. I have been writing this description in order to draw attention to two important points. The first is that each substance obviously has an electro-magnetic field of force, which is discernible with a pendulum with the correct length of swing. This length can be measured accurately. If the balls and pendulums were standardised, a complete table of rates could be worked out, which would always be constant. It would be as reliable as a table of boiling points of liquids, or any table of that kind. The second point is that it will not work by itself. It needs the human body, or rather the human electro-magnetic field, to make it work. This supplies the current and turns it into a machine. I do not know whether it would work for everybody, or whether it is subject to the same variations as the divining-rod; but, as far as I have seen, anybody can do it. It may be that each person might have to work out his own table of rates according to the potential of his field, in the same way that each person according to the quality of his eyesight has to vary the focus of the eyepieces of his binoculars. But for a given person, a given table is constant or appears to be so.

Now this alone surely lifts the subject of dowsing out of the world of magic, straight into the realm of physics. It may be magic; but if so, this kind of magic is also part of science. There is no trace of superstition about it. It is 'honest to God' experimental science and probably as important in its way as any atom-splitting that was ever done. For it shows that there are completely unknown possibilities in the human make-up. A person can locate hidden objects without using any of the five senses. The dowser does not see, hear, smell, feel, or taste the hidden object. He finds it by some other means. He has, in fact, a sixth sense. Mankind has always maintained that some people have a sixth sense, and why not? There evidently is one.

Some water diviners can find water without a divining-rod. Their hands tingle. So did I tingle when I met the Ladram ghoul. It is a passing of a current of some kind. And since your current is being used when you experience the emotions of the ghoul, you feel with it, horribly cold, like you feel before a heavy gale. But in my dowsing my rough hazel ball has told me so far all I want to know. I have made at least two dozen of them for friends and so far everybody has been able to get some results from them. But perhaps it should be noted that young people are better at dowsing than their elders. They either have more current to spare, or are less constricted by their thoughts.

Dowsing for objects is sometimes very useful too. On 2 August 1962, we had a good example of this. My wife wears a gold signet ring which belonged to her great-great-uncle, the Cambridge theologian, Dr. H.B.L. Swete. The ring is always known as 'Uncle'. On this particular morning, my wife found something bad in the larder, the cat's breakfast no doubt. She took it out in a hurry and flung it up the bank at the back of the house, where the gull which spends much of its time on the roof would find it. Away, with the piece of rotten rabbit, flew Uncle. She called to me in considerable distress, 'I've really lost Uncle this time.' And so, to all obvious reasoning, she had. The bank, into which the back of the house is cut, slopes up at about 45 degrees. It is covered with tussocks of grass, brambles and stinging nettles, which had been cut about two months before. They were all about a foot high. I climbed up through a bed of nettles and stood on the steep slope above her head, while she indicated where she thought Uncle might have gone. I found the lump of rabbit, but could not see the slightest hope of finding Uncle without stripping and searching the whole slope. I sent her for the pendulum. We tuned it in for the rate of gold, and in less than five minutes had located and found the ring. We are getting so used to the accuracy of this instrument that it hardly seems remarkable at all.

The twig, or the pendulum, has no magic power. It is simply an indicator, like the needle of a meter, or perhaps like the float of the fisherman sitting frozen on the banks of the Cam on a cold March day. I am sorry if I look like being a spoilsport and for removing some of the gilt and mystery from magic. But then I believe all the gilt can be removed from magic which will then remain as solid scientific fact. I think we have reached the stage in learning when it is possible to do this, if anybody can be bothered to try. I believe too that all the mystery can be removed from ghosts and ghouls and that their formation will be accounted for by simple scientific laws, acceptable to both boffin and ordinary man alike. I do not say that we will get very far in this book; but do hope that by the time it is finished, we will have got far enough with the study to be able to foresee what may be expected if it is taken further.

Curiosity, of course, would not let us leave the pendulum at this stage. What are these fields which are detected by using it? As I think I have said already, I am deliberately avoiding looking for, and reading, publications on this subject, so that I can be quite free to observe facts, uncoloured by other people's views.

Well then, the first thing to determine is the shape of the fields. Since we are living in an age in which everybody talks about rays of this and that, I rather naïvely supposed that each small object was at the centre of a sphere, from which rays of something radiated in all directions. I visualised a sort of cosmic sea-urchin. I also thought that there must be some relationship between the length of the rays and the length of the cord of the pendulum. A few simple experiments showed that the second idea was perfectly correct. The pendulum rate for lead is 22 inches for me, for gold 29 inches, for copper 30·5 inches and for iron 32 inches. These measurements are those of the radii of circular fields at ground level, if the object is resting on this. In other words, if you put a piece of brass or copper on the floor and measure its surrounding field at that level the result will be a circle 61 inches in diameter. It does not matter whether the object is a tiny brass pin or a heavy ash-tray; the circle will be the same size.

However, if you try to find the top of the supposed hemisphere above the object, it is not there. Even if you climb on a chair, you still cannot reach it. In fact you cannot do so without a fireman's ladder and perhaps you cannot do so then.

I put a brass ash-tray on the floor of the hall and went upstairs. I found it perfectly easy there to pick up the field of the object on the ground below. I plotted the circle this field gave at floor level. Its limits could be judged to within about an inch. Instead of being 61 inches across as it was on the ground, the circle was now one of 48-inch diameter. I was clearly dealing with a cone and not a sphere. All our measurements are very rough, but this cone must be about 50 feet high. What is more, by putting the ash-tray upstairs and working the pendulum on the ground floor, one finds that there is a downward pointing cone as well as one pointing upwards. The two cones are joined base to base and the field as a whole is at right angles to the surface of the earth. A perfectly fantastic 'science fiction' world is beginning to emerge from our simple study. The whole surface must be covered with invisible and interlocking cones. Since such things as streams and waterpipes also have their fields, these must be high walls, curving or straight, which pass through the mass of cones.

I am not going to fossick about in this invisible world at the moment. The idea is quite enough to make one giddy. The thing which surprises me is that it is so ridiculously easy to find this world and no one seems to bother to examine it.

Of course to me, as an archaeologist, its implications are enormous. You have only to work your pendulum correctly to be able to find any brooch, pin or coin that was ever buried in the ground. I may be rather better at it than some, but I have yet to test a person who cannot work a pendulum at all. There is no possible excuse for leaving important objects behind on the spoil heaps of excavations, or for not going deep enough to find such things beneath your dig. You should be able to tell what kind of ornaments are buried with a skeleton before you unearth it and find the graves themselves by the fields of the objects hidden in them.

The question of finding the depth of an object in the ground is also important to the archaeologist. The pendulum can do this; but it is probably more trouble than it is worth to attempt it in detail. However, it is absolutely easy to work out a series of tables which give the answer for any particular substance. The rate, which is the same as the radius of the circle at the base of each cone, is known. By plotting the circle formed by the cone at a given height above the object, one can draw a simple figure and measure the reduction in radius of the circle formed by the horizontal section of the cone at any height. To take two examples (Table 5).

Table 5

| Metal | Radius | Depth | Reduction |
|-------|--------|-------|-----------|
| Copper | 30·5 in. | surface | 0 |
| | 29·5 in. | 2 ft. | 1 in. |
| | 28 in. | 4 ft. | 2½ in. |
| | 25 in. | 6 ft. | 3½ in. |
| | 25 in. | 8 ft. | 5½ in. |
| Lead | 22 in. | surface | 0 |
| | 20·5 in. | 2 ft. | 1½ in. |
| | 19 in. | 4 ft. | 3 in. |
| | 17·5 in. | 6 ft. | 4½ in. |
| | 15·5 in. | 8 ft. | 6½ in. |

Of course it is easier to measure the full diameter of the circle, which shows the reduction more clearly. When a copper object is 4 feet deep in the earth, the diameter of its circular field on the surface is no longer 5 feet 1 inch but only 4 feet 2 inches. This is quite appreciable. A very short examination will show whether an object is deep in the ground or not.

There are other interesting points to be noted in this study. For instance there are various substances which completely intercept the link between the operator and the conic field of the object. As far as I have progressed, it seems that these are mostly metals. But one must understand that every element in a compound appears to have its own rate and cone. Thus calcium carbonate, the constituent of a snail shell, has two rates and probably three. There are calcium 22, carbon 12 and presumably oxygen also. But calcium is an interruptor. So are lead, sodium, potassium and magnesium. So also is rubber. If any of the salts of these metals are placed against something whose rate you have on the pendulum, the reaction stops instantly. Remove the interruptor and the circular swing starts once again. You can see this by tuning-in over some objects, while holding a piece of lead in the hand not holding the pendulum. Tune in until the circular swing is obtained and then pass the piece of lead over into the other hand. The circular swing stops dead and a back and forth oscillation takes its place. Change the lead over again to the other hand and the circular swing will begin once more. Why this should happen I have as yet no clue. The cones of force are there all the time. They are just prevented from being appreciated by your sixth sense.

Another phenomenon is even more unexpected. By placing an object on the ground floor and plotting the circle where the cone of force cuts the floor above and repeating this experiment several times in the course of a day, it is easily shown that the cones are not rigid. The apex of a cone of lead swings round a circle of at least a foot. At first I thought this must be the well-known phenomenon observed when flowers follow the sun, but this is not the answer. Cones appear to swing ahead of the movement of the moon. This needs much more investigation, but is not difficult to watch. I have neither the time nor the patience to spend years just measuring things in the hope of producing proofs through statistics. I work by simple reasoning from data, which I have observed myself, and cut out all elaboration derived from other sciences which, although it may look learned to include it, simply clutters up the reasoning. We may use the conclusions from other studies and yet avoid their technicalities. It is open to anyone to find fault with my reasoning; but it is not so easy for them to laugh off the data on which the reasoning is based.

The cones are certainly very high and I have not as yet been able to reach the apex of even the ones with the smallest radius. That for sulphur is only seven inches, but I cannot find the apex of its cone. It seems to me that each cone may in reality be drawn out into a single thin ray. If so the ascending ray probably passes out into space, while the descending one extends to

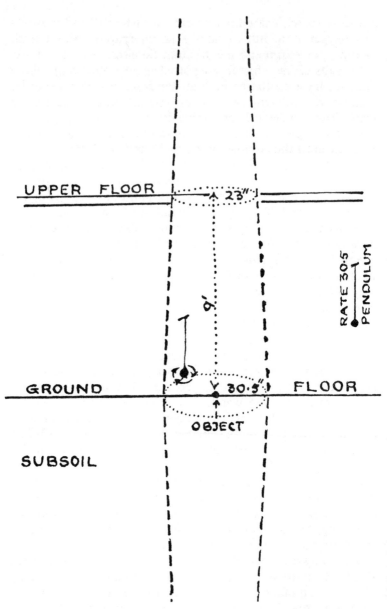

Figure 7. Simple diagram to show ascertainable portion of the double cone of copper and the relationship between its radius and the rate for the pendulum.

the magnetic centre of the earth. I suspect that we are really dealing with something in the study of Harmonics and that these things resemble the figures formed by plucking taut strings, except that the vibration of a taut string only takes place in one plane, whereas our fields vibrate in all directions. Should there be any sense in my suggestion, one can appreciate two things. The first is that the ascending rays could perhaps come in temporary contact with the fields of the sun, or moon, and secondly they might form paths by which the force of gravitation could travel.

There is another possibility. Since you can with a single pendulum find only one point on the surface of a cone at any one time, there is no means of telling whether the whole cone is always there, or whether it only exists in one plane at one moment. The contact between your psyche-field and the field of the object might be similar to the plucking of the taut string and the conical appearance might be due to a succession of contacts round the perimeter. In other words the apparent cone may be an illusion and all that is really there be a single ray of indefinite extent, agitated into conical form by a series of shock contacts. The way to test this is to have several operators approaching a given object at the same time and each oscillating a pendulum calibrated to their own rate for that substance. We have found by using two pendulums and two operators that the cones appear always in position. From whatever direction they are approached, the result is the same.

As far as this investigation is concerned, it is not of great importance what form the field of the object takes. The important point is that one's own field can discriminate between the infinite and interlocking fields of a variety of substances. It can without hesitation pick out the ascending field of a buried pin, or bead. This is something which none of our five senses can do unaided by elaborate mechanical contrivances. It is what is popularly known as magic; but television is in just the same category. The fields of objects may be cones, or they may be rays of considerable complexity; but, invisible and intangible as they are, we can make contact with them by employing our sixth sense and using a pendulum as an indicator.

Since we have our own fields, composed of a considerable collection of ascending and descending cones, or rays, it seems

53

probable that we may be ourselves influenced by magnetic forces from the moon and even from far distant planets and stars. It is possible that the study of astrology is not so improbable as it might appear. I heard the late Professor Joad once proclaim that 'astrology is bunk', but later he became a professing Christian, accepting many dogmas which seem far more improbable. I can accept most of the facts recorded in the Gospels, there appear to be some interpolations, but I cannot reasonably believe much of the dogmatic theory based on the interpretation of the Gospels. Having spent much of my life trying to disentangle the scanty facts about the Dark Ages and struggling to make sense of the contemporary chronicles, I find it very hard to believe that the interpretation of Christ's teaching, produced by the Christian fathers during that epoch, is likely to bear much relation to what He really taught. I do not know whether astrology is bunk or not, but seeing what Joad would accept, I do not think he was in a position to condemn astrology without deeper study. I cannot be bothered to study its intricacies myself, but I begin to see how it might work. The moon, for instance, is known to pull the oceans and make the tides; vegetable growth has been shown scientifically to be affected by the phases of the moon — although it is scoffed at by many, observers see changes in mental patients as the moon waxes and wanes. It presumably exerts a pull on any fluid and so alters pressures in the human circulatory system. If the moon can exert such an influence, the planets might well do so too. I do not know the answers, but feel it wiser not to scoff at an unstudied subject without proper study. Joad was, I feel, very conceited to do so.

The human field is clearly not restricted to its vertical axis. We have seen that it can be extended by using a pointing finger to search for buried objects. With a view to getting some idea of the range over which this searching can be carried out, I have tried extending it by holding a light cane in the left hand. Although it is difficult to extend one's arm for any length of time and hold the pointer steady, it is clear that the ascending cone of a copper pot can be registered at a distance of 150 yards and that of a sheet of corrugated iron at 300 yards. This is getting near that of the ranging procedure of our cat, who can sense a fellow cat 450 yards away and on the other side of a two-foot wall. My wife and I watched him do this one warm autumn evening while out for a walk.

After all, this radar-like proceeding is not very unlike what is known to happen with bats. The bats are believed to use their highly specialised ears to send out a beam whose 'echo' returns from any solid object in its path; but who shall say whether it is the solid object which returns the echo or its electro-magnetic field?

# Chapter 3

Some years ago, we were having afternoon tea in our Cambridge drawing-room with the french windows open on to the garden beyond. We were chatting about this and that when suddenly there was a loud buzz and a large object passed over our heads, settling on a plate at the farther end of the room. I got up and walked over to the plate, which hung on the wall in shadow, to see who our visitor was. To my surprise I saw it was a privet hawk-moth, one of our largest insects. It sat on the plate with its wings closed, not quite in the middle, but nearly so. I went rather too close and disturbed the moth. It buzzed out of the window again and flew down the garden. Then it turned round a rose-bed and came straight in at the window again, landing on exactly the same spot on the plate. It did not hover: it just went straight to the chosen place.

Privet hawk-moths are not rare, but the behaviour of this one seemed very curious. I did not disturb it again, but noted carefully its position with regard to the pattern on the plate. It remained there quietly all evening and did not move when the lights were turned on, but in the morning it was gone. I was much puzzled by this performance. Why had the insect flown twice to a particular plate and chosen a particular spot to rest on?

The plate is an old blue and white one, which has been in the family very many years. It is some 14 inches across and elaborately painted. I had thought it was Chinese, till a friend, who had made a study of such things, told me it was Korean and of early seventeenth-century date. I had not been greatly interested in it till this incident with the moth took place. Then I looked at it carefully.

On the spot where the moth had settled there was a very small dab of paint slightly lighter in colour than the blue of the plate itself. I could not think why this was there, so I took it off its hook to examine the back. The plate is mounted, after the manner of plates which are hung on walls, in a ring of wire. This particular wire ring is wound round in a binding of thin bamboo strips. I had forgotten anything I might have once noticed about the back of the plate, but I now saw that it had a crack, which I believe is called a shake, in it. Someone had feared that the plate might break in half and it had been riveted to make it good. The reason for the dab of paint was that one of the rivet holes had been drilled too far through the plate and the point of the rivet had pierced the glaze on the other side. The paint was put on to hide this mistake. The paint was so well chosen that it needed a close look to distinguish it. However, it was very slightly lighter in shade. This was the spot chosen by the moth. It had been able apparently to choose it from a distance of about 25 yards. Why did a little dab of paint have any attraction for the moth? It could hardly have been a question of colour. It was conceivable of course that the insect might have mistaken the plate for a large blue flower, but it hung in shadow and indoors. This did not seem to be a likely solution. The colour of the dab of paint differed so slightly from that of the rest of the surface that, if the moth had made this mistake it would hardly have returned to exactly the same spot twice.

The attraction then did not appear to be the colour. The plate was in shadow and not shining in the sun, so the attraction was not bright light. I could only think that it was the rivet itself which was the cause.

A number of my friends have been keen on moths. I have not been much interested in them myself and have never collected them, although I know many of the larger species. I have watched friends attracting moths to light-traps at night. I know that collectors put out female specimens of certain moths to attract males from a distance. I have even noticed a female emperor moth in the heather on a moor and, when bending down to look at it, observed a male of the same species fly in, right under my nose, and settle beside its mate. I do not think it

O   1   2   3   4
I N C H E S

Figure 8. Privet hawk-moth resting on a rivet on a seventeenth-century Korean blue and white plate. The two fore-legs are on the rivet.

is known what causes this attraction. Some speak of it as 'radar', others as 'resonance'.

I turned the plate about in my hand looking for a clue. Then a possible answer came into my head. I was really looking at a very simple and primitive electric coil. The rivet was the soft iron core of the coil and the bound wire ring the coil itself. It seemed probable that an infinitesimal current would be generated in this coil and the rivet act as a minute magnet. Purely by chance the force exerted by this coil might be just equal to that exerted by a female hawk-moth to attract a male. For, if my inferences from this incident with the plate are correct, this is what must happen in nature. I feel reasonably certain that this is the correct answer and that the male emperor moth for instance experiences a series of minute electrical tinglings from the electro-magnetic field of the female. To him they might be quite large and obviously attractive (Figure 8). I recall that I have on occasion experienced this myself. It is known as a 'thrill'.

I now seem to begin to understand why the antennae of many male insects differ so greatly from those of the females of the same species and often remind me of the strange forest of television aerials in a town. They apparently answer the same kind of purpose. The vibrating leaves on the antenna of many male moths strike the eye at once. As the moth turns them this way and that, it may happen that these leaves pick up the radiation, if one may call it this, of the female. Then the male has only to fly down the beam to find his mate. Apparently the male always flies to the female.

When I tested the plate on which the hawk-moth had sat, the pendulum immediately responded strongly to the 29-inch female rate. There were also rates of 14 inches for the glaze, 30·5 inches for the cobalt blue of the paint and 32 inches for the iron rivets. Quite by chance then the plate was emitting the female rate, which might be expected to attract a male moth. Unfortunately I was not sufficiently versed in sexing moths to know whether our example was male or female. However it seems most probable that it was a male and very disillusioned by its experience.

But this sex ray is presumably only one of many. It seems certain that the antennae of the *Lamellicornia*, the scarab group of beetles, must be used also for locating dung. How often on a warm summer's evening has one not heard the drone of a big *Geotrupes* going overhead to some distant heap of droppings? Obviously the beetles might have to walk for days without finding any. But they have this 'radar' device, which homes them straight on to their target. I have watched them arrive; sink a little mine shaft; roll up a ball of dung and then manoeuvre it into the hole where it is used as a store of food for the grubs, which hatch out of the eggs laid in it. Here again, as in the case of the plate, it is not like calling to like, but dung calling to beetle, something very different. It is easy to visualise an electro-magnetic attraction over a short distance between male and female of the same species; but not a distant attraction between a beetle and some partially digested grass. Here mystery begins.

One evening, a few years ago, I happened to find a small beetle, which had drowned itself in a drink I had prepared for my wife and left on the windowsill. Now this beetle was named *Bolboceras armiger* and it is very rare; only about a dozen had ever been found in England and one of those had been knocked down by an entomologist with his walking stick. *Bolboceras* is supposed to live in dung, and so I searched for more in one of my fields, the only field for half a mile with cowpats in. I must have turned over and examined hundreds of cowpats, for the field is five acres in extent and my tenant's cows had been in it for some time. I found hundreds of beetles, mostly species of *Aphodius*, including many of *rufipes*, which comes into our bedroom. But there was no *Bolboceras*. I did not think I could have missed it.

Since my experiments in the field had proved abortive, I had to think again. The house faces somewhat east of south and only from this direction could a light from the chink of curtains in our bedroom have been visible. For a fortnight before *Bolboceras* was found, the wind had been fresh and steady from the south-east, straight up the gap from the sea. I wondered whether the beetle could have been blown over from France. I looked at the charts, and found that a beetle taking off from the Cherbourg peninsula, the nearest point, and carried by the then prevailing wind, would have arrived direct at the bedroom window. With the house standing 300 feet up, the light would have been visible a long way out to sea. Even though it was a hundred miles, it seemed highly probable that *Bolboceras* had blown across from France.

Meanwhile I wrote to the Entomology Department of the British Museum at South Kensington, to find out more about our visitor. They told me that *Bolboceras* was not, after all, a dung feeder. All the cowpat turning had been in vain. It seemed that in America at any rate he had a predilection for truffles.

But as he had not been recorded in Devon before and there was considerable uncertainty about his real habits, the Museum was anxious that I should try to find some more specimens. This was easier said than done.

Henri Fabre, in his book *Social Life in the Insect World*, published by Fisher Unwin as long ago as 1911, tells how he found that the beetle then named *Bolboceras gallicus* collected tiny truffles, which at that time were known as *Hydnocystis arenaria*. It seems probable that Fabre's *Bolboceras* is but little removed from our *Bolboceras*, for there is a continual process in zoological museums in which names are changed to suit the fancy of some expert or other. This beetle collected the truffles, then bored a mine shaft about a foot deep, took the truffles down and ate them at the bottom.

Obviously I had to try to find the truffles on which our *Bolboceras* might be expected to feed. I needed, it seemed, a sandy soil; and I had to look out for little bore holes, or mine shafts. I spent a long time out in one of my fields where there are patches of sand, and found nothing. So I decided to look for the truffles by the diviner's art. But did truffles have a rate on the pendulum? The only thing was to experiment with some bits of known truffle.

Truffles are scarce and very expensive. The only thing that Sidmouth could produce in the truffle line was a small tin of Swiss *pâté de foie gras*. On opening this we found that the truffles in it had been minced into tiny black specks, smaller than shot used for shooting snipe. The only thing to do was to lick them out of the *pâté*. When about a dozen of these specks had been licked out, washed and dried, we tested them with the pendulum. It was soon apparent that they had two rates. One of 21 inches appeared to be common to all fungi; but another rate of 17 inches seemed peculiar to truffles. Presumably these rates are those of chemicals found in the composition of fungi; but at this stage I have not attempted to find out what they might be.

The hillside at Hole slopes steeply up to the right of our gate. Along its side stretch fifteen acres of woodland above a lane running half a mile into Branscombe village. This wood though largely bare of undergrowth harbours quite a variety of beasts and birds. Having found the pendulum's rate for truffles, my

61

wife and I went through the gate and standing outside of it, started surveying the wood with the pendulum and a pointing rod. From where we stood, we covered a stretch of perhaps 125 yards. We soon found several reactions to the 17 inch rate, but most of them were on the steepest slopes. We chose the farthest one away, more than a hundred yards, because at that point we knew there was an old sand pit with a fox earth in it. We took the bearing carefully and moved along to where we thought it was until we could take a cross-bearing. This gave us the approximate position of the object inside the wood. It was above the fox's earth and on a comparatively level space.

We found our central point by plotting out our reactions from several directions, and began to move the old beech leaves with a trowel. We took them away and began to scrape off the earth beneath. Perhaps 3 inches from the original surface there was a small spherical object. It was about the size of a large green pea, and the colour of old dried blood. We thought that it must be some kind of truffle. It was obviously a kind of fungus; but we had never seen anything like it before. It was harder than a puff-ball.

Next day I sent our find to the South Kensington Museum and asked if it were the kind of thing on which our *Bolboceras* might feed. They told me it was certainly of the right family and was known as *Sclerogaster compactus*. The letter added: 'If your method of finding the fungus could turn up a few more specimens, the museum would be glad to add them to the collections here. Rather like *Bolboceras*, it is not commonly recorded.'

This began to appear to be a most unusual story. First a rarity appeared in my wife's glucose drink and then, when we went to search for its food by unorthodox means, we found the correct kind of food, but it was also a rarity. Then to our great indignation a hard frost set in. We had to abandon the search till another year.

In September 1965, a year after the first appearance of the beetle in the glucose, I began to investigate once more. There were several reactions to the pendulum as there had been before. Two or three were in the neighbourhood of the place where we had found the truffle. Either I was too early, or there were no truffles this year, for there had been very few mushrooms for which this district is famous. In each case I found the white mycelium threads on which the truffle grows, but no truffle was on them.

There were at least two other places to investigate. Exactly beneath the central point of the circle of one of them was the caterpillar, the larva, of a beetle of the chafer family to which *Bolboceras* belongs. I removed it and put it in a tin with some of its surroundings and then tested the place again. The 17-inch rate of the pendulum had gone. But the tin with the caterpillar in it reacted strongly to the rate. In looking for a truffle, I had found a beetle grub with the truffle's pendulum rate and no truffle. I tried the second spot, but only found a dead larva of the same type.

At this stage I had not the slightest idea whether I had found the grub, or larva, of *Bolboceras*, or not. All that I really knew was that the grub and the truffle reacted to the same pendulum rate of 17 inches. This was in itself remarkable. But I was not bothered particularly whether I had found the right beetle or not. I was thinking more in terms of how any beetle managed to locate its food supply. Fabre in his *Social Life in the Insect World* clearly realised that insects arrived at their desired destination by following some rays which we could not appreciate. He thought that these were unsmellable smells. I did not think he was right, but here was an obvious way of beginning to investigate this problem. If insect and food reacted to the same rate on the pendulum, then we might learn something of considerable interest; that *Bolboceras* and his kindred beetles appear to be linked to their food supply by a ray, or the same pitch of resonance.

But something quite unexpected happened. We found that the 17-inch rate belonged to beech trees and beech nuts as well as truffles and beetles. Perhaps this is not surprising. The dung beetles, we found, have the rate for cowpats on which they feed and in which they go through their life cycle. Why should not *Bolboceras'* larva feed on beech nuts? The mycelium of the truffle grows on rotted beech nuts and the perfect insect, the imago of *Bolboceras*, enjoys the truffles; even the land-snail, *Cyclostoma elegans* reacts to 17 when under beeches. It all makes sense. We had to wait to see if the larva hatched into *Bolboceras*, for if it did we could probably have discovered the whole story. In the event, it did not do so. It was the larva of another beetle of the same family, *Serica brunnea*, whose food is unknown.

Mr E.H.S. van Someren of Cambridge very kindly sent me four offprints by Philip S. Callahan, recently published by the Entomological Society of America. These are highly technical reports and theories dealing with the flight of insects to their food supply and to their mates. As far as I understand it, Callahan has gone a long way beyond Fabre's theory that insects are drawn to their food and to one another by unsmellable smells. These unsmellable smells come into his theories but only at the last stages of the attraction. The main pull (and that over long distances) is comparable to radar. The wing beats of the insect are thought to generate enough heat to produce the electricity necessary to send out a vibration, which contacts the desired object. When the insect has flown down this beam to within a relatively short distance of its objective a second built-in reaction to scent waves brings it dead on target. The technical details of the whole elaborate process are of no importance here; the point is that it seems to be unmistakably the same as that which has been deduced from the study of the behaviour of insects by using the pendulum. The pendulum also appears to demonstrate the existence of a numerological scheme at the back of these vibrations. For the first time we begin to see direct links between so-called magic and orthodox science.

As far as we can observe at present, the distance to which these rays, if that is the right term, can extend is relatively very great. To the cat a distance of 450 yards appears to be nothing. The moth comes in to its mate over unbroken miles of heathery moor. The shearwater flies something like 3,000 miles to its chick. Distance has, unlike mechanical electricity and magnetism, apparently nothing to do with it all. The power of the transmission ought in theory to decrease in relation to the square of the distance. Our transmissions apparently do not conform to this law. But why should the laws which man has worked out for his mechanical products conform to the rules set by nature? We are probably trying to study an attribute of life itself.

This is becoming an extraordinary and most difficult picture.

It seems that our electro-magnetic field and those of animals, can project a ray to an unlimited distance, through a forest of other ascending rays, and will with this single out a particular ray and record it by a gyration of the pendulum. To get any idea of what appears to be happening, we must now go back to the short pendulum for a little.

Take two small objects of the same material and put them a foot or so apart. Do not take a modern penny and an old one, for they are of different metals. Swing the pendulum between them. It will oscillate as long as you can be bothered to hold it there. There is no obstruction. The pendulum swings freely backwards and forwards. Now substitute an object known to be of a different substance for one of the originals and swing the pendulum again. It swings out of the line between the two objects and with me goes into a complete gyration. Presumably the current, which at first flowed freely between the two objects, has now met an obstruction and can no longer pass freely. But is not this the object of the bat's radar? Things are not observed by affinity, but by the turning back of rays, or whatever they may be, against an obstruction. This is how our pendulum works. It records an obstruction to the flow of some kind of current between you and what we must presume to be the earth's field. The flow of the current could presumably continue unchecked if there were no obstructions. But there always are obstructions and you can identify which they are by tuning in to their own particular rate of vibration.

With the short pendulum you can show apparently what opposes the free flow of current between you and the earth's field. Some substances seem to encourage this flow, others oppose it. This is like nothing in man-made electricity or magnetism. It is far more varied and of wider scope. It is not only apparently intensely selective, but it also appears to be free from the limitation of earthly distance. As we go on I hope to show how it is independent of earthly time also.

Naturally it really needs a great number of trained experimenters to work at this subject; but it is quite surprising how much can be learnt in complete simplicity. Rates can be found by inference, which in theory could only be obtained in a laboratory. For instance gases can yield up their rates by a pendulum analysis of several of their compounds. One seldom has an oxygen cylinder available in a country house, nor the apparatus for separating hydrogen. But the pendulum shows that in a compound the rates for the various chemicals composing it do not merge. Each has its own particular cone of a particular size. Therefore, if you wish to find the rate for oxygen, all you have to do is to take a few of its compounds, their names often end in -ate, and see which unknown rate is common to all of them. By this method it is soon shown that the rate for oxygen is $26 \cdot 5$ inches and that for hydrogen 30 inches. Water thus has two rates $26 \cdot 5$ and 30 and you can test this without difficulty. With the divining-rod you can only find water because it forms an obstruction of some sort.

But here we come to another interesting matter. Witches, by which are meant those who cast hostile spells against others and not just devotees of an old religion, are by common belief in the countryside unable to cross running water. So are ghosts for that matter. If there is anything in the belief, then running water is presumably an interrupter.

It is not difficult to test this. Stand on one side of the sink in the kitchen. Elder is thought to be hostile to man, so put a piece of it on the opposite side of the sink and test between yourself and it with the short pendulum. At once the pendulum gyrates. The opposition of the elder to an even flow of current is clear. Now turn on the tap so that water runs between you and the elder and test again. The pendulum does not gyrate. The hostility, if it may be so termed, of the elder does not pass the running water. Presumably this is due to a field of force caused by the friction of the running water against the bottom of the sink, for there is no such interruption with standing water. In any case, if the active malice of magicians can be sent out as a ray between one personal field and another, running water would interrupt it. Of course I do not know whether it really can, but it seems probable that this popular belief originated in some similar kind of experiment. There is something in the idea.

Nature apparently always consists of a balance of opposites. Where there is night there is also day: where there is evil there is also good. Positive and negative, male and female. So it is not surprising to find in our study that it is not one-sided. Although you can tune in on what appears to be a repulsion rate to substances, there are other substances which act, like the running water, as a complete obstacle to this. I call them interrupters, but this is not the right term, for they are really conductors and counteract the repulsion effect which gives us our rates.

The first interrupter I found was lead. Lead has the same, or nearly the same rate as several metals; but while it is an interrupter, silver with the same rate of 22 inches is not. The effect of an interrupter is instant and quite dramatic. If you tune in to a gold object and, while the pendulum is gyrating put a piece of lead beside the gold, the gyration changes in a moment to a back and forth swing. If you hold a piece of lead in your left hand while the pendulum, suspended from your right hand, is gyrating over the piece of gold, and then transfer the lead from the left hand to the right, the gyration stops at once and oscillation begins.

If I have reasoned correctly before, we find the rates of substances because they cause a block in a circulatory system of electric current, which includes your personal field and that of the earth. This may be wrong, but the current must flow between you and something of that sort. The pendulum oscillates because the pressure tries to get through and on that particular rate there is an obstruction, which forces it aside and round through a circle. It makes the water-diviner's rod turn over for the same reason. The rod is in unstable equilibrium with the current passing through its apex and the obstruction of the flow causes it to turn aside and rotate. The force is very great and breaks the rod if you try to hold it tight and prevent its rotation. This is not difficult to understand, perfectly reasonable and within the bounds of science. It is also magic, for divination is one of the magic arts. I think that all magic arts could be interpreted in terms of science, if it could be bothered to study them.

Now our lead somehow neutralises the obstruction. In man-made electricity it is an insulator and prevents current leaking away from copper wires. Why it should do so, I do not know. Presumably it was found long ago that it did so and it may have been used without question ever since. It may be known why it works, but I do not know. An archaeologist cannot be expected to have a wide knowledge of physics. Yet an observed fact in physics is the same as an observed fact in our study. Lead is an insulator in both. In our study the very presence of a lump of lead, within the radius of its pendulum rate prevents current flowing from our electro-magnetic field into that of a piece of gold.

Thinking that since gold has a rate of 29 inches and a conic radius at the base of 29 inches, there might be a zone outside the 22 inch radius of lead in which the gold rate could still be found. I tried this. There is no such zone. The lead neutralises the field of gold at its centre. There are not two double cones of force one inside the other, with a dead lead cone inside and a live gold one outside. The effect of the lead is complete.

However, lead is not by any means the only interrupter. But of metals it appears to be the strongest. Aluminium is another; although it is weak compared with lead and has a different rate.

A friend complained to me that he was unable to find a gold watch when it was hidden from him. In theory the gold case should have reacted to the 29 inch rate. But it did not. This would have seemed insoluble if we had not already learnt of the existence of interrupters. But having got so far, it seemed clear that something was getting in the way. I tried other watches. It made no difference what the case was made of. None of them reacted to the appropriate wave-length. Since their works only appear to contain iron, brass and the bearings for their wheels, it seemed clear that the interrupter was in these bearings. I had always heard of the bearings being spoken of as rubies. One had seen lists of stolen articles: 'A gold watch jewelled in nine holes, and a gold Albert (meaning a watch chain)', and so on. What were the bearings made of? A search revealed that they were either made of indifferent rubies, or a hard form of garnet. Both were complicated compounds containing the metal calcium. I had some garnets, which came from a glen on the south side of the head of Loch Morar. These showed at once to the pendulum that they were interrupters. But they were relatively weak. Still interrupters they were and whether the bearings were of ruby or garnet, this was the reason why my friend could not find his hidden watch with the pendulum.

Iron was frequently put above cottage doors to keep evil away. It was also a common practice to put a single iron nail beside a dead Romano-Briton when he or she was buried.

Presumably this was to prevent the powers of evil from carrying off the spirit of the departed. Anyway it was done. I have found such nails in Roman graves, just as one sometimes finds a bronze coin put in the mouth of a skeleton to pay Charon's fee for taking the spirit of the dead across the Styx. I think I have only twice found the coin out of some 300 cases of Roman inhumation burial. But the single iron nails are quite common. So magnetised iron was widely believed to be protective and the pendulum shows that it is an interrupter. Is magnetism the answer?

I took a bar magnet and put it on the floor. Assuming that what I had been calling sex rates were perhaps in reality simply positive and negative, I tried the bar magnet first with the male and then the female sex rate on the long pendulum. There was no answer to either of them, either directly above the magnet, or at each end where the poles are. So the pendulum did not appear to react to magnetism on either of these rates. It does react to about $20 \cdot 25$ inches, slightly longer than electricity.

I took a piece of rusted blacksmith's iron, which I believed to be the remains of a round file and tested that. It gave an instant and very strong reaction to the male rate and none to the female. Furthermore it had no poles and investigation showed that it was enclosed in the now familar double cone of masculinity. Modern machine-made iron is of course without this attribute. The masculinity is no doubt induced on the fields of the iron objects, which he forges, by the blacksmith himself. In medieval times men believed that diseases kept away from the blacksmith's forge. When we look at other interrupters, neither lead nor rowan wood can be classed as magnetic. In any case the ordinary magnetic field of a bar magnet has never, as far as my slight learning goes, been considered as a double cone, but rather one in a single plane with poles at either end. This is hardly a correct picture. The field must be more like a dumb-bell, but in any case our cones are at right-angles to the ordinary magnetic plane.

Although there are resemblances, it does not in fact seem possible that the pendulum simply reacts to magnetic variations. When I first started to dowse for water with a hazel fork, I thought that it must be reacting to variations in the earth's magnetic field, due to such interruptions in a continuous flow of current as might be caused by a stream of water, or a seam of different rock protruding through a crack in other rocks. Our experiments with the pendulum make this idea seem quite improbable. As far as we know magnetic variation does not exist between two pieces of twig. It seems most improbable that it exists between the cast of the inside of a sea urchin, which died 100 million years ago and a living human being. It seems even less probable that it could indicate sex and thought rates in these long dead fossils. This is nothing really comparable with magnetism as it is understood. Just as you can compare the flow of water through a pipe with the flow of electric current through a wire and yet know that the two flows belong to entirely different subjects; so we must, I believe, assume that the resemblances between our study and magnetism are quite superficial. We are dealing with something distinct and apparently both simpler and more comprehensive.

The same piece of blacksmith's iron gave reactions at 32, 27, 26·5 and 24 inches with the long pendulum, which should be the rates for iron, thought, oxygen in the rust and male rate from the blacksmith. Salt interrupted each of these rates in turn. It also interrupted the rate for lead, 22 inches, and lead interrupted the 22-inch sodium rate in the salt.

Salt appears in old superstition in a curious double manner. It can bind people together and yet it is unlucky to spill it ashore, or mention its name at sea. It seems to have been regarded as very powerful and yet uncertain in the exercise of its power. It had to be guarded carefully or it might get out of hand and do you harm.

I tested some salt with the long pendulum beside a copper object. The field of the copper was neutralised. Salt is an interrupter. Then with the short pendulum, I tested it against myself. Here the result was unexpected. For a moment or two the pendulum oscillated showing affinity and then suddenly this changed to a violent circular swing. It was more strongly obstructive than elder. I tried salt against rowan. The salt interrupted the rowan. It interrupted the male rate for elder on the long pendulum.

This is very remarkable, but the behaviour of graphite, ordinary pencil lead, is more so. Graphite reverses the rate given on the pendulum for sex. It turns female into male and male into female. It will do so for animals and human beings and for the objects, such as pencil drawings, which human beings impress with their sex rates. Further than this, it can over-ride salt as an interrupter.

I have some skulls of whitings which are useful for experiments. Some give male rates, others female. A piece of graphite put down beside a male skull at once changes the rate to female and vice versa. Now, if you take a male skull and put salt beside it, you can get no reaction on the pendulum. Masculinity is blotted out. You do not get anything and no reversal of the sex rate. Even the smallest scrap of pencil lead, however, not only gives a marked reaction, but that reaction is on the female rate and not on the male. Graphite completely overcomes salt as an interrupter, and it goes on to reverse the sex rate also. Of all the strange phenomena we have met, this seems to me to be the oddest. Graphite is not lead; although it is often spoken of as being lead. It seems to be a semi-vegetable fossil material.

We will leave the interrupters for a moment and go on to another facet of this study, which also happens to contain the same problem. My wife was entirely responsible for this and I doubt whether I should ever have thought of it. She remarked, when we were getting a meal, 'Why do you think that some trees are considered unlucky?' On my grunting that I had no idea, she continued: 'Do you think you could find out with the pendulum?' Her question opened an entirely new line of approach and I do not suppose that anyone has followed it. Whoever in these scientific days would ever believe for a moment that a tree could be unlucky? This was some superstitious nonsense, which could not possibly have any foundation in fact. Nevertheless the beliefs are most widespread. I have long grown up past the stage of scoffing at such things.

I started to recall what I could remember of folk-beliefs. Of course elder was most unlucky. You must never cut it down without asking its permission. You must never burn it, or somebody would die. An alternative version had it that you burnt the Devil and so presumably irritated him. So widespread are these superstitious beliefs that you might say that they are everywhere in the country. Elder was evidently believed to have an inveterate hostility to mankind.

Yet elder has its uses. Its flowers make a kind of bubbly wine sometimes likened to champagne. Its berries are mixed with various pies to add flavour. The yellow inlay in marquetry furniture is often elder. Incidentally elder when freshly cut stinks. Some say it smells of corpses.

Now rowan, mountain-ash, is just the opposite. From East Anglia to the Isle of Skye, I have heard rowan spoken of with great respect. A sprig of it over the door will keep evil magic away. A friend, who runs a pack of beagles, told me that when some disease struck them, which the vet could not cure, she surrounded the kennels with pieces of rowan and they recovered at once. I do not know whether the wood is used for any particular purpose, but my aunt used to make a good jelly from the berries.

Here were two common trees credited with absolutely different properties. Could there be any possible reason for these beliefs?

I cut pieces from each tree and tested them with the long pendulum. Elder gave a male reaction and rowan a female one. The short pendulum indicated repulsion between elder and myself, while rowan showed attraction.

This started me off on a search for other samples. I cut a piece from Zeus's own tree, the oak; and others from holly, thorn and elm. Oak has, of course, been a most useful timber for thousands of years, but I was really thinking of the elm. Kipling was a good folklorist and not for nothing did he write:

> 'Ellum she hateth mankind and waiteth till every gust
>    be laid
> To drop a limb on the head of him who any where
>    trusts to her shade.'

But he had the sex wrong. The pendulum said the elm was male.

Elm is not much used inland except for floor-boards and coffins; although there is some elm furniture and I have an old sideboard made from it. But from Kent to the Scilly Isles boats are still planked with elm. It builds very sturdy boats for beach work. Nevertheless elm is regarded with some suspicion.

Oak reacted to the female rate on the long pendulum and showed attraction on the short. Thorn was the same, but the reaction was slight. Holly was weakly male and hostile.

In all I tested fourteen trees. Six were male and indicated repulsion. Eight were the opposite as Table 6 shows.

Table 6

| Tree | Pendulum Male | Reaction Female |
|------|---------------|-----------------|
| Elder | x | - |
| Rowan | - | x |
| Oak | - | x |
| Ash | x | - |
| Elm | x | - |
| Thorn | - | x |
| Hazel | - | x |
| Holly | x | - |
| Fig | x | - |
| Pine | x | - |
| Willow | - | x |
| Apple | - | x |
| Ivy | - | x |
| Beech | - | x |
| Total: 14 | 6 | 8 |

Now from a botanical point of view this was all nonsense. Many trees are hermaphrodite and bear both male and female flowers. What sense could there be in what the pendulum appeared to be telling us?

I took a branch of elder and pulled it to pieces. I had flowers, fruit, bark, pith and wood. I tested these separately. Only the wood was male and hostile. I have yet to think of a reason why this should be so.

Remembering the belief that, although elder was hostile, rowan was protective, I tried another experiment. I put a sprig of elder opposite myself and swung the short pendulum between the two. The pendulum went into a circular swing, indicating, according to the ideas I have already described for inanimate objects, that there was an obstruction to the flow of current between my field and that of another which I have guessed as being the earth's field. Then I placed a sprig of rowan beside the piece of elder. Immediately the previous gyrations stopped and a back and forth movement began. Therefore the rowan masked the elder's obstructive power and restored a normal flow of current. The same thing happened when the long pendulum was used. The rowan obscured the elder's male sex rate and the pair together became female. So rowan in the vegetable world has the same property as lead in the mineral one.

Thinking that magnetism probably had some say in this curious phenomenon, I placed a horseshoe magnet opposite myself with its ends open and swung the short pendulum. The pendulum gyrated. When the ends were closed, the oscillation began. In a sense then the rowan sprig when applied to the elder could be compared with a soft iron bar placed across the ends of a horseshoe magnet. If this comparison is permissible it looks as if these interrupters somehow close the electro-magnetic fields around objects in the same way that the soft iron bar joins the ends of the horseshoe magnet and forms a closed circuit.

In any case we seem to see that if elder can exert any deleterious influence from its field, rowan can stop this. But it can only do so within the 29 inch radius of its field. Within this radius its feminity is too strong for the elder. Something of this situation appears to have been appreciated by less sophisticated persons than those of the present day. Somehow they learnt that rowan could close the gaps in their protection from hostile influences. How it could possibly do so we have yet to find out. It does not seem in the least credible, but very little in this study did when we began it.

The comparison with terrestial magnetism as it is understood is probably far too easy. In the first case we have the perfectly simple matter of closing a circuit in one plane. The horseshoe magnet is only a bar magnet bent round in a half circle and all that the soft iron rod does is to join one pole to another. A piece of soft iron joining the two ends of a straight magnet would have the same effect. But in the case of the fields we are exploring a small object placed beside another appears to swamp a whole biconical field with its own. The field of a human-made magnet is imperceptible to the five senses. That of an object is so also. Neither magnetism nor electricity are directly perceptible to the five senses; although their shocks to the body can be appreciated. The biconical fields surrounding the objects we are studying can only be appreciated by indicators of some kind. The electro-magnetic fields of the inanimate objects may come into the normal curriculum of physics. The fields of human beings and animate objects are not so easy to study. We are probably trying to investigate a facet of life itself and the means available are quite inadequate. Electricity and magnetism no doubt come into it, but are only a small part of the whole. The life itself appears to be four dimensional. Therefore we have no idea how powerful these biconical fields may be, nor what effect they may have on the human body. Without knowing this, it is impossible to say that elder is not hostile to humanity nor that rowan is friendly.

# Chapter 4

If you cut off a lock of your hair, it is then, in theory, dead. It certainly does not live for very long. Take the lock of hair and put it in a sterilised glass bottle. It certainly was grown on your body and in that sense is part of you. But it is no longer growing and is now dead and isolated. Now, for at least 2,000 years, it has been maintained that a bit of your body, a lock of hair, a finger-nail paring, a drop of blood, or even a gob of spit, remains in contact with the person from whom it originated. Those who practised witchcraft believed that they had only to obtain possession of something of this kind to be able to influence the body of the originator for good or evil. The modern mechanical healers with 'The Box' go entirely on this assumption and in practice it seems to work.

I began to wonder, then, how much effect time and such matters had on the rate of an object. So to return to our lock of hair shut up in its sterilised bottle, after a week or two it must be completely dead. But then test it with the short pendulum against the body of its former owner. The answer given by the pendulum is an oscillation. Not only is the living body pleased to contact its former possession, it appears to be delighted. The oscillation increases and almost becomes violent. Anyone who can work the pendulum at all can test this and see that I am right. The dead object retains a field and this field is in agreement with the field of the body which grew it. Test the hair in the bottle for sex. It will react to the sex rate of the former owner.

It occurred to me to try to find out how long this sex rate

persisted in a dead object. It seemed most improbable from a materialistic point of view that it could persist at all. The thing is dead and that ought to be the end of the matter. Nothing should remain of the life that once animated it.

I have a pernicious habit of picking up fossils whenever I happen to see them, and, having a sharp eye, I find quite a number of them. I bring them home and they lie about on window-ledges and so on, collecting dust and spiders, till someone puts them in a box in justifiable indignation. Although I did not expect to get any results, I thought it would be interesting to test a few fossils. On looking round the house I found that I had thirteen specimens of the chalk fossil *Mieraster cor-anguinum,* which is generally known as 'the shepherd's heart' and down here as 'the heart of flint'. Twelve of these fossil sea urchins are casts in silica of the inside of the shell, 'test' as it is called. One is the test itself, which I had dug out of the actual chalk. The silica, which formed the casts inside the tests, is said to have been collected from the water of the ocean as the animal inside the shell decayed. How this was done, I do not know; but you could surely not have anything much more dead than these casts of the insides of sea urchins, which, at a rough estimate, perished in the deep water of the Cretaceous Seas some 100 million years ago.

I took these thirteen fossils into the hall and placed them one by one on the slate floor, which is relatively free from interruptions. I tested them in isolation for sex with the long pendulum. Six gave a reaction for the male rate. Five, including the specimen with a real shell gave the female rate and two gave both male and female.

The most astonishing thing about this experiment was that there should be any sex rate, or magnetic rate, or any rate at all except for silica, from the casts of sea urchins which had been dead for such a stupendous length of time.

I had forgotten anything I might have learnt about the sex life of sea urchins while an undergraduate at Cambridge and did not know whether you could tell a male sea urchin from a female, or whether they might not be hermaphrodite like earth worms. I took the fossils and examined them with care (Figure 9). It was clear at once that there was a great difference between the casts which the pendulum said were female and those it

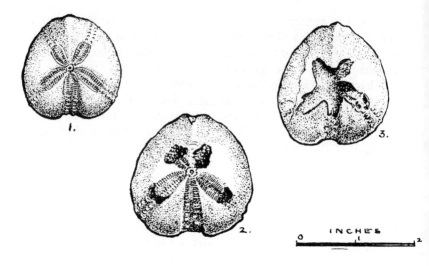

Figure 9. Cretaceous fossil sea-urchins. Flint casts of the interiors. These give sex rates on the pendulum. 1. Male. 2. Male and female. 3. Female. Species is *Micraster cor-anguinum*.

designated as male. The one with the actual shell in place was of course different from both, because one was looking at it outside, while all the others were impressions of the inside of the shell. We will leave it out of the study and deal only with the casts.

In the case of the male casts there is a beautiful five-pointed star on top like a picture of a leaf. This shows what are known as the ambulacral grooves, through which little tube-like feet once projected giving the animal both motive power and a breathing apparatus. The base of each foot is clearly marked on the cast giving an elaborate and attractive pattern. In the case of the casts, which the pendulum calls female, little of this pattern remains. The places where the feet used to be are taken by five deep hollows. It was evident to me that when the urchins died there were swellings extending inwards from the ambulacral areas into the body of the animal. These were naturally reproduced in the cast as hollows. The shell above had not gone, but was obscured. It seemed to me that the

78

swellings, which produced the hollows, must have been bunches of eggs. The casts, which gave both male and female reactions on the pendulum, appeared to show that the swellings were just beginning to form. The male pattern had begun to break down and hollows were starting to form on top of the cast. A very small specimen, which I found later, showed little sign of the ambulacral areas and gave no sex reaction at all.

Without knowing more than this, I inferred that this kind of sea urchin began its life without sex. Then it became male. When it had shed its male seed, which in the case of a oyster is known as spat, I assumed that it produced eggs and was then female. When the eggs were fertilised, I presumed that the organism had finished its life cycle and died, for there is no further male stage. The female fossils are roughly a size larger than the males. I guessed that this cycle took two years to complete.

Although it had little to do with our main subject, I was now interested in the sex-life of sea urchins. I consulted a number of handbooks both zoological and geological; but although there were several theories as to how they were thought to have developed down the aeons of geological time, no one seemed to have considered their married life worthy of much consideration. The nearest I could get to an answer was in *Wood's Palaeontology.* Here it was stated that *Echinoderms,* an order which includes sea urchins, are as a whole generally sexual, but that no one can tell the two sexes apart. Ah well! Perhaps my books are out of date and there is now some easy way of telling the sexes. In any case the pendulum appears to be able to do it with no trouble at all.

Now, to return once more to our lock of hair in its sterilised bottle. It is, of course, dead in the normal sense, but it gives a reaction to the male sex rate. I tried both my living self and the bottle of dead hair opposite the dead casts of the sea urchins. In each case the tests gave the same results. If living male body, or dead male hair is placed opposite a fossil regarded as male by the long pendulum, when the short pendulum is swung between them, a gyration, or disagreement is indicated. When a supposedly female fossil is substituted for the male one an oscillation, or agreement is shown. This was constant and has to be accepted as a fact. Current passes freely between male and female. Between male and male or female and female there is an obstruction. We saw, however, that with inanimate objects current apparently flowed between like and like and was obstructed when the composition of the objects was different.

The very important point which comes out of this simple series of experiments is that some trace of the original sex life remains in fossils after a period of some 100 million years. The original inmate of the fossil shell has been dead all that time and yet a detached portion of his field obviously still remains and can be detected through our own field and our nerve-endings by a pendulum.

Not only is this the case; but a sample of our dead hair is apparently able to talk with the dead sea urchin. Something must be still alive surely and outside our notion of time.

To find out more about this strange matter and attempt to make sure that I was not exercising thought and influencing the pendulum, I thought out another experiment.

This needed two dowsers in different rooms, each with a pendulum. My wife went upstairs taking with her a pendulum, a male and female fossil sea urchin and a bottle of my hair. I remained below in the stone-flagged hall, while she conducted her operations over a concrete fireplace in the bedroom. I tuned in my pendulum to the 24 inch male sex rate of my hair in the bottle upstairs. My wife swung the short pendulum between my hair and a fossil sea urchin of which I could not know the sex rate. Watches had been synchronised. At a given moment I began to swing my pendulum in the hall downstairs, while she swung hers in the bedroom.

I am really a terrible disbeliever. I did not for a moment expect a tangible result. However, after a few moments, the pendulum began to oscillate with much greater fervour than usual. Apparently the double 'voltage' had increased its reaction considerably. 'Good heavens!' I thought, 'she must have been trying my hair against a female sea urchin.'

We broke off for three minutes and then I swung the pendulum again. Instantly, and with great violence, it went into a circular swing. It was so strong that I felt a sharp tingling in my finger-tips and could not keep them steady. 'A displeased male,' I thought.

My wife joined me. I had got both answers right. It was

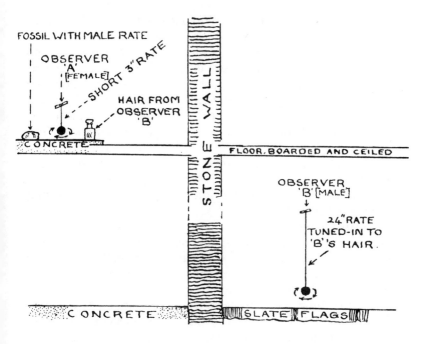

Figure 10. Simple diagram to illustrate transmission between two pendulums in comparative isolation. Observer B's pendulum downstairs will take up with vigour, the oscillation, or gyration, obtained by observer A upstairs. The link appears to be the sample of B's hair.

perhaps only one answer; although my wife might have tested the same sea urchin twice (Figure 10).

We then changed everything about. I went upstairs with a bottle of her hair, one pendulum, a male and a female sea urchin and considerable surprise. She went into the hall and tuned her pendulum to 29, the rate for her hair in the bottle I had taken with me. She got both answers right, but with rather less violence than I had experienced. Of course we did not stop at so few trials, but it is unnecessary to do hundreds of them at this stage.

One point is at once clear. Two operators with two pendulums in tune add greatly to the ease of observation. Also it is evident that the necessary force to work the pendulum comes from the operator himself. We both felt tired after these experiments.

Of course curiosity would not let me rest. Was this reaction peculiar to sea urchins, or were other relics of dead organisms involved? I had a few fossil urchins, *Echinobrissus,* from the corallian beds at Upware, between Cambridge and Ely. These too reacted to a sex rate. But I could get none from a few specimens of what must have been young examples of a modern urchin, *Paracentrolus lividus.* This is a small relation of the edible sea urchin, well known to many, round our coasts, *Echinus esculenta,* whose eggs are very good with sherry. I thought the *Paracentrolus* specimens were probably too young to have developed sex.

I turned to fossil mollusca, the ordinary shells of the sea shore and also the pond and land shells. As a general rule I could get no sex reaction from the shell of any dead mollusc, fossil or recent. Large oriental cowrie shells had no more reaction than that of a dead snail on the garden path.

Since nothing could be learnt from shells apparently, I went through my drawers of relics, which I had collected in boyhood and boxes of things picked up in more recent times. I had skulls of various birds; hawks, crows, jays, pigeons, puffins, shear-waters and herons; wonderful examples of mechanical contrivance and things of beauty in themselves. Nearly all the owners of these skulls had been dead for at least forty years, and yet each one responded to a sex rate.

Then there were bones of mammals; stoats, weasels, moles, the skull of an artic fox picked up in Jan Mayen in 1921, and the complete skeleton of a very old badger, which my wife had found lying in a lane in 1959 and I had buried until the bones were clear of flesh. I had had flu when she returned with this prize. The business of skinning made me giddy, and, having no alum to preserve the skin, it had to be rubbed with wood ash. But I had the body buried before I returned to bed. I say this to show that there could be no doubt that the badger was really dead. The bones were not dug up again for over a year.

Now all the skulls responded to either the male, or the female rate for the pendulum. Although, however, I had the complete skeleton of the badger, only the skull had any sex rate at all and this was male. There was not even any response

Table 7  Table of various bones tested November 1963

| Species | Specimen | Pendulum rate | Remarks |
| --- | --- | --- | --- |
| Arctic fox | Skull | Female | Young. Found dead in Jan Mayen 1921 |
| Badger | Skull | Male | Very old. Teeth worn right down. 1959 |
| Badger | Pelvic girdle | No reaction | ,,            ,, |
| Badger | Other bones | No reaction | ,,            ,, |
| Stoat | Skull | Female | Found dead 1919 |
| Weasel | ,, | Male | ,,            ,, |
| Mole | ,, | Female | ,,            ,, |

to the sex rate from the pelvic girdle where, if anywhere, such a response might have been expected. It appears that with mammals this sex rate is confined to the skull alone.

I have quite a collection of other mammalian bones. For instance I have a series of metacarpal and metatarsal bones of sheep, which I have picked up on various excavations. They range in time from the Bronze Age, about 1500 BC right through the Iron Age, Roman, Saxon, Viking and Medieval times to the recent bones of soay and black-faced sheep. I collected them because I wanted to find out why and when the legs of sheep changed from thin deer-like types to the relative thick legs of today. No interest could be raised among the experts on ancient sheep; but, as far as my evidence goes, the change appears to have taken place in Tudor times, or even later. These bones give no sex reaction on the pendulum; neither do those of horse, red deer, ox and so on. Lower jaws of various animals do not react. In fact the skull alone appears to do so.

It is the same story in the case of birds. I make a point of picking up bird bones in order to be able to identify specimens from ancient sites by comparing the bones with modern ones. Only the skulls give the sex rate (Table 8).

The pendulum is in touch, apparently, with something that has the right equipment and can signal that parts of the fields of sea urchins persist for 100 million years. It can signal the answers to many other questions as well.

Table 8   Tested November 1963

| Species | Pendulum rate | Remarks | | |
|---|---|---|---|---|
| Kestrel | Female | Found dead | | 1919 |
| Kestrel | Male | ,, | ,, | 1920 |
| Jay | Male | ,, | ,, | 1920 |
| Crow | Female | ,, | ,, | 1919 |
| Pigeon | Female | ,, | ,, | 1919 |
| Puffin | Male | ,, | ,, | 1919 |
| Manx-shearwater | Female | ,, | ,, | 1919 |
| Heron | Female | ,, | ,, | 1943 |

We are confronted obviously with a subject which has not been included in the information we have been taught since childhood and to understand anything about it we have to begin from the beginning. Now we have heard all this before. This is something one remembers from the Christian Gospels. 'Unless you become again as little children ye cannot enter the kingdom of heaven.' Well that may be so indeed. Unless you can appreciate that there is a part of your make-up which lasts indefinitely and knows much more than your brain, you are stuck in the world of materialism and atom bombs. But if you can appreciate that this something exists, a completely new view of life opens up. We can regard our body as a caterpillar and expect to go on through a chrysalis state to that of an imago, or complete eternity. For the whole is the sum of its parts. If part of the whole persists for 100 million years, the whole must do so too. We must try to find what else can be transferred to the electro-magnetic field in order to see what might survive indefinitely.

Bearing in mind the claims of the people who go in for psychometry that they can extract memory pictures from inanimate objects, it seemed hopeful to attempt to find a pendulum rate for memory. But, although it was not particularly difficult to find a rate of 27 inches which apparently corresponded to memory, it is not so easy to distinguish memory from thought. In practice almost all thought is more or less dependent on the memory of something or other. My wife and

I tried the 27 inch length rate over one another. If one of us vividly recalled a picture of some incident or place, the pendulum held by the other gyrated as it would do for the sex rate. If then, by an effort of will, the victim managed to switch his or her attention on to a coal scuttle, or some other triviality, the pendulum instantly went into an oscillation. But if the victim tried to think of something else, such as how to set a mousetrap in the shed, then memory was once more involved and gyration took place. It did not seem that one could separate thought from memory very easily. Thought does appear to be able to affect the pendulum. However there seems to be a distinction between thought and memory which could be useful if it could be employed.

This also showed how right I was to be cautious about reading other people's work on this subject. Despite the sage advice of critics, I am deliberately avoiding the study of the works of others in this line. There is a very good reason for this. It is not known how much thought, conscious or unconscious, may not influence the results which we appear to obtain. If you know what others think the results ought to be, your thought may then influence your own results. We are dealing with a subject which is remarkably intangible. It was a branch of this study which caused Jung to say that he had to raise a revolution before science would look at it. He said, and I have also said, that it is mental laziness and a lack of the scientific approach to neglect it.

All science is based on observation and reasoning from this observation. The observation may be incorrectly interpreted, but without observation there can be no science. Newton's apple was an observed fact. So was our privet hawk-moth landing on a plate, as I described in the last chapter.

In the last chapter I also described how the pendulum appeared to be able to detect traces of the human beings who had made or used various objects. These traces, showing as pendulum rates, survived for very long periods in things which had been deliberately fashioned by man. Elizabethan ironwork gave the male sex rate (24 inches) of the blacksmith who had made it and a rate of 27 inches for the thought he had put into his work. The rates had persisted for four hundred years. Flint implements, made perhaps 3,500 years ago, also gave male, 24 inches, or female, 29 inches, rates for their makers, or users. I decided to try to see what happened to objects which man had used, but which he had not made. Entirely natural objects that is to say, which man had used without altering them for the purpose. Could the pendulum tell us whether, for instance, a particular pebble had been used by prehistoric man as a sling-shot, or not?

This was rather an interesting point to me. About ten years ago I became involved in a controversy as to whether a large figure of a giantess and her horse, which I had found just outside an Iron Age hillfort at Wandlebury near Cambridge was a natural product of the Ice Age, or had been made by man. The chalk surface of the figure, under the turf, was found to be covered with small rounded pebbles, mostly of quartzite, which had stuck in it when it was wet. I collected about two thousand of these; weighed about 1,400 and brought the remainder here to Hole, to be weighed if I felt like it. It was reasonably obvious that they were sling-shot, flung from the rampart of the fort, both in practice and also possibly in war. If they were sling-shot, it was clear that they had fallen on the surface of the figure when it was exposed to view turfless and it could not possibly have been any Ice Age freak. I don't think as a matter of fact, that the people who doubted the man-made character of the figure had any idea either of what happens to exposed chalk, or what goes on near an ice-field. But it is not worth the trouble to get too deeply involved in the dogmatic intrigues of people who make their living by posing to the public as specialists. Any serious loss of face ruins their chances of advancement.

So I left the subject, knowing well enough that sooner or later it would have to be re-opened, when the professors had either retired, or were in their graves. It was of little importance to me. After thirty years of experience in digging on this kind of chalk, I knew what it was and I was supported by two archaeological knights and a professor who really knew their subject. The whole thing could wait. But it would be of interest to see if one could demonstrate that the pebbles were sling-shot.

Fashions in the art of war are interesting. For some reason, although the bow had been known from very early times and Early Bronze Age flint arrowheads are commonly found all

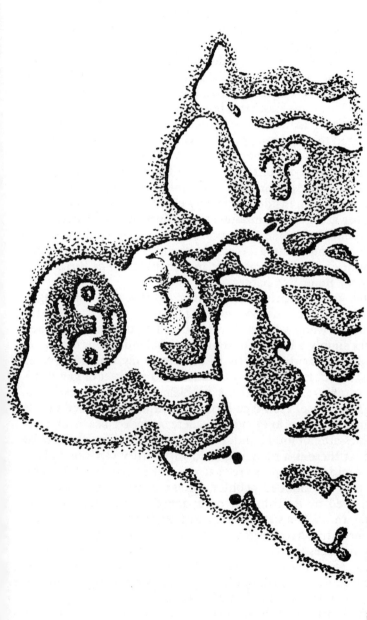

Figure 11. Giant figure of a goddess on horseback (probably Epona), found by sounding and excavation at Wandlebury, Cambridge.

over the country, nobody in England seems to have thought of using a massed force of bowmen till the Welsh evolved the long-bow in the Norman period. This great ash bow would, as Giraldus Cambrensis tells us, drive an arrow through a six-inch thick oak door, or through a knight's mail, his leg beneath and kill the horse on which he rode. There were smaller bows, used for instance against the Saxons by William the Conqueror at the Battle of Hastings; but, although the bow must have been known to them, the Iron Age peoples in this country preferred to use the sling. Somewhere about 200 B.C. many big Iron Age forts had to be modified by additional ditches to keep hostile slingers out of range. The difficulty with a more or less circular Iron Age fort was that, unless you had a very large number of men inside, the enemy could always mass a greater number at a given point outside and overwhelm the defence at that point by massed fire power. Then they could rush the defences and make a breach in them. There is a very good account of how this was done in Xenophon's *The Persian Expedition*, Book V, Chapter 2.

One great advantage of the sling was that it cost nothing to make and its ammunition, except for professional troops in the employ of Rome who used cast lead bullets, cost nothing either. It was simply a bag full of rounded pebbles of about the size of a walnut. Our difficulty is to be able to say whether a given natural pebble is a sling-stone or not. As a matter of fact this is not usually a very difficult problem, merely a question of common sense. Iron Age forts are frequently perched on the summit of some lofty down, where rounded beach or river pebbles are not found, unless they have been taken up there by man. If there is a ploughed field within fifty yards of an Iron Age camp, the chances are that you will be able to walk over it and pick up rounded pebbles, foreign to the soil, which have been used by its Iron Age occupants for sling practice, or in actual war. When such pebbles are found scattered about inside the fort, they have been presumably shot into it by an enemy. The numbers found are often very great and on occasion little heaps of ready-to-use ammunition are found inside the defences. It is absurd to think that the two thousand rounded pebbles found on the Wandlebury giant could have possibly reached this site in the normal course of nature. You might be

Figure 12. Giant figure 100 feet high found by sounding the area of rotted chalk beneath the turf at Wandlebury, Cambridge.

1. Torque. 2. Shield. 3. Sling stones? 4. Old trackway which destroyed the legs. The top of the head has been excavated. Incredible though it may seem, and despite the fact that Roman pottery, many modern shells and upwards of 2,000 sling-stones were found in the rotted chalk of the three great Wandlebury figures, some archaeologists still believe that they were made by frost action in the Ice Age! (5. Modern pipe-line).

able to pick up half a dozen in an acre of neighbouring field. These Wandlebury pebbles must have been sling-shot and they must have been collected in sacks from some beach, or old river gravel, a long distance away. But you cannot prove this by any ordinary means. It is only inference based on Inherent Probability. In fact very little in the study of archaeology can be proved. The whole structure must be based on inherent probability, because man is not a machine and what he did can seldom be correctly inferred from the information produced by excavation. Archaeology is far less reliable than history, and everybody knows that the inferences drawn from history are subject to the whims of the historian.

There are still two unexcavated giants at Wandlebury, which I plotted through the turf by using a stainless steel sounding bar. One of these (Figure 12) appears to represent a Celtic god dressed in a torque and leine, warding off sling-bolts with a small round shield. This idea was suggested to me by a kindly correspondent; but I regret to say that I have forgotten who it was.

We will leave Wandlebury to prove the existence of its own giants and turn to other Iron Age hill-forts. These were probably seldom forts in the accepted sense of the word; but they were protected places where cattle could be driven at night to secure them from rustlers and wolves. A 'creagh', a cattle raid, could not be successful in a Celtic community if the beasts were inside a stockade and there were not enough raiders to overcome the defending herdsmen. These, when armed with slings, made the entrance of anything but a large body of raiders costly and difficult. Some hill-forts were of course the places described as 'towns' by the Roman invaders. But even so they were in no sense the towns which grew up in Mediaeval England. Most hill-forts were far more like the shielings of Scotland, where the beasts were collected for milking and cheeses for the winter were made. The population lived on its farms outside, in houses which are seldom excavated.

I have for some time been interested in an Iron Age hill-fort named Blackbury Castle which is not far from our house at Hole. Blackbury Castle, a translation into English of Dun, or Dinas, dubh, is the first of four sites in the district where sling-stones are found. But it appears to have been built before sling warfare came into fashion. It is a single banked oval earthwork of considerable strength with a kind of barbican protecting the gate. When it was designed, the most formidable onslaught it might have been expected to receive was a rush of men armed with spears and throwing stones. The object of the barbican seems to have been to keep the attackers as far from the main gate for as long as possible. But Blackbury Castle has been excavated and the main point of interest, which resulted from this work, was the discovery of very great numbers of sling-stones, brought apparently from Branscombe beach, inside the barbican and round the main gate itself. The fort had been attacked in a manner which it was not designed to receive. Perhaps it was stormed. Who can tell?

Whatever happened, and it is most unlikely that anyone will ever know, I was interested to see whether the defenders of Blackbury had used slings in its defence. About twenty-five yards from the barbican is a field, which is sometimes ploughed and is bare in places. It is full of angular flint nodules; but looking over its fence at the bare patches we noticed several round stones of suitable size for sling-shot. They were not beach pebbles, like those inside the camp, but spherical flint concretions enclosing fossil sponges. Not knowing whether these were sling-shot or not, we tested them with the pendulum. Rather surprisingly three of them gave reactions to rates other than 14 inches for the silica in flint. They gave rates of 27 inches 'thought' and 24 inches for 'male' sex. Others, which were just as suitable for shot, did not give these reactions. Not knowing how far anything of this sort was to be trusted, it yet seemed probable to my wife and myself that the defenders of Blackbury had used slings, but had not bothered to go the distance to Branscombe beach to get the far better pebbles to be found there.

In the summer of 1965 I was asked by Peter Gelling, who used to come to my archaeological lectures at Cambridge, to come over to see his excavations in the Iron Age camp at Pilsdon Pen in Dorset. Pilsdon is a spectacular hill, rising abruptly for nearly a thousand feet and dominating the surrounding district of Marshwood. It is a magnificent defensive position, but was, I think, more of a shieling than a military work. To me the low circular structures inside suggested more the rings round the bases of Eskimo summer tents than the houses of a permanent garrison. The excavators had found very many rounded flint beach stones scattered inside the camp. They were calling them sling-stones.

It had been raining torrentially before we went and the path up to the rampart was scoured by the rush of water. On the way down this I picked up a couple of these pebbles and brought them home to examine. They were very highly rounded sea pebbles and must have been brought at least five miles from the nearest shingle beach. I tested them with the pendulum. They gave the now familiar rates for thought and male sex as well as that for flint.

This was becoming interesting and a check was now necessary. To avoid handling, a number of pebbles of suitable walnut size were picked up from the shingle on the beach with a pair of tongs and immediately dropped into a container. They were never touched by hand. When tested with the pendulum, none of them gave any reaction except the 14 inches for silica. How did the other rates for thought and male sex become attached to other similar pebbles, which man had handled perhaps two thousand years ago?

I took one of the untouched pebbles and held it in my hand for half an hour. Then I tested it. It gave the 14-inch rate for silica as before; but now it reacted to the 27-inch rate for thought as well. There was no male sex rate as there was with the sling stones. I thought it over for some time. Perhaps the male rate was induced in the field of the object by some feeling of violence on the part of the slinger. I took the pebble out into the garden and flung it as hard as I could against a stone wall. I picked it up and tested it again. It now reacted to 14, 24 and 27 inches. My violence had apparently induced my sex rate into the field of the pebble. Of course the term 'sex rate' may well be incorrect. It is simply a term of convenience. It is a rate common to males when it is 24 inches and to females when it is 29 and it is different from what I am calling a thought rate of 27 inches. Memory, as distinct from thought, is 7 inches. 20 inches is the rate for living things. Thought on the pendulum appears to be memory plus life. The experiment was then repeated by my wife. She took two untouched pebbles and threw them in turn against the wall. When examined they reacted both to the

27-inch thought rate and to the 29 inches for female sex. They would not react to the male rate.

I then took half a dozen supposed sling-stones from Wandlebury. Of course these had been excavated and picked up by man. If the thought rate is easily induced, one might expect them to have a 14-inch rate for silica and perhaps 27 inches for thought from the modern excavators who dug them up. But they should not have a 24-inch rate because this is apparently only induced by violent treatment. All six pebbles reacted to 14, 24 and 27 inches. Violence had apparently had its effect on them and as we had not treated them violently, it seemed that this 24-inch male sex rate must have come from the prehistoric slinger and have been with each pebble for two thousand years or so.

This is only the start of a lengthy series of experiments. Many more stones have to be tested in various ways. But we are beginning to see here something which is well known to the students of parapsychology as psychometry; an art by which a medium, now called a sensitive, can hold an object and give information about the past life and actions of its former owners. This is not the first time in which I seem to be rediscovering pyschometry by attempting to approach the subject in general in a scientific manner. The art undoubtedly exists and it can be most impressive to listen to a sensitive when holding an object; unfortunately many factors may interfere with its accuracy.

Of course the pendulum cannot give us the vivid pictures obtained by a sensitive. I have been told by one that she saw something comparable to a minute cinema film; so small that it was difficult at times to be sure of detail. But when used in an entirely matter of fact and down to earth manner, the pendulum will report bits of information relating to the object. We have seen this already in the case of *Bolboceras* and the truffles and it becomes evident again when we are dealing with sling-stones. It can reveal a great variety of objects buried in the ground and also at a considerable distance. While one naturally doubts the rather mystic performance of the sensitive, one cannot doubt the mass of pins, nails, old spoons, glass, china, pottery and so on which the pendulum can find for you. We will see presently if we can increase the information it can give about the former users of objects.

However, the first thing to be found out was to see what percentage of the Wandlebury sling-shot reacted to what appears to be the personal sex rate of the slinger. Were there female slingers? And so on. I had meant to take a round number of a hundred stones, but made a slight mistake and examined a hundred and ten. It does not matter in the least, but does not look so tidy! Of these 110 stones only 9, that is only just over 8 per cent did not react to the male rate. These were also the most irregular specimens and the least likely to have been used in a sling. Some were too big. No pebble gave a female rate. Amazons apparently did not function at Wandlebury. However, there was a large percentage of stones which seemed too small to have been used by grown men in war (one half to one and a half ounces). These no doubt represented the practice shots of children being trained young in the use of their weapons. When it is realised that several hundred stones remain to be examined here, that there are 1,407 in the University Museum of Archaeology and Ethnology at Cambridge and that the whole lot were found within the outlines of a figure 105 feet long by 80 feet high, it is obvious that the stones as yet uncovered must run into many more thousands. Practice must frequently have been carried out from the Wandlebury ramparts and the children made to work hard at it. The hillside would have been scattered with pebbles as thick as 'hundreds and thousands' on a sugar cake.

We now have to deal with our second experiment. Do pebbles always take up the sex rate of the thrower if they are projected with force? For this experiment we collected about a hundred rounded pebbles from Seaton beach. They were picked up with a pair of iron tongs and dropped into buckets. The pebbles we each picked were kept separate, but this apparently was not necessary, for when brought back and tested there was no reaction to anything but the 14-inch rate for silica from any of them.

The pebbles were then thrown in groups of fifty, one by one, at a wall in the garden. Table 9 shows the result. This experiment could be conducted by anyone who can use the pendulum.

It appears evident that the sex rate of the thrower can be impressed on the field of the object thrown. Once impressed it seems to remain there indefinitely.

Table 9 Pebbles from Seaton Beach, untouched by human hand except that of the thrower

| No. | Thrown by | Pendulum examination by | Result | Comment |
|-----|-----------|-------------------------|--------|---------|
| 50 | Male (TCL) | Male (TCL) | All react to 24-inch rate (male) | No reaction to female rate |
| 50 | Male (TCL) | Female (MEL) | All react to 24-inch rate (male) | No reaction to female rate |
| 50 | Female (MEL) | Male (TCL) | All react to 29-inch rate (female) | No reaction to male rate |

Not long ago, my publisher, Colin Franklin, wanted to know whether the reproductions of pictures still retained the sex rate of the painters of the originals. To enlarge it somewhat, one might ask whether a book carries with it part of the original field of force of the author, which struck me as being a very interesting possibility. I did not believe it for a moment.

My idea was to test first an original drawing for the sex and thought rates and then to test the reproduction made from that drawing in a completely new and unopened copy of the book itself.

I tested some of my original drawings on the slate floor of the hall, where there should not be much interruption from anything but the slate. In a state of considerable interest, I put the first drawing on the floor and tested it for the rate for male sex of 24 inches and then for thought at 27 inches. It responded strongly to both. Then I opened the new copy of the book at the figure made from the drawing and tested that. There was no reaction of any sort to either rate. The figure appeared to be dead. My wife and I went solemnly through all the drawings and prints made from them. All the drawings responded to the sex and thought rates. Nothing at all happened with the prints. There was no reaction to either rate from the book itself. There was not the slightest indication that any fragment of the author's personality passed to the book, except that the printed word might mean something to the person who read it. There was no direct contact at all. The book was not a link in any parapsychological sense between the author and the reader. There was nothing passing between an artist who painted a picture and the reproduction of that picture. The quality of the reproduction, however good it might be, is something entirely mechanical and lacking in the life force which has been impressed by the artist on the original.

This experiment was rather a relief to me. I had not been able to see how anything could really pass from original to reproduction. Whereas everything we had investigated before followed a logical course, however strange that course might appear to be, this transference of something to a reproduction seemed completely illogical. Yes, I was relieved, we had managed to put a brake on.

I tested a number of new books. They were all blank. Then I tried an almost new book, which, as far as I knew, had only been read by one man. This gave a strong reaction on the thought rate and one on the male rate. It also rather unexpectedly reacted to the female rate. Then I remembered that the book had been given to me by a woman friend. She had probably looked at it first. Library books all reacted to the thought rate and most of them to both male and female. However one only gave a female reaction, although several people had taken it out from the library. It did not look the kind of book that men would read. This of course is in reality what people call psychometry, but we are only doing it in a halting and uncertain manner.

# Chapter 5

As one studies the rates the conviction that we are getting a glimpse of a master plan becomes firmer. Look at a wasp for instance. Why is it coloured black and yellow? Everybody knows that black and yellow is a warning colour scheme. Somehow man recognised that black and yellow spelt danger. Before the days of Nelson ships of war were painted in variegated colours. But Nelson, who was something of a mystic as well as a great sailor, insisted that all the ships under his command be painted black and yellow. His enemies have left on record that nothing they had ever seen was so daunting as the slow approach of the two lines of British ships at Trafalgar.

But why is this colour scheme a warning? The rates give an answer at once: 29 inches, the rate for yellow, is also the rate for danger; while the 40-inch rate for black is the same as that for death. The wasp says plainly, to those who know, that they are in deadly danger if they meddle with it. And so they are. Fatal casualties from wasp stings are not unknown among human beings.

Or there is the sinister and beautiful black, glossy berry of Deadly Nightshade. I have not often seen this trap unwary children; but, if any plant flaunts its deadly property, this one does. It glares at you malignantly in the woodland glade, almost daring you to eat it. Even if you did not know what it was, there is something about it that shouts a warning to you. The black berries of the yellow honeysuckle are poisonous and everyone knows the pain inflicted when accidentally sitting on a tuft of yellow gorse.

Then there is the laburnum tree with its lovely drooping sprays of yellow flowers, from which come its little black bean seeds. These are a great soporific and, I believe, can kill. Forty inches is also the rate for sleep. Danger and sleep are both shown by the colours. Many yellow plants are poisonous; even the buttercup, with its bulbous root, can poison. But when we come to purple it is a different story.

Many of the purple *Labiatae* are useful herbs. Thyme and sage, balm, self-heal, and mint all have their uses, along with others of this family. The purple autumn crocus alleviates gout and the purple opium poppy soothes pain. For purple, with a rate of 9 inches, stands for safety. But here we see an apparent paradox, for the flower of Deadly Nightshade is purple, which seems like a contradiction till we remember the use of Belladonna for the eyes.

Of course I began by tabulating such rates as had been discovered. But a table as such is not particularly helpful. As I studied the table, a rather remarkable feature caught my eye. Certain basic concepts were found together at 10, 20, 30 or 40 inches (Table 10).

Table 10

| 10 inch | 20 inch | 30 inch | 40 inch |
| --- | --- | --- | --- |
| Light | Life | Sound | Death |
| Sun | Heat | Moon | Cold |
| Fire | Earth | Water | Air |
| Red | White | Green | Black |
| East | South | West | North |
| Graphite | Electricity | Hydrogen | Sleep |
| Truth | | | Falsehood |

All these were of such importance that it seemed obvious to me that I was dealing with some completely fundamental plan. It could be no accident that, with a table beginning at 0 and ending at 40, each 10-inch rate should carry with it so many matters of vital consequence. Some intelligence must have constructed the scale and fitted everything into it. I looked at what I had found in astonishment. It seemed quite impossible to believe that so simple a thing as a pendulum could tell such a remarkable story. The rejected study was giving the evidence, which all other studies had failed to produce. Materialists were materialists simply because they could not observe a basic plan behind the other studies.

Was I imagining the whole thing? Did some layer of my own mind produce the whole gamut of rates? Everything might be a fantasy. But it could not be a fantasy. The concrete objects produced from beneath the earth by an application of their particular rates were plain for all to see. And many people had watched me find them. No it could not be a fantasy. Therefore it must be fact. Furthermore it was not the Earth's magnetic field which gave rise to the whole system of rates. You can take your prismatic compass, lay off the line to magnetic north on the ground, point at it and swing the pendulum. The pendulum just goes on swinging backwards and forwards. But if you make the correct allowance for compass deviation and point to true North, the pendulum gyrates at once. Therefore, if the Earth has any say in the arrangement of these rates, it is the Earth's mass which determines them and not its magnetic field.

Here we get into even more difficult problems; but we will do no more than notice them now. Is everything, man, beast, bird, fish, tree, and rock directly under control by the Earth itself? Does the Earth arrange how they shall be formed and how they shall develop? Is the Earth, as some have believed, itself a living organism with great intelligence? Are we in fact simply cells in the Earth's structure, just as the cells in our own bodies are each one individual? To these questions, the answer for the moment appears to be that some great intelligence has evidently devised a scale, a framework perhaps, in which everything is controlled by rays appreciable to a sixth sense by means of a pendulum. This framework is arranged in relation to the Earth's mass and not to its magnetic field. Magnetism, in fact, has a rate of its own, not the same as electricity at 20 inches, but very near it. The magnetic rate appears to be 20·25 inches. It is not one of the cardinal points on our compass-rose of rates.

I plotted out this compass-rose, the term for the circular card on which the sailor observes the bearing of the head of his ship in relation to magnetic north. I had the four cardinal points, North 40 inches, East 10 inches, South 20 inches, West

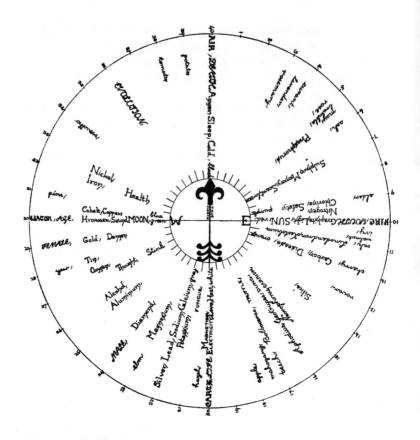

Figure 13. Diagram to show distribution of pendulum 'rates' on a 'rose' of 40 divisions. Different types of printing used to differentiate differing conceptions. The figures round the circumference show the number of inches for each rate. Each of these is actually a ray at least an inch in width. The positions of the rays on the diagram are thus relative but not exact. TIME, 60, is outside the circle.

30 inches. There were 40 divisions on the rose; not 360 or 32 as on the mariner's compass. If you plot the rates in any other manner, say 36 or 32 divisions, it will not fit (Figure 13). And there I stuck in my thinking for a very long time. What qualifications had I for getting on even as far as this? The only hope

you have of finding anything out in a new subject of this kind is to admit to yourself that you know nothing. It is perhaps comforting to know that nobody else knows much anyway.

Having the four cardinal points of North, South, East and West; Air, Earth, Fire and Water; Black, White, Red and Green, or whatever series of four we like to choose, it is a simple matter to draw out our compass-rose of 40 segments. On to this can be marked all our known rates in their correct positions. Other pairs of opposites at once become apparent (Table 11).

Table 11

| 5·5 inches | Phosphoros | 25·5 inches | Alcohol |
|---|---|---|---|
| 7 inches | { Memory <br> Scent <br> Sulphur | 27 inches | { Thought <br> Stink |
| 9 inches | { Purple <br> Safety <br> Chlorine | 29 inches | { Yellow <br> Danger <br> Gold <br> Female |
| 12 inches | { Carbon <br> Orange <br> Disease | 32 inches | { Iron <br> Health |

At 32·5 inches we went outside the range of any inorganic substance whose rate had yet been found. But when attempting to obtain a rate for Evolution, I seemed to get it at 36 inches, which is the opposite of the 16-inch rate for dung and dung beetles, which we have discovered earlier in this book. I think both these rates are probably correct and if so that for Evolution takes on a considerable significance. What is Evolution but a step forward? A step forward is 36 inches. An attempt to study the 16-inch rate suggested that it referred to regression.

I have no confidence in what appears to hang on the 36- and 16-inch rates But, suppose you take this scale to be the foundation of all earthly happenings, then Death is 40 and full Life 20. Suppose you think of this, not in inches, but in years. At 40 man dies; at 20 he is in his full vigour. This is not comprehensible now, because man lives much longer than he used to do. In a hunting community, in which the earliest form of man found himself, he seldom lived much longer than 40 years; because, after that age, his reactions became too slow to avoid death from the fangs, claws, horns, or stroke of the tail of the beasts he hunted in order to feed himself. The Eskimos, who I have seen in West Greenland, were the most cheerful people I have ever met. Yet they seldom lived over the age of 45 years. We know why they did not do so. The men grew too slow to cope with hunting the white bear, the walrus, or even the grey seal. They were killed by the polar bear's mighty paw, or their kayak was smashed to splinters by the walrus. Suppose there is some sense in what I have been saying; what happened at 16 years? Why then surely man and woman had become fully and vigorously involved in sex and, instead of being evolving mental beings, reverted for a time at least to the more animal side of their nature. So too when this side had been satisfied and worked out, at 36, they began to wonder what life was all about and some of them started to climb the ladder of mental evolution. This idea of mine may be the purest nonsense. But nevertheless it has some observation to make it worth consideration. The 40 year life span may have been the one originally devised, by whatever intelligence devised the whole original plan, to be that of man himself. Life for early man was always so hard that 40 years was quite long enough. It is now so soft that man does not wear out so quickly.

To me at any rate it seems that all development may have been designed to fit into this 40-divisional scale. It was perhaps no more than a blue-print and now the time scale has nearly doubled. Man has passed the 36 mark again and is lifting himself slowly higher. But one cannot help noticing how many men and women stick in their evolution at about the age of 36. Unless they pass this mark, then their minds appear to be dead at 40. I have more than once heard artists say that they will have to do all their best work before reaching this age. It is nonsense of course. Caesar was 45 when he began to make his great career. Before that he was just a smart 'man about town'.

In all of this kind of research one has at times to be one's own guinea-pig. Where would Jung have got had he not used his own dreams in his studies? So I will look at my own case. From about 23 to 36 I was almost entirely taken up with archaeology.

Everything revolved round it. Old brooches were far more important to me than political upheavals, or getting an extra thousand pounds a year. As a matter of fact, although living at Cambridge and doing the excavation work for the University Museum of Archaeology and Ethnology and the Antiquarian Society, from which this museum grew, I was a volunteer and not a paid servant of the University. I worked for love and did so for a generation with great delight. The Museum was a sort of International Club. One met and got to know everybody in Western Europe and America who was interested in the archaeology of Britain. But about 1937, when I was 36, this kind of existence began to pall. Archaeology was not a big enough subject to occupy one's whole life. It was very interesting; but it was trivial. An archaeologist was simply a species of public entertainer. He gathered scraps of information about the behaviour of men long ago which occasionally served to liven the tedium of the lives of his fellows for a few minutes at a time. That was all he ever did. I did not lose my interest in the subject, but began to look round for something to do of greater importance.

In 1937 I went on my third Arctic Expedition, after a gap of thirteen years. It was a very successful expedition. I was able to dig many ancient Eskimo houses in West Greenland and Arctic Canada and so added a knowledge of Eskimo archaeology to that of British archaeology. But that was not enough. Two subjects of the same kind were no more enthralling than one. I became involved in studies concerning the whole North Atlantic coastline, the voyages of the Vikings, the early peoples of the Hebrides, the Celtic missionaries, the pagan Saxons, early boats and seafaring, everything which had to deal with this northern area came into my picture. Then began the years of the war, which nearly severed my link with archaeology completely. When 40 years, or 40 inches, or whatever 40 it may be, had passed, I was in a new life. The old one died at 40. The new one began to grow and is still growing. Wife, home and occupation are all different and I find myself no longer trying to interpret a few facts about some ancient pot, or brooch, but about those of life itself. I think I can safely say that so far as this particular guinea-pig is concerned, the 40-divisional compass has told a true story. What happens to other people I do not know. It would need a social survey to get the information; but it could be very valuable. It might well show that, to get the best out of a man's powers of mental evolution, he ought to change his occupation when he is 40 and not wait to be retired at 65.

I am by no means sure that the next step I intend to try is right. It seems so simple and yet my knowledge of mathematics is relatively small. Never mind; the simpler the whole thing is the more likely it may be to be correct. I came upon it as usual by chance. I had drawn out my compass-rose of rates as I described before. This is simply a circular card of 40 divisions. It is not the mariner's compass card of 32, or the geographer's card of 360 degrees, but one derived from the pendulum rates. These start at 0 and end at 40, but it is obvious that they must go on again beyond this point. Why do I say this? Well, having obtained my compass-rose, it seemed interesting to me to see what happened if I measured out the appropriate distance along each line representing a 'rate' on the rose. Sulphur would be 7 inches along its ray, silver 22 inches and so on. The end of each measurement from the central point, which was the fixed position of you, or me, the observer, would then be the centre of the base of the biconical field of force around the object observed. It is perfectly easy. It is simply the story told by the pendulum. There is nothing there to be seen. But it can be plotted with no difficulty, on a sheet of paper.

I plotted it out. My shortest rate, remembering that I have by no means studied these rates exhaustively,was $5 \cdot 5$ inches for phosphorus. My longest was 40 inches for death, sleep, cold, black and so on. This was perfectly simple. You measured each pendulum rate along the appropriate ray on the compass card. Nothing could be more easy. But when the figure had been drawn out to these reasonably accurate measurements, I was at once confronted with an Archimedean spiral. This is a perfect geometrical figure. There is nothing in the least unusual about it: but it is not the spiral which would have been produced had the divisions of the compass-rose been 36 instead of 40. With this 40-divisional spiral, the opposites noted earlier fall naturally into place. With any other scale they do not. The 36, or 360, scale derived from degrees of longitude, does not fit. But what reason is there to suppose that the degrees of longitude are arranged round a scale of nine divisions? Why should the division not be into ten? Why a 90° right angle and not 100°? I don't know the answer to this question. There may be a very good reason; or it may be some dogmatic idea. It would be very upsetting if it were not correct. The whole conception of the measurement of the globe would be upset. Why was a right angle divided into 90° instead of 100°, which seems so much easier?

All through this research work, which I have been doing now for some years, I have never had any idea what will be round the next corner. One must reason from the information given to you and not from preconceived theories, on opinions given by others. But in no work that I did before was the Biblical saying: 'Ask, and ye shall receive; seek, and ye shall find; knock, and it shall be opened unto you' so clearly demonstrated. Every clue leads on to another. Loose ends become picked up and tied in and at any stage one can stop for a while and draw a picture, but all the time it is an unfolding story. Who would have guessed when we started with our simple experiments in finding the rates of this and that, that they might presently lead us to something which looks remarkably like a cosmic plan with an intelligence at the back of it? It is the complete negation of the Darwinian School of Evolution on which I was educated. Evolution is still there, of course, but instead of being a haphazard affair, it seems to be revealing itself as a most elaborate scheme worked out in minute detail from a prearranged series of tables. Whoever put, or puts, it into operation could, or can, work out his blueprint for an organism so that it would function correctly in every detail. We have only found the most minute fraction of these tables and there are innumerable gaps in what we have found. But we have found enough to show that the tables must be there and there must be an intelligence to put them into operation.

There is this spiral. Presumably you would always find it if you started from 0 and ended at 40 whatever you were plotting. So much in nature is based on a spiral. Look at the spiral twist on the trunk of a fir tree when it has been felled and barked. Or at an ordinary snail shell on the path. If anything rotates about an axis and, at the same time moves sideways at right angles to the point of rotation, a spiral is formed. The tree grows upwards, or the point of the snail shell grows outwards. But the natural spiral goes on growing. It is not just one single twist. Our table of rates yields one single whorl when you plot it out (Figure 14). It starts at 0 and ends at 40, which is the rate for death. If you look at the drawing of the spiral, it is clearly not complete. It must go on beyond 40 somehow. The obvious thing for it to do would be to go on growing in the same way in which it had grown before. But I was too devious in my thinking. I saw it reach the point of death at 40 and then said to myself: 'It must go on, but nothing can be the same after death. Perhaps it swings out in a wider curve and returns again to its own axis.' I wasted a lot of time and thought on this. The figure had to look right. I was thinking in terms of Irish Art of the Dark Ages. If I made a second and reversed twist four times as big as the first, it made a satisfying figure. You worked out the reversed spiral from a point four times 40 inches away and plotted it with rates four times as big as before. But, although the figure then looked right, there was something wrong about the whole matter. I had in my head the idea that the first spiral represented some form of mental evolution. It expanded right up to the point of death. According to the new figure, it went on expanding for a time and then began to contract, ending up once again at 0. This seemed nonsensical. If the point of all life was mental evolution then why should it go into a decline? Of course in the end I came back to the obvious. The spiral had to go on getting larger.

If the spiral grew, how did it grow? Nobody knew what happened beyond the point of death, unless they accepted the information derived from sensitives in the form of visions, automatic writing, spiritualism and so on. But I was not working in this way. I was trying to approach the subject in a scientific manner. It was already becoming apparent that whatever produced the rates was not confined to three-dimensional laws. It appeared to be outside both time and distance. The pendulum was surely working in another dimension, the fourth or perhaps the fifth. Could it then record rates beyond the point of death at 40? If it could record such rates, what relation would they be likely to bear to those which we had already discovered? The obvious solution was that the 40-inch rate for the first completed twist, or whorl, should be added to the original rate.

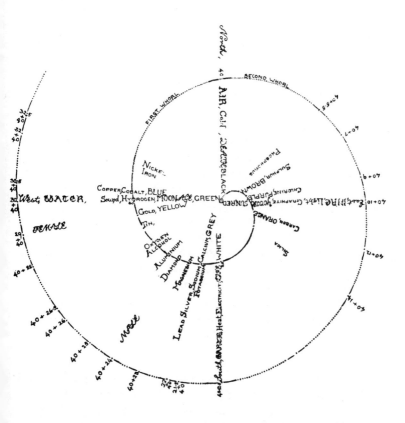

Figure 14. Diagram to show how the central point of each force-field, as indicated by the pendulum, lies on a spiral track. The numbers are in inches. The force-fields are biconical and at right angles to the spiral. The circumference of each basal circle cuts the central point of the spiral. This applies to both first and second whorls. The radius of each circle equals the rate on the pendulum.

I took some sulphur with a 7-inch rate, put it on the floor, measured a 40 + 7-inch rate on the pendulum and swung the pendulum at the spot 47 inches from the centre of the 7-inch field round the sulphur. The pendulum went into a gyration. There was a 47-inch rate for sulphur as well as the 7-inch one; but it was noticeably weaker. The same was shown to be the case with silver. There was a rate for 22 inches and one for 62 inches.

Of course this was most exciting. Whatever the rates really meant, they did not stop at the point which they themselves had indicated as being death. And they went on in the same order. If this 40-inch rate was really death, then everything beyond it was in the same sequence as it was before. Sulphur was still sulphur and silver was silver. As high as one could reach up the pendulum told the same story. The second whorl of the spiral was a larger facsimile of the first one. You need not, if the pendulum was to be trusted, be confused in your navigation in the next world. Red is still red and green green. 'Green to green and red to red, Perfect safety. Go ahead.' So says the old seaman's doggerel.

But this spiral is not a concrete thing at all. It is simply the curve along which the central points of the circles at the bases of biconical fields of force appear to lie. We have found the rates, the radii of these circles, by a series of experiments. We have found the double cones, standing on the central point of these radii, by experiment. But the spiral has only been found by plotting the results in an arbitrary manner. However, each stage led to the next. First we found our table of rates. Then we were led to construct our compass-rose of 40 segments, and on this rose we built up our spiral. You could not have made the rates into any other figure and you could not have made a spiral to fit the rates other than this one of 40 divisions. So it is quite reasonable to assume a spiral of this kind as being a kind of path on which a larger number of biconical fields of force stand vertically.

It is extremely improbable that the spiral is flat. Although it is difficult to demonstrate, it seems that it is an ascending spiral comparable to the rates. At the 40-inch point, it is probably 40 inches above the base point. In this again it is like a snail shell. One is accustomed to think of a snail as being a point upwards and moving point forwards. In fact the point is the dead end of the whole affair. As the snail grows, so does the lip of the shell become larger, and, as it moves, the point is backwards or downwards. So it is with our spiral. 0 is far away and forgotten, and the whorls continue to grow larger round a central axis.

The central axis appears to be the vital factor, for it seems to be the axis of the individual himself around which the whorls grow and the rates are arranged. It is at right angles to the

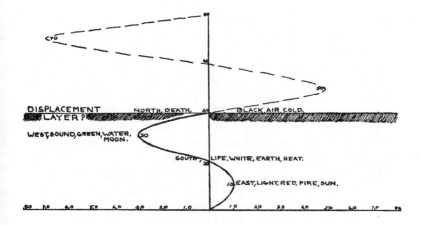

Figure 15. Diagram to show side view of the spiral of rates. The angle of climb is conjectural. Numbers in inches.

spiral, but parallel to the axis of every double-cone based on the spiral. Round that axis the double-cones swirl. They and the axis are not confined to the three-dimensional world, but are something beyond it. The whole thing must always be moving through time. You are not always standing in one spot just swinging a pendulum. You move about in space and everything moves in time. You can move in any direction in space, but in only one direction in time. Therefore any diagram we may attempt to draw of our spiral will only be true for one exact instant, the present moment. A second forward, or a second back and the whole pattern will have moved. No one can tell in which direction it may move except someone who can appreciate all movement from outside. But some part of our make-up can apparently do this, as was shown in Prof. J. B. Rhine's now famous card experiments and by those seers who frequently prophesy correctly about future events. I have even done it myself.

Now, if there is a part of ourselves which is both outside time and also distance, why cannot we use it always and what is it? Of course the answer to the first question must be that we are not meant to use it, for its use would remove the point of the whole experiment of living on this earth plane. We cannot use it because something happens at 40 which cuts 39 off from 41. After 40 the rates appear fainter to us on this plane, but they may well be much stronger on the next. The answer to the second question is that it is a level of our mind and mind is distinct from brain, as I have tried to show in other books.

Let us return to our spiral again and notice a most remarkable phenomenon. I have the handle of a William IV silver teaspoon which I use when making experiments with silver and the pendulum. I found it on a path in the kitchen garden where some ashes from the greenhouse boiler had been spread. I have never used the boiler and when we got here and fought our way through a jungle, we found the greenhouse with an elder tree just pushing off the roof. The boiler had burst and we removed it and the elder bush, making the place usable once more. There is a crest on the teaspoon handle, but after its experience in the boiler, which burnt off the bowl of the spoon, I cannot really say what it is. So this is a useful object to throw on the floor for experiments.

Now, as I have said, you can put this object on the floor and by approaching it from different directions, find the 22-inch circle of its double-cone. You can also find, standing on the 22-inch circle, that there is a 62-inch circle also. But if this circle was centred round the teaspoon, why did you not find it 40 inches outside the smaller one? You walked towards the spoon with the pendulum swinging, anywhere inside the 22-inch circle the pendulum will gyrate, but it did not gyrate inside the 62-inch one. The answer appears to be that the two circles are not concentric. You can approach the 62-inch circle from any direction and find that it is truly there, but it is not around the spoon. It has a centre of its own (Figure 16). Now in the three-dimensional world this is impossible. The spoon could not be in two places at once as these rates seem to indicate. We are faced with an incomprehensible situation. Either the whole pendulum story is nonsense, or there is an explanation.

Now, over a period of years and through a very large number of experiments the pendulum appears to speak the truth. If it is speaking the truth now, what does it mean? There is the object on the floor with the circle round it. You are at the rim of the circle. The object is in its appropriate place 22 inches from the axis, or spindle of the spiral. Suddenly another centre of another circle appears 62 inches away at the correct spot on the second whorl of the spiral and it has its own circle round it as you can easily test. More than that, it also has a weak 22-inch circle

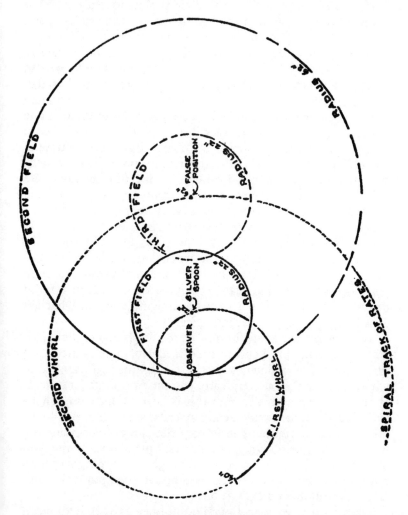

Figure 16. Diagram to show how the field of an object appears to become displaced after the 40-inch point on the spiral of rates. It can be shown that there is a third whorl of the spiral which presumably adds two more fields to the picture.

round where its supposed centre lies (Figure 16). It seems that there can be only one explanation. We are dealing with a displacement of some kind. Something happens which has the same kind of effect as when light is bent at the surface of a sheet of water and you see a fish in a different place to that in which it really is. As we stand on the hall floor we see the silver spoon handle in one place, but, as we test its field of force with the pendulum, we find it is in two places. If we walk round the rim of the original 22-inch circle around the spoon handle, we can find as many centres of 62-inch circles as we can be bothered to fix. All are mock positions of the spoon handle. But if we remain in one position there is only one. However, all of them at one moment of time lie on the track of the spiral. As you move, so does the apparent position of the object. But you take time to move. The object itself does not seem to move. From whichever direction you look at it, there it is inert on the floor. We will not consider that the floor itself is moving in space and time as we all are. But there is an extra movement of the apparent position of the object once you have passed the 40-inch mark. This is a horribly complicated situation to those who, like myself, do not like juggling with dimensions and higher mathematics. Shall we just note that after passing the 40-inch mark nothing above it will appear to be in the same position as it did below. This surely has a very great significance in what are called psychic, or parapsychological studies.

You cannot find a rate for time on the first whorl of the spiral. This is presumably because time is always passing here and you cannot pin it down with the pendulum. On the second whorl, beyond the rate for death, you can find a rate for time. It appears to be static, although this is beyond our comprehension. It is the same as the second whorl's rate for life, 20 + 40. In other words, if you happen to pass the point of death and are living on the second whorl, it takes no time to do anything you want to do. If that is so, anyone engaged in creating a species has only to draw up his design and he can then put it through all its evolutionary stages at once.

There is a third whorl outside number two. It is rather a trouble to investigate, for its rates are those of the first whorl plus 40 and again 40. This makes a very long cord on the pendulum, which is difficult to measure and awkward to use. I use the well of the staircase for experiments. As far as I have investigated, number three is again a replica of number one; but on it there is once more no rate for time. Events are evidently once more in time sequence as they are on the first whorl. There for the moment I must leave it, for I have nowhere suitable to look for a fourth whorl. It seems most probable that there is one and that what we have been examining is a measured demonstration of the Buddhist belief in the endless repetition of life and everything else. If so however, there seems to be something left out in what is reported about their belief, for I have never heard of timeless intervals between the lives.

Of course I may have reasoned incorrectly from the information at my disposal. I do not trust my powers of reasoning. But others must experiment and see that the facts are there as I have told, for this appears to be something of vital importance.

Let me say once more, as I always do, that I am not qualified to deal with this. My reasoning may be quite infantile. But my observation of what seems to happen is reliable. Otherwise I could not have found a specimen of *Sclerogaster compactus* and sent it to the South Kensington Museum. I can observe and do so. I trust my own observations. If the reader does not do so, there is no point in his reading this book. But if he does not do so, his opinion is of no more value than that of a plumed Papuan of New Guinea. Professor or layman, his mind is governed by superstition, a dogma which will not allow him to look facts in the face. What is more, this dogma is of quite recent growth. At the most it can hardly be two hundred years old. Before its creation the bulk of humanity knew that these odd things happened. Those who believed fervently in their Bible accepted them as a matter of course.

People as a whole do not realise to what extent many of the learned men they listen to on the wireless, or see on television, are parrots. A very large proportion of them are only the parrots with the best memories. What was taught by Professor X, two or even three generations ago, has still to be served up to get the best marks in an examination. The whole system of promotion, and by that of bread and butter, depends on being a good parrot. But what if the man, who taught the parrot to say: 'These ideas are absurd', was in himself wrong? Don't let us question it. Science is so marvellous. It can shoot a rocket to the moon. Very well, perhaps it can; but so can a small boy shoot a rocket into the sky. But what use is either effort? Is it any good if you are suffering from a serious disease to know that somebody has photographed the back of the moon, or even landed on it? Of course it is not. What you want to know is what happens when you die. Do you continue as Mr Jones, or do you simply disappear? Most Mr Joneses hope that they may go on being Mr Jones, but science tries to persuade them that they do not. Life begins and ends with the brain. When the brain is dead there is nothing left. Mr Jones has gone and *Necrophorus mortuorum* flies in to try and eat him up before the undertakers can get him shut up in a box.

Well, as far as it goes this scientific view is correct. Mr Jones's body is of no more use. It is worn out and has to be returned to earth again to provide in the end more food for the building up of another Mr Jones. But even by using the pendulum we can see that something has been left out of this scientific idea. Materialism, as it is called, has forgotten one vital point. Brain and mind are not the same thing. Mind can work in many dimensions. Brain can only function in three. Since science by its terms of reference can only deal with these three dimensions, length, breadth and thickness, it is not the slightest guide to what happens when you have to deal with four or even more. A scientist has no more qualifications than a stevedore to talk about this matter.

All we have learnt from our experiments tends to refute the materialistic belief. It tends to show very clearly that a part of our mind is not bounded by the Earthly three-dimensional bonds of time and space. It also knows far more than does our earthly one. Yet the two portions of mind are linked, although prevented from close co-operation by something comparable to the refracting layer between air and water. Everything we know in our earth life appears to continue on the next, but there are certainly additions. The biconical fields of force with which every fragment of matter seems to be surrounded, are evidently perceptible to our other mind. It can single them out with no difficulty and pass back the knowledge to us by the simple pendulum contrivance.

To understand why this should be so, it is necessary to see if we can appreciate a little of what the pendulum has been telling us about our mind (or is it our spirit?) beyond the 40-inch rate. It has told us that this mind, as I shall continue to call it for convenience, can sense things hidden from us by a veil of matter whether they are beneath a layer of soil or behind a stone wall. It can also jump across thousand of years of our time and do this both forwards and backwards. It has a further qualification which is quite beyond our earthly conceptions, for it can apparently appreciate objects in two places at once. Now the faster anything moves the closer it becomes to being in two places at the same time. If it moved at an infinite speed it would be in all places at once and appear to be at rest. We can surely infer therefore that to our mind beyond our earth life, things move very much faster than they do here. Everything, including ourselves, vibrates much faster on the next plane than it does on Earth. Green is still green and red red, but it is probably more intensely green or more vividly red.

Owing to this greatly increased rate of vibration, things which are solid and impenetrable to us are no longer so on the higher plane. Someone on this higher plane would be able to pass through the solid obstructions of Earth with as great ease as television vibrations pass through walls of houses or steel decks. This is more than half-way to understanding the mysteries we have been trying to investigate. Solids on the next plane are vibrating so fast that we cannot sense them at all, but they are solid enough to the individual on the next level. Just as everything is now known to be in constant movement here, so it is on the higher plane. The only difference is the speed at which things move. There is nothing unnatural about the next level. Things simply move too fast for us on Earth to sense them.

So much too depends on what we have been brought up from childhood to see and feel, or what we have been taught to observe later. The more varied that instruction is, the easier it becomes to appreciate unfamiliar matters. Early specialised training is bound to lead to a narrow and rigid outlook. I am most grateful to my mother and the old men of my boyhood for starting me off with a wide variety of interests.

Both my wife and I make a point of observing things, and trivial social things can sometimes be very interesting. I have been trained by my wife to notice what kind of clothes are worn by women I meet when she is not there. I am fairly good at it now and when she says, 'What kind of clothes had Mrs So-and-So got on?' I can reply with a description. 'Oh, she had on a hat made of grey curls like the back of an old-fashioned retriever and she had a plum coloured woolly coat and a skirt like a patchwork quilt.' That sort of thing. So I noticed our friend, Mrs X's, outfit when I sat opposite her at coffee. She and my wife sat side by side. Mr X sat beside me facing them. Well, I observed Mrs X, even though my wife was there. I don't suppose I had seen her for over a year and never very often.

After coffee we were shown various things about the house. I was often within a foot or two of Mrs X and talking to her. There was no change in her appearance even when they came to their front door to see us into our car.

On the way home, my wife remarked: 'Poor Mrs X, how terribly strained she looked. Her hair has gone so white and she looked much older. Of course that white jumper did not help.' 'What?' I said. 'A white jumper?' 'Yes,' said my wife, 'with a modern silver Celtic brooch in the front of it.' 'That is not how I saw her,' I said. 'She had on a smart, silk I call it, light chocolate-coloured dress. I noticed it particularly and wondered if we ought to have come in old tweeds. In the front of the dress was an openwork, round, gold brooch with some kind of yellow stone in the middle. I wondered if it was a topaz or a cairngorm. Her face appeared smooth and unlined and her hair was only slightly salted.'

We realised at once that this could not have been a mistake in observation by one of us. It was a definite slip in time of some sort. Either one of us was seeing Mrs X as she had been; or the other was seeing her as she was going to be. But to each of us she was there talking, drinking coffee, eating cakes, pointing out various things about the house and seeing us to our car.

It is not easy to determine what had happened. If it had been only a phenomenon in the sitting-room, then one might think that this was only a matter of thought transference and I had been seeing Mr X's memory picture of what his wife used to look like. But it is most unlikely that he would have gone on carrying this memory picture about all over the house and outside to our car. This cannot be the correct answer.

What happened with our spiral and the end of that silver

116

spoon? When you had passed the 40-inch mark, you found a new position for the object and in fact the spoon appeared to be in two places at once. Something similar it seems took place with Mrs X. She seemed to have been in two places in time. It was a fourth-dimensional displacement. I rather think that the displacement was mine and I had been seeing a television picture of Mrs X; although she was alive, well and talking to me for an hour. It was a perfectly natural phenomenon and may happen far more frequently than anyone observes, for, if only one of us had been present and there had not been two to check what we had each seen, no one would have noticed anything out of the ordinary.

This is, I think, one of the best cases we have observed. Unless someone can suggest a better explanation, it seems to be a perfect example of seeing a ghost; but the ghost was alive. I had seen some part of Mrs X displaced in time. In fact it looks as if I had seen her fourth-dimensional aspect, younger altogether than her present-day third-dimensional one.

This term 'dimension' is most unsatisfactory and irritates me, but I do not know what other expression to use. As far as I can estimate the position, it seems that the mind, our mind, exists on many planes and at many rates of vibration, which in itself is a term few can understand. Our present state of living, or shall we say the stage at which our mind happens to be using a machine called a body, apparently to obtain information about conditions in a denser medium, a slower rate of vibration, or what you will, is three-dimensional. Above it, actually in it perhaps, the mind has become accustomed to four dimensions and is able to handle matters which cannot easily be dealt with in three. But it is still our mind. To make the experiment of living under denser conditions seem to be real at all, it is necessary to have some kind of block between 3 and 4. If you knew quite well on this third-dimensional level that you were only using a body as an experiment, you could not give the same personal touch to your feelings as you do when you think you and your body are one and indivisible. You can almost do this when you watch a really good film. And this film in itself is probably a pale copy of the kind of thing your mind is actually watching, observing and noting through the brain in its body.

Since the experiments with the rates, which produced the

117

spiral, appear to show that green is still green, red still red, copper still copper and so on, after you have passed the rate for death, it appears that your mind still has a body once it has passed this 40-inch rate. On the fourth-dimensional plane this will seem as solid as the body we use on the third-dimensional earth. But the two cannot be cognisant of one another because of the apparent refraction at the 40-inch level. However some people seem to be able to slip from one level to the other without particular difficulty. As I visualise it, they slip up the spindle of the spiral, or down again like a fireman sliding down a pole to his fire-engine. When they are up, the fourth-dimensional world appears as real as earth does to us. When they are down they do not usually observe the higher level.

This whole thing is becoming so remarkable that I often feel that I ought to abandon it, or hand it over to the churchmen or philosophers. But when I meet specimens of both disciplines I usually think: 'Well, I don't believe they know more than I do, and most of them have far less general knowledge.' They may earn a reasonable income at their trades and mine does not cover the price of stamps for answering the flood of letters from people who do not even buy my books, but write with pride to say that they have managed to borrow them from libraries. Well, you know this is a bit tough on the author who is expected to pay the postage on the answers. Why I answer them I don't know. I give them the benefit of thoughtlessness and on rare occasions rise a good trout who becomes a pen-friend for years. A very few extremely intelligent and thoughtful people put a stamp in with their letter and they often become pen-friends too. But I know only too well how many people have later written to say that I was the only archaeologist who would answer their letters.

I have wandered off again, but I was brought up to the expression, when a gale was screaming round the house and the rain pouring down the chimneys: 'Pity the poor sailor on a night like this.' Pity the poor author too. He may work for many years on a serious book and practically the whole of what he earns does not cover the lowest paid operative of the Printers' Trade Union in wages for half a year. Why does anyone write books at all? The answer is that they are compelled to do so by the natural urge to create. They cannot make a living at it. It wastes enormous energy. But they have, like the lemmings of Norway to obey the call which drives them to the sea.

# Chapter 6

Radiaesthetic healing appears to work through the repulsion of some kind of force from the channel in which it had been accustomed to flow. What this force is, nobody knows. But it is clearly the same force which we have been trying to understand. It is something different from all the forces which scientists have spent enormous time and trouble investigating. It is not electricity as we know it, and it is not magnetism; because the pendulum clearly shows that it is related to true North and not magnetic North. But it is extremely powerful. One can pull it out between one's fingertips and see it faintly, like the spark between two terminals of an arc lamp. So strong is it that, when holding the pendulum, it can make one's hand judder like a car that will not take a gradient. It is some force which we have not as yet studied. But it is a force which was known and controlled by men long ago. They knew how to generate it, and how to store it in the fields of trees and stones. In our rather simple study we can see that we ourselves can do the same. I cannot be expected to know much about it, but I call it the Life force. It is the force which makes all nature work. It is not nature itself, but it is the life force of nature. Furthermore it is not confined to our earthly time scale, or to our earthly scale of distance. We have only to look around us to see that there cannot be a fixed time scale for living things. A raven may live a hundred years, a blue-tit one and a mayfly a day. Also consider how far a mile would be for an ant. Nowhere in nature is there a fixed scale.

The operator of the Box diagnoses what is wrong with a

patient by tuning in to a blood-spot on a circular scale. In place of a pendulum he uses an upright magnet. The scale is divided into 360°. When tension, stickiness, is observed on the rubber plate, this is the rate for the illness affecting the owner of the blood-spot. Healing is applied by simply reversing the reading on the dial by rotating the magnet. Thus if the rating for the disease was 130° the healing rate would be 310°. This is how I understand such descriptions of the performance as have appeared in print. There is probably more elaboration than this, but it need not concern us here. We see at once that, although there is a resemblance between dowsing and the operation of the Box, there is one big difference. The use of magnetism is essential to the Box, but the pendulum tells us that its orientation is concerned with true North and not magnetic North. The pendulum also shows us that its scale of rates is divided into 40 divisions and not 36 or 360. Is the healing force derived from the Earth's magnetic field, or from its mass? If the second proposition is correct, then the Box will often only be healing by near misses and also its value will vary in relation to the Earth's magnetic poles. If someone operates a Box in Greenland the variation between magnetic North and true North may be of the order of 90°, a quarter of a circle, while here the difference is about 7°. You may be nearly right in England, and almost right on the equator, but furiously and hopelessly wrong in Baffin Land. The variation decreases about half a degree in four years.

There are healers who use a pendulum, but do not use the Box. I do not know if any of them use the long pendulum and obtain rates with it like we do; but I rather think they do not. I had not thought of investigating this kind of thing; then, quite unexpectedly we became involved in it. Some months ago my wife saw a friend of ours, who had hurt his toe which was painful. More or less jokingly he dared her to heal it. Naturally, being dared like that, she took up the challenge and then expected me to know how she ought to do it. I had not the slightest idea how to begin. But I did have two rates, which were apparently those of Health and Disease. They were opposites on the 40-divisional circle, 32 and 12 inches respectively. We had no blood-spot; but we had a specimen of the man's handwriting. Going by intuition rather than reason, it seemed to us that if you tuned in on the right rate for health over this letter you might produce the same kind of result as with the Box. Since my wife had been challenged, she had to be the magician. She measured the 32-inch rate on the pendulum and swung it gently over the letter lying on the stone floor. It gyrated strongly and she counted 120 revolutions. Then it stopped and returned to a back and forth swing. At a second count later in the day the number of revolutions fell to 96. Two counts next day gave 72 each time and the following day two of 60. Then one of 44 and lastly one of 32, which was the same

Table 12

|  |  | Pendulum counts | |
| Date | Time | 32 inches | 27 inches |
| --- | --- | --- | --- |
| 24.xi.65 | 12 noon | 96 | |
| ,, | 6 p.m. | 120 | |
| 25.xi.65 | 8.15 a.m. | 72 | |
| ,, | 6 p.m. | 72 | |
| 26.xi.65 | 8.15 a.m. | 60 | |
| ,, | 5 p.m. | 60 | |
| 27.xi.65 | 9 a.m. | 44 | |
| ,, | 5 p.m. | 32 | |
| 28.xi.65 | 9 a.m. | 32 | |
| ,, | 5 p.m. | 32 | 27 |
| 29.xi.65 | 9 a.m. | 32 | 27 |
| ,, | 5 p.m. | 32 | 27 |
| 30.xi.65 | 9 a.m. | 32 | 27 |
| ,, | 5 p.m. | 32 | 27 |
| 1.xii.65 | 9 a.m. | 32 | 27 |
| ,, | 5 p.m. | *96 | 27 |
| 2.xii.65 | 9 a.m. | 50 | 27 |
| ,, | 5 p.m. | 32 | 27 |
| 3.xii.65 | 9 a.m. | 32 | 27 |
| ,, | 5 p.m. | 32 | 27 |
| 4.xii.65 | 9 a.m. | 32 | 27 |
| 5.xii.65 | 9 a.m. | 32 | 0 |
| ,, | 5 p.m. | 0 | 0 |
| 6.xii.65 | 9 a.m. | 0 | 0 |
| ,, | 5 p.m. | 0 | 0 |

*Patient had bad fall at 8 p.m.

as the rate on the pendulum. We thought it was probably similar to the 'normal' of a clinical thermometer, but we were wrong. For three and a half more days the 32 count remained steady and then an evening count suddenly gave 96 followed next morning by one of 50. There were then five consecutive counts of 32. At this point the count dropped to 0 and remained so.

We were, of course, most interested to know whether anything at all had happened to our friend. Then six days after the curious jump in the table, my wife saw him and talked to him about it. His foot had apparently recovered, which it might have done in any case, but the jump in the counts was far more interesting. At 5 p.m. on 1 December 1965, the count was taken and written down in a notebook following those which had preceded it. At 8 p.m. on the same day our friend was standing on a chair doing some building work when it collapsed and threw him on to a heap of rubble. He was not much hurt, but it was a shock.

This is once again not possible in three-dimensional study. Three hours before the accident took place, the pendulum told us that something had upset our friend's health count. It happened approximately fifteen miles away from here. It was a relatively trivial matter, but there it was, indicated in the notebook, three hours before its time. Not only is it remarkable that a pendulum can tell you anything at all about somebody fifteen miles away by just swinging over a bit of his handwriting, it can tell you what is going to happen to him. Mind you, we find this just as hard to believe in as you do. It is just utterly impossible, yet it happens.

If you take a letter from an unknown person written in ink (pencil will give some faulty answers) and test it with the pendulum, it is easy to find whether it comes from a man or a woman. You can also find if the writer is in good or bad health. If the pendulum says that the writer's health is not good, you can easily work out a table of rates for the different parts of the body and find out what is wrong with him.

Of course, to prove this, the experiment ought to be performed hundreds of times. A warning is, however, necessary here. All pendulum work entails the use of some current from the operator's body to project the ray through the pendulum.

123

As far as our work goes, we find that a great deal of current is in fact used up and the operator soon becomes tired. After testing for sex and thought rates in 110 sling stones, I was very tired. I think it is most probable that, if you did more than a couple of dozen of these telepathic experiments at one time, the operators would become tired and errors would start to creep in. I do not know and the number is a guess. However I think that this would happen.

People whose nerves are bad cause great exhaustion to the operator. In fact we now test the nerve rate first when testing for health and, if it has a bad reading, have no more to do with it.

Probably the way to test whether the operators are becoming tired is by using the psi rate of $9\frac{1}{2}$. By the psi rate I mean the rate for psychic ability. This I regard as a measure of potential, and you measure it by counting the number of turns made before the pendulum ceases to gyrate. We have tested 84 people for their psi rates. This can be found from their handwriting just as well as by reading direct from the actual person.

Fifty-four persons had what we may perhaps speak of as psi potentials of varying values. They range from 0 to at least 50, but they are not constant. They go up and down according to the person's bodily condition. During bronchitis, one guinea pig's potential dropped from a normal of about 45 to 30, and remained there till the illness was over. People with a potential of 15 and upwards can usually work the pendulum quite well. The only professional medium whose writing we were able to test was no higher than 18, whereas we had about a dozen of 45 or over. From around 30 and upwards people seem liable to have more extra-temporal and other unusual experiences than most of their neighbours.

There remains more than a third of the selected group who have no reading on $9\frac{1}{2}$. Instead they have one on the opposite side of the circle at $29\frac{1}{2}$, which we are calling minus psi. It is seldom very large, and when small fluctuates to the positive side and becomes $9\frac{1}{2}$. When we tested the few minus psi persons who had a reading of 30 or over, we found that they were in poor health according to what the pendulum reported. This showed as rather bad readings for the nervous system in particular. There were generally traces of something else wrong as well. By no means all persons with bad nervous readings have minus psi potential, but it is something which is worth bearing in mind.

Animals have psi readings and such cats as have been tested mostly have a potential of about 45, as high as any human in fact. Dogs we have not yet tried.

It seems evident that a psi potential is really a necessary part of the human make-up, but in many cases it is becoming weak, or converted into something else. Since examining nervous cases with the pendulum is intensely exhausting, it seems probable that the minus psi draws current from plus psi and these people become, in a sense, vampires. Many readers must have experienced a feeling of exhaustion after being in close company with another person. This is, I think, due to the leakage from plus psi to minus psi. It flows from the highest to the lowest and those persons whose psi is normally under about 10 probably never experience this phenomenon at all. With much practice in pendulum work your normal psi rate appears to rise, but this does not warrant too much use of the instrument at any one time. This leads to exhaustion. Should one suspect that another person is draining power from you, it can be checked to some extent by being outside the range of the rates, that is 40 + 40 inches.

Although psi is in many ways similar to electro-magnetism, it is by no means the same. For one thing, we have seen that it does not diminish with the square of the distance. For another, it can pass up from the three dimensional plane into a second and a third. Psi is not bounded by time, or distance, as we know them. As I have suggested in another book, it may well be the same force as that which operates gravity. It also appears to be related to ultra-sonic sound. This is the force which has to be considered when thinking about both telepathy and psycho-metry.

Of course you cannot have one without the other. Telepathy has to be used by the psychometrist to extract impressions from an object in such a way that they may be comprehensible to the mind. We usually think of telepathy as being the process where a single idea appears to arrive almost simultaneously in the minds of two people. This seems to be a chance happening and it is often difficult to establish which mind originated the thought. But telepathy is much wider than this and in the case of animals it is clear that individuals of differing species can carry on conversations by its means. In the case of birds, whole flocks operate as one, wheeling and diving with no word of command. Telepathy, in fact, is an alternative method to speech as a means of communication, and can be quite deliberate.

I said that the psychometrist must make use of telepathy and this may seem an inaccurate statement. But telepathy has to be the means by which the information stored in the field of an object can be transferred to the mind of the operator. The information may be pictorial, or in sound form, but whatever form it takes it cannot pass into the operator's mind by its own action. Telepathy provides the beam on which it passes. The beam can, as we have seen be broken down into various rates and these we are beginning to appreciate, even if we do not know what they really are. But then does anybody honestly believe that he understands electricity? He may know all there is to know about harnessing the force, but what it really is remains an enigma.

It is the same with telepathy. We may know that it can transfer thought forms from one mind to another, or from one object to one mind. We may soon learn to control it in the manner that electricity is controlled. Yet it may never be possible to say what it really is, beyond the vague statement that it consists of high velocity vibrations.

There we will leave telepathy for the moment, having demonstrated, I hope, that it can be utilised mechanically in the manner that electricity can be so utilised. We can, moreover, note that we have now two branches of parapsychology, telepathy and psychometry, both of which seem capable of being studied in a normal scientific manner, but both of which are evidently outside the range of three-dimensional science.

It is by paying attention to animals that we can get perhaps a better idea of how psi works than by looking at our neighbours. With animals psi still functions as it is meant to do, for their minds remain unhampered by long ethical training of one kind or another. Each one is out for himself and no nonsense. Cats are the least 'civilised' of the domestic animals; but they certainly have a sense of friendship and of humour. However, to think that you own a cat is ridiculous. It owns you and on occasion, with great kindness on its part, it will bring you a mouse, mole or bird as a present; particularly if it knows by its psi that you are worried or unwell.

The cat's psi is a most efficient and unexpected faculty. Although their eyesight is not good in daytime and they find it difficult to distinguish stationary objects unless they convert them into moving pictures by rapidly sliding their eyes from side to side, they have a way of locating things which is far superior to any of our normal five senses. Of course dogs have it too and, being less selfish, are more ready to make use of it to help human beings. I think the cat's private radar seems more efficient. It is noticeable too that it works very well when they are asleep, which apparently indicates that, like human beings, they live on other whorls of the spiral. It would seem that the cat is as immortal as the Pope, or the Archbishop of Canterbury; though I doubt whether they would be pleased to have this proved to them.

We have a Siamese cat and this almost completely wild animal is a great hunter. On most mornings before we get up she comes into the bedroom and goes to sleep on the end of the bed. One morning she sat up with a jerk and began to scan the corner of the room. She seemed to fix a bearing, jumped off the bed and ran out of the open door. In about three minutes she was back with a short-tailed field vole, which she devoured with horrid noises under the bed.

Now, on her line of bearing, there is a grassy bank beside the lane, about twenty-five yards from where she was sleeping. To get there she had to run along a passage in the opposite direction, across a big bedroom, down the backstairs, across the kitchen, out of the window, through a small court, round two sides of the house and then across a yard. It seemed clear that she had picked up the position of the vole in her sleep and then fixed this on her waking mind. At least two mental levels were involved. She kept that bearing in mind through several changes in direction and knew exactly where the vole was. It had no chance of escape. This has happened several times since then, and the same revolting ritual feast has taken place beneath our bed.

It seemed probable that the cat's whiskers acted like divining rods and I decided to try and find out their co-ordinates in our pendulum code. There is more work in this than anyone might think, for not only have you to rate the whiskers but you have to find out to what thought forms these co-ordinates also belong. Actually the cat has at least four sets of bristles. The longest and furthest back have a rate of 16 inches for sex, which is not a surprise. The next group is on 20 inches. Man comes on this rate, with love and life. The smallest and farthest forward of the groups is on 24 inches. On this rate you also find mice. Finally, its eyebrows are on 10 inches. On 10 inches you also find heat, explaining surely how a cat knows with unerring certainty where to find the warmest spot in the house.

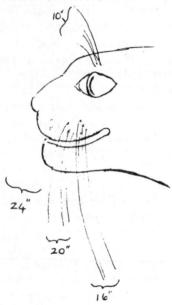

Figure 17. Diagram of a cat's face to show the rates of its whiskers as indicated by the pendulum: 10″ =heat and light; 16″ =sex; 20″ =living things and man; 24″ =mammals.

These four groups of bristles, then, seem to explain a cat's vigorous sex life; its fondness for mankind; its passion for mice and its love of warmth. This can hardly be either chance or coincidence, but looks like a carefully planned arrangement. If you were asked to describe the characteristics of a cat, surely these four would come high on your list.

Look at the way a beetle or moth finds its food. On its head it carries an instrument which acts like the diviner's twig, but in reverse. There are two antennae with a built-in response to the vibrations from the plant which its children have to eat. It is all perfectly simple and apparently most carefully thought out. This could never have taken place through any accidental evolution.

Of course no one with the slightest curiosity in his make-up can resist experimenting with the information freely presented to him by the writers of letters. We saw that something of the personality of an Iron Age slinger remained for two thousand years in the field of the stone he slung. It is just the same with a letter. Something of your personality remains in it, which is beyond what you said in the words you wrote on the paper. This is in accord with some modern theories of how memory functions, and although these have not yet been presented to the general seeker-after-truth, it seems evident to me that they must be nearer the correct answer than anything which has gone before. The holographic function of the mind is the coming idea.

What do you want to know about the people who have written to you? As this is, I hope, a scientific investigation, you want to catalogue them under various headings. We had over a hundred cards at Christmas and this seemed quite a big enough sample to learn something, although I might not believe what the pendulum said. Again and again I have to stress that I approach all this with complete disbelief. I am a most down-to-earth person and have had a scientific upbringing and training. I just do not accept anything the pendulum says without a struggle in my own mind. You must understand that we have worked out a table of rates, which comprises many things, and it seemed reasonable to try some of these in relation to others. I chose $9\frac{1}{2}$ inches, which appears to represent the psychic potential of a person, and which I call the psi rate, 16 inches which apparently indicates the sex potential, $19\frac{1}{2}$, which stands for blood and may show something about its character, and 30 inches, which stands for age. It soon became clear that the age rate had no effect on the sex or psi potential. Nevertheless this is the one I am going to discuss now.

In all, we tested 120 specimens, and whenever we knew a

person's age the pendulum was right within two revolutions. The method was to start the pendulum gently swinging over the specimen of handwriting when it had been set at the 30 inches rate for age. Then, quite arbitrarily, but apparently correctly, we counted one year for each turn the pendulum made. It is not easy to be sure when the revolutions start and when they stop and this is why one is liable to an error of a year at either end. Critics of this method must try it out for themselves before they are in a position to form any judgement of its accuracy. It sound complete nonsense and yet it appears to work. The proof of a pudding is not in what it looks like, but in how it tastes.

Now I am an archaeologist, and all archaeologists spend much of their working lives trying to fix the age of things. Much of what you read in books and newspapers about these dates is complete guesswork. At the best it is the result of elaborate calculations of the possible resemblance between one thing and another. It is built up on the apex of an inverted pyramid, whose point is one object whose date appears to be reasonably fixed. The pyramid is always wobbling about and sometimes falls, disastrously. There is a method of analysis known as Carbon 14, but this is only of value for very ancient things and is known to be liable to considerable error. It may be of use for objects three thousand years old, but is useless for those of three hundred.

It seemed to me therefore that anything which only seemed to have a possible error of two years would be of vast importance to the archaeologist. Even if it could be shown to be right, I knew very well that it would take at least twenty years for other archaeologists to believe it, for they will hardly believe that they have a nose to their faces unless they are feeling it continually and seeing it in a looking-glass many times a day.

I tried out an experiment tentatively and in complete disbelief. I took a link lost from brass chain armour, which I had picked up long ago in the sand hills at Sanna Bay on Ardna-
‹murchan. I had always wanted to know its date and rather thought it was Roman, although it was larger than any Roman mail I knew. I put the link on the floor. Mail links are unmistakable because there is a tiny pin hammered through to fasten together the ends of each ring, a rivet. Then I set the

pendulum at 30 inches. I swung it gently over the ring and it started to gyrate. I had greatly underestimated the tediousness of this process and how tired and mesmerised one would get. The wretched ball revolved eight hundred and twenty-four times. I took the figure 824 from the year 1968 and arrived at a date of AD 1144. Yes, it could well be right. The object was not Roman, but belonged to what we would call the Norman Period in England, when mail of this kind was the normal armour of a man-at-arms. Sommerled, the ancestor of the MacDonalds, was King of the Isles at that time, and was frequently involved in fighting. The answer might be true, but I was not convinced.

Through the years I have picked up old coins from time to time in various places. I keep them in a box, each in an envelope, in case they may come in useful for reference purposes. I went to the box and took out one envelope. I did not know what was in it, but guessed from the size that it was either a bawbee of Charles II or a farthing of Henry III. I put the envelope on the floor, and went through the whole operation again. The pendulum made 642 revolutions, which gave a date of AD 1326. I took out the coin and examined it. It was a silver farthing of Edward I, or Edward II, whether it could be dated more closely I do not know, but the date of Edward II's murder was AD 1327. The pendulum was apparently just right and if I had miscalculated the number of turns by two, it was well inside the limit.

It is very tiring doing these long counts, but it would be perfectly simple to devise an instrument for recording the number of turns if it should prove worth it. Supposing it is right, what about finding the date of Stonehenge? Nobody really knows this, within hundreds of years. You could date any earthwork without digging it and then guessing the date from the lost objects you happened to find.

I had to go on with this investigation. As it happened, I had what I thought would do nicely. In Moidart, on the north side of Ardnamurchan, there is a place called Cul na Croise, on Kentra bay. There are actually four little sandy bays, but only one concerns us. Above it is a wooded ridge known as Creaghan theach, 'the raven's crag'. One day in the autumn of 1924 I was in a boat off this bay, having with me a couple of cousins and one of the local Camerons. We had set a long line for flounders, with perhaps a hundred hooks baited with lug worms, and were waiting for it to fish. The Cameron presently looked up and remarked that there had once been a battle in the sand-dunes ashore. At once I was interested, and asked when it had been. 'Ach, I don't know,' he said. 'It was in the time of the Danes.'

Kentra bay is a lovely place, even now after the commandos were trained in landing there during the Second World War. A burn with little green flats beside it runs down from woods of scrubby trees to the dunes on the edge of the sea. Westward are the blue, jagged peaks of Rum and Eigg, and to northward the hills of Skye. This is a splendid place for beaching boats when the wind is off-shore and it is the best place for this purpose for many miles. It is not surprising therefore that local tradition tells of battles there.

However, local tradition is difficult to extract, and still more difficult to interpret. One heard of the 'Red Rover', whose name may have been something like Dewing, fighting on the beach and that its real name was 'traigh a raever' — meaning the 'rover's strand'. Whoever the Red Rover may have been I have never been able to discover. He is said to have been driven off, and to have died on an island near Dublin.

There was a tale of a second raid carried out by a dozen Irishmen, who were also driven off, chased to Skye, captured and their ship taken. But again no one knows who they might have been, and all that remains is the echo of a story of the bravery of a local weaver, a Cameron apparently.

My insatiable curiosity took me to the Rover's Strand on many occasions. Sometimes I walked for some miles through the woods from Acharacle on Loch Shiel, and sometimes I landed from a boat. I have hunted those wind-blown dunes till my back, bent from peering at the sand, ached so much that I had to give up the search. The sum total of my efforts was very small by archaeological standards, but it was also most intriguing. I found an early Bronze Age land-surface on which were scraps of 'Beaker' pottery and flint implements. Then I collected quite a number of glass beads, four black, three yellow, one blue and one white. I could not date them, although I have made a study of beads. There were fragments of at least ten barbed and socketed iron arrow-heads, and parts of four small iron knives, probably arm-pit knives. There were at least 100 iron clinch nails from a boat. All these iron objects and the beads might have belonged to 'the time of the Danes', for the Scottish crown did not obtain the islands till the thirteenth century, when it bought them for 4,000 crowns in 1266. There was a little brass ring-brooch, which perhaps belonged to this age too. But what was one to make of many lead musket and pistol balls, and a brass button embossed with a crown and the words 'Argyleshire Volunteers'?

I decided that this was a fitting series on which to try the pendulum. If what it said made sense, then I would be prepared to accept its statements, with due caution, of course. I did not really know the date of a single object, except perhaps that of a little copper bawbee of the reign of Charles II.

There were a lot of musket and pistol balls, but I had only kept two of the former and one of the latter. I tried these first. Remember, for it becomes more important in a moment, that I know I can be two years out in the counting. According to the pendulum, these balls were shot away and lost at the following dates:

> Musket ball, AD 1785
> Pistol ball, AD 1784
> Musket ball, AD 1795

The button of the Argyleshire Volunteers was apparently lost in AD 1785. Now if the pendulum was telling something like the truth, it was obvious that no Red Rover, or boat-load of Irish pirates, had anything to do with this collection. The most probable solution appeared to be that the Volunteers had used the dunes for musket practice and one had lost a button off his uniform.

I knew nothing about the Volunteers. I had heard of the militia of course, and of the difficulties encountered by authority in enrolling them at the time of the Napoleonic Wars. I looked up what I could find.

It appears that Volunteers were a by-product of the Militia Act of 1757, and that by the next year officers were permitted to accept volunteers instead of compulsorily enrolled militia men. By 1778 there were Volunteer companies and corps formed independently of militia units. In 1783 with the political stupidity to which we are long accustomed in Britain, the Volunteers in England and Scotland were disbanded. They had to be hurriedly raised again on the outbreak of war with Revolutionary France, and in 1795 the invasion scare was in full swing. In 1798 the Volunteers were formed into 'armed associations' and the word 'Volunteer' was dropped. From this it is clear that the musket ball dated by the pendulum to 1795 is exactly right, and all the other three objects are within the two years margin of error due to the difficulty in deciding the exact moment at which the gyratory movement begins and stops. Perhaps the most impressive thing of all is that the gap of ten years during which the Volunteers were disbanded is reflected in the dates given by the pendulum. There are too few specimens of course, but my incredulity had received a knock.

Now ten arrows are not lost by accident, for anyone can see a 'clothyard' shaft sticking in the ground. These must have been shot away in action and never picked up again afterwards. We can infer then, that whoever shot them cannot have lived in the district, or they would have returned when all was quiet again to pick up what they had fired. Therefore I take it that these arrows had belonged to some force landing in the bay and that their landing had not been successful. Here we have some confirmation of the Red Rover tradition, but what was the date of the arrow-heads and were they all contemporary?

Through the years I have made a number of attempts to establish the dates of iron arrow-heads and have had little success. Although the name Red Rover suggested the Vikings, I was well aware that these arrows might have been of any date between perhaps the years AD 1000 and AD 1600. Bows were used by the English against the Spanish Armada in AD 1588, and probably much later in the Hebrides.

The tedious business of counting long runs of revolutions now began again. It was so tiring that I could never do more than two arrow-heads in one day. After a time, while watching the ball slowly swinging round, you begin to wonder if you are counting fifties or sixties. It is impossible to let your mind wander to anything else, and quite difficult to remember whether you are in the four hundreds or the five. You certainly cannot carry in your head the number of turns which had been

134

made by the last specimen. It took twenty minutes to do each count.

The pendulum's answers for the date of loss, when the number of turns had been subtracted from the present year in 1968, were as follows:

AD 1340
1344
1341
1344
1342
1341
1343
1341
1344
1343

Two knives, which I still have here, both gave readings of AD 1343.

It seemed clear, allowing for the possible error in some of the counts of two years, that an average shows that all these arrows could have been shot away, and the knives lost, in the year AD 1342. This ought to be the historical date of the Red Rover's abortive landing.

To anyone who had spent much of his life trying to fix dates by observing minute changes in the shape and ornament of objects, this result was fantastic. I was not sure that I liked it. If the pendulum was right, any child with a high psi count could be far better at estimating the date of an ancient object than the most learned professor of that particular subject. Still, one was trained as a scientist and so had a duty to record what one observed. However important an idea may seem to its originator, he must have the honesty to give it up when discovered facts prove it to be wrong. Some well-known people today have prostituted their art by not obeying this principle. I may not like what the pendulum appears to be able to do, but I must accept what I find.

There is no end to the study. When you think you have come to a place where you can leave it and do a little mild gardening, up crops another puzzle and off you go again. Where I have perhaps two hundred rates, there must be thousands, if not millions. Even the four cardinal points and such things as life and death, sun and moon, red and green and so on are enough to make us wonder why they are numbered and who numbered them. 'The very hairs of your head are numbered', Jesus said and to this the pendulum replied: 'Yes, they have a rate of eleven and a half inches.' This is not meant to be blasphemous; it is an observed fact.

# Chapter 7

The question of the meaning of time is going to figure largely in the investigation, for it appears to be a key, which may unlock many boxes of secrets. Time, as we know it in daily life, is just a convenience for the observation of sequences of events. It is not the time which interests us but the sequence. It is obvious that there is no such thing as a fixed time scale for all living things. Time to a blue tit is quite different from time to an oak tree and to us. Our respectable time scale does not really work and what is happening in the observer's mind need not have any relation to it at all. Two people may travel to America by the same plane. For each the same number of divisions of the scale are occupied by the journey; but for one, who wants to get there in a desperate hurry, the time will drag and seem much longer than it does to the other, who does not wish to get there at all.

In my lifetime there has only been one man who could really bring home to people the importance of the study of Time, for he saw that it carried with it the answer to whether there was a plan in life and whether it continued beyond the point which we call death. When Dunne's first book, *An Experiment with Time*, came out, it caused the greatest interest and thrill all over the world.

Dunne was greatly surprised to have a series of dreams which were about matters which had not yet happened and he felt compelled to investigate this theoretically impossible matter. I shall not quote from him. If the reader is keen enough, he will get a copy of *An Experiment with Time* and read the

exciting account himself. They are remarkable: volcanic erup-
tions, terrible fire and other dramatic events, all dreamed of
before they took place and mostly derived from newspaper
reports as yet unprinted. One indeed contained a numerical
error, which was to be in a newspaper when it came out later.
In his sleep Dunne was obtaining information about things he
was going to read in the papers days later. It was all recorded
and timed in a way which could not be shrugged off. Dunne's
future memories were as much fact as the landing on the moon.

In brief, Dunne's theory was that every person was built up
of a series of observers, each watching the actions of the one in
front. The only observer who ever died was the first one. The
others continued to observe.

It seems now that, though there may be a series of observers,
each is not a replica of the preceding one. They appear to have
become more learned and intelligent in succession. The point
here is that Dunne had apparently altered our conception of
time, but the thinking world was too lazy to take it seriously. I
am kind in calling inaction 'lazy', for it is obvious that many
vested interests were involved also. The Church might have to
rethink its explanation of the doctrine of free will.

Accustomed as scientists were to dealing with one world in
which they need only trouble with what could be weighed and
measured, how were they to regard memory which they could
not measure? And a world of sleep was beyond their terms of
reference. There must have been a considerable number of
people on both sides who felt guilty about all this. But the
younger ones would realise that their bread and butter was at
risk if they admitted taking an interest in such outrageous
matters.

But the one vital question, which mankind wants to know, is
whether his personality, individuality, or whatever you like to
call 'himself', is extinguished at death. Solve this and then all
the exploits of atom splitters and astronauts are simply light
entertainment.

I can say at once that there seem to be two main types of
dream. Apparently one type is a cut from a true dream, brooded
over and extended by a sleepy mind. This is probably the kind
of thing which interests psychologists. Over it the dreamer's
mind seems to have some kind of control and to a professional

it may give some indication of the state of the patient's mentality. The second type appears to be a true dream, beyond the control of the earth mind. It is clear and vivid and may not always belong to the dreamer at all, as at times it seems to be something transmitted by telepathy from somebody else.

Although many people may deny the possibility of seeing ghosts, it is quite absurd to say that no one experiences dreams. It is now supposedly possible to tell with instruments if a sleeping person is dreaming. Dreams are respectable: ghosts are not. Yet there seems to be much in common between the two phenomena. They both belong to a different level of awareness from the one normally used in waking life. However, scientists will accept somebody's story of what he dreamt and be blankly incredulous if the same person describes a ghost which he has appreciated. It is a curious blind spot in the scientist's own make-up and the reverse of the true scientific outlook. A witness should be believed until he can be shown to be wrong. If a scientist can pick and choose what observations he will accept, it makes others wonder how much reliance they can put on his reports of his personal findings. What has he left out because it did not fit in with some preconceived theory? One knows of several cases where this has been done and which thereby created a completely false picture. Fortunately we are now about to deal with dreams and so there is a reasonable chance that what we report may be believed.

As I said before, there are two main classes of what may be called dreams. Over one our waking mind seems to have some measure of control and, by its imagination, it can mould the progress of the dream. The second class is a true dream and appears to be completely uninfluenced by the waking mind. It is an experience on another level of consciousness and from these experiences we can derive a great deal of unexpected information. Here is one, which at once attracted my attention.

On 23 October 1970, I had a clear dream in colour (as most of mine are). I appeared to see, for in reality it was pitch dark, something like a brown, furry snake coming into the room beside my bed. The snake was followed by a brown lump attached to it and perhaps nine inches above the floor. Very soon a complete brownish cat had come into the room backwards. I memorised the furniture and when properly awake

139

drew a picture of the whole incident (Figure 18). Of course cats do walk backwards along window ledges and things of that sort, but it is not their normal method of locomotion. The more I thought of it, the more probable it seemed that the dream cat was not coming backwards into the room, but was going out of it. When I reversed the drawing of the furniture in the looking-glass, it was clear that I was looking at a slightly distorted picture of our own bedroom as seen from my bed.

A                                    B

Figure 18. The dream of the reversing cat. From memory: A. The tail appears. B. The whole cat comes into view.

The cat was our Siamese, Hecate. Others have experienced reversal dreams of this nature and this reversal is evidently reasonably common. But it raises problems. How does one's mind run backwards? Every natural phenomenon must have a natural explanation and the reversed picture of Hecate became in the end a most important clue.

The recording of dreams does make us take trouble, for what one appears to be observing passes very quickly, like a picture on a cinema or television screen. It is shot apparently on one mental level and appreciated, like a memory, on the next. The observer has to cultivate the art of catching it, like the good

140

portrait painter catches the fleeting expression of his sitter, and this may be a very difficult art to master.

Apparently the dream is a sequence on a different level of mentality from that used in earth life and it probably passes much more swiftly likewise. If you study a lot of dreams it appears that the same sequence takes place on each level. One is a replica of the other, even if there are some differences in observation. We see here that we are getting very close to Dunne's series of observers; but there is a difference. In dreams each observer does not see exactly the same picture as the first one does.

I could report many unthrilling future dreams also, for I have them all written down and dated. Some were things I was going to see in newspapers in a few days' time; some are shots from future television and so on. Generally there is some slight difference between the two experiences, but the identity is clear. Dream memories can be and frequently are in future time. I am afraid this is a fact we are all saddled with and, upsetting though it may be, it needs a rational answer. I do not know whether everybody has future dreams, but all the people I have asked to note their experiences have had some in future time. It is certainly more common than the reversed type.

We have been confronted with two types of situation, which to our grandparents would have appeared utterly impossible. How could an event happen backwards, or how could the future exist? But these things are fact, not imagination or delusion. One suspects at once that, in some way which we cannot for the moment see, the dilemma's horn of time is poking into the picture. One remembers the extract from a pilot's log during the 1914 war: 'Passed a seagull flying backwards!' Something must have made our cat appear to walk backwards, because the observer is in some way moving faster than the cat appears to be doing. But the observer is apparently asleep, or nearly so, in bed. It appears that the observer on the next mental level must be going faster.

At present we know nothing about this observer at all, except that he seems to be so tightly linked to our earth personality that he apparently experiences the same sequences of events. Which comes first, the egg or the chicken? Or are both sequences identical? They cannot be identical or the cat would not progress backwards. But they might be like identical strips of film exposures starting at the same moment and run through at different speeds.

If this were so, it would account for both the cat (like the seagull in the report) and for occurrences in future time. It would depend on the speeds of the two projections. This is rather difficult to visualise but I think most people today will understand what I mean. From this we can surely infer that during sleep our minds are still operating, but at a different speed from what they do when we are awake on earth. The body may be at rest but the mind is still busy. One imagines that it is playing through the strip of film, which the earth consciousness was experiencing while it was awake. One might think it was checking the thing through in the same sort of way as that in which an author corrects his proofs. This seems to me to diminish greatly the importance of the brain, for this is not apparently being used. The whole operation is in the mind and there is no evidence that the second observer has any connection with the brain at all. He may have very little connection with the observer on earth, except to use the film, which that observer has made for him. Or that observer may be a projection of himself and sent out to gather information. I incline towards the second view, but let us see what happens as we go on with the investigation.

I have a pen friend, Mrs V. Beresford, who lives in the Beaconsfield area. I have never met her. She is a very keen and efficient research worker in all these odd subjects. On 30 November 1969, I woke to see a small highly-coloured bird of the parrot family peering out of some box or hole. I did not take much notice of the bird, for a strange voice was speaking. I could hear the words, which seemed to be: 'Budgie is very peeved. His sole of rubber . . . has been spotted.' That morning I wrote to Mrs Beresford and told her about this dream. By return of post, sent on 2 December, I had a letter from her saying she had received mine and had been very surprised by what it said, for on 1 December a strange budgerigar had flown in through her window. She had put it in a spare cage and remarked to a neighbour: 'A budgie, he's pleased. He knew somehow he'd have a safe harbour here.'

This was even more remarkable than the other two dreams.

First I had experienced a dream memory of future time. I got this memory at a different time of day from that at which the incident really happened. Therefore it could not have been a case of ordinary telepathy, or thought transference. Then, although the words I apparently heard were not the same as those which were spoken a hundred miles away in Beaconsfield, their sound, probably not remembered exactly by either of us, was so similar that one can hardly doubt that they were the same. Since my earth observer was asleep, the whole incident appears to argue some kind of telepathic communication between Mrs Beresford's observer two and my observer two. Further than this, the whole thing suggests a very great deal of activity on the part of the observers on the second level. The incident was so trivial that clearly much else must pass between the two observers. One might think that they study each other's films. I am inclined to think that those who believe that they are to enjoy a period of laziness and rest when they die are in for a considerable surprise.

Mind is perhaps eternal and the part of it you use in daily life just a very small fraction of the whole. Of course I am guessing now, but as we go on we may come upon more clues, which may help to make the guesses more informed. Guesses, even if they are wrong, are useful, for they stir up people to think out what is wrong with them. It is the lack of original thought which has left us with this dilemma for so long. People are afraid to think and even more afraid to try out their ideas on others.

Dunne worked out an extremely complicated explanation of this strange phenomenon. The explanation, which did not seem to make the question any easier to understand, tended to obscure the basic fact. Time did not always go on ticking in one direction for ever. Sometimes it ticked backwards and effect came before cause. The egg was there before the hen laid it; the man was killed by the bullet before it hit him and so on.

Whatever the explanation of this phenomenon may be, it will not be obtained by denying the facts. Too many have found future elements in their dreams for that attitude to be considered. We have to admit that these apparently impossible things occur, and then see whether there is not some relatively simple, natural explanation to account for them.

Over and above everything else there appears to be an external system and we have only touched the fringes of it. This system seems to be so detailed that it is possible to recognise the food plant of a particular insect by the length of cord on a pendulum and the number of times it rotates. It is possible to trace the movements of a person round the world, observe when he is ill, and appreciate the part of his body affected. We have by divination also learnt of the accident to a friend, fifteen miles away, three hours before that accident took place. This appears incredible, but it is all down in my notebook. We are dealing all the time with the apparently impossible and there must be some natural reason for the results.

All these measurements and experiments took years to perform and there is probably no limit to what you could find out. We have one fixed point in this problem, which is that dreams often contain elements drawn from future time. This cannot be evaded. Dunne tried to get round it, but not very convincingly. The explanation must be quite simple and not need an elaborate system of observers. A possible answer is that this earth life is not real and we are now going over something which has been lived already. If this were so, then it would perhaps be possible to go into the place where the film was projected and look over it for both forward and backward shots (just as you can unroll a cinema film and examine it when it is not being shown). Could this be what happens when we go to sleep? Do we just go into the projection room and look over the film? If so there must be an infinite number of people looking over an infinite number of films at the same time.

If we take this idea and examine the flash and strip types of dream, there appears to be some confirmation. So many of them seem to resemble the results of people trying out stills and little strips of film on projectors of some kind. They often appear to do it inexpertly and shots stick or come on back to front.

If there is any truth in this idea, it could begin to give us remarkable thoughts of what may be happening in the next zone, for it suggests that there may be mechanical projectors there not very different from those we know here. This is a long way from the old idea of people sitting on wet clouds and

144

twanging harps, yet it seems to be a more practical possibility.

I have seen a large number of stills of people and there are several strange points about them. They are like ordinary earth pictures (photographs, drawings or paintings). They are always strangers. There are others of dogs, but never of dogs the dreamer remembers. There are stills which can be appreciated as coming from photographs or postcards. When seeing these you get exactly the same impression as when watching somebody operating some form of projector. There is a yet more remarkable point. Two of my stills did not come on properly. One stuck in the left corner and I could not see the whole face. The other came more than half way on and there stopped with a hard blank end just as if a lantern slide had stuck in the 'gate'. I feel reasonably certain that these were indeed lantern slides. If so where and how are they being put on? Who is doing it? Other people often tell me that they have dreams of this kind.

Are we seeing projections taking place in the next zone, on some private kind of television projector? If so (and people will call me crazy for making the suggestion) these stills might be call-up signs to attract the attention of a particular person.

Obviously if these things are call-ups, then it is only by chance that we happen to see them. We perhaps are changing our rate of vibration from sleeping to waking, or back again, and for an instant happen to be on the right length to pick up a particular sign. An alternative possibility appears to be that (since there is no time in the next zone) when we get there in sleep, we may be able to pick up transmissions from some form of apparatus not yet produced on earth.

However, we must remain obstinately curious in all this study. When everything is so nebulous it is only too easy to believe anything which looks like making sense. I think it is clear from working over the dreams that our imagination does add to some extent to what is actually dreamt.

Now if our earth time is moving on a straight line, the time on the next mental level must be something quite different. It is not moving at all. But there is a sequence on this second level and so there must be many series of events stored somehow on it. Since we experience these sequences in dreams, it is clear that they can be put on to a moving time scale, just as one can put a cinema film on to a projector; but until this is done they are meaningless and inert. It seems to me that a sequence on the second mind level must be represented not by a line like a ruler but by a dot. I visualise each sequence as an infinitesimally small globe composed of what we must call 'onion skins' of experience.

I think it must be clear now what we are finding. These dots are memories. Our second mental whorl on the spiral becomes a vast library of memories. The memories are not tied to our earth time and so 'future' events can be revealed but, owing to the expanding of the spiral, they will not correspond exactly with what happens on earth. More than this, we can see from a study of dreams that these memories in the library are available in some telepathic manner to people other than those who experience the sequences which the memories store.

One would expect this to be the end of it all and assume that after death a person just browses in a vast storehouse of memories until it becomes such a bore that he cannot be bothered to continue his existence. However, the pendulum shows that this idea is wrong. There is a third whorl above the second and a fourth above the third and on both these whorls time is as it is on earth. You walk out of the museum into a new life of time and sequence. I say 'walk' because the pendulum indicates that there is no death beyond the first one.

I think we must assume that when we experience memories during earth life, we have already got a foot on the second level. The memories come to us by chance and in no particular order. We have just taken a particular dot out of the collection, which some incident in earth life has brought to our notice. We can even do it deliberately. The block between the two levels is not very solid.

Many races have taught that after death a person has to review his past earth life. It seems that this may well be the truth of what happens on the second whorl, where there is succession but no movement of time. On the third plane, time begins to move once more. It seems possible that the Roman Catholic idea of Purgatory originated in some knowledge of what appears to happen on the second timeless whorl. The more one looks into these subjects, the clearer it becomes that far back in the Ages men knew much more about them than they do today. One has only to look at the teachings of Jesus,

146

Buddha and the Kahunas to see that this must be so.

It is hard to visualise what happens on the second plane. But perhaps it is not particularly inept to picture each particular incident as a stone thrown into quiet water with ripples spreading out in all directions (see Figure 19). There will be an infinite number of these points and the ripples will have no troughs between them. The earth level time will pass through a particular point in a straight line; whichever way it passes through, it will hit the same successions. However, some will go forward and some backward. If you happen to concentrate on the backward ripples, you will return from sleep with an impression of things moving backwards. However, if you concentrate on the forward series, you will at first get ordinary memories of events which have already happened in earth time and then, as the point on the second level does not move, you will receive impressions of things which have not yet happened.

Man exists on many mental levels, of which the earth life appears to be the lowest. On this level he gathers information to be used by his real self on levels above. He is not an animal but is compelled to use an animal body to be able to exist on the low level. He is not the equal of any other man. He is entirely independent and his method of development is peculiar to himself. On this level he is completely alone and all his decisions are his own, to forward his own development. Only when he can realise this will he rise at all in the scale of evolution. Higher in the scale he is probably not so much alone.

In sleep your mind appears to go right out through the second level and has no recollection of what happens when it returns; but during its passage on to a still higher grade, it passes through the second zone and there it picks up its dreams, which are memories. These, as we have said already, can be past or future and may belong to you or somebody else. They are real memories and not imagination. One morning as I was waking I thought I saw a bottle of Gordon's gin standing by itself on the bedside table. In reality the table was heaped high with books. When I went to bed that night I noticed that on a second table, which was now beside the bed and otherwise bare of objects, there was a copy of a magazine lying face downwards. The whole of the back cover was an advertisement in colour for Gordon's gin and in one corner of it was a large picture of a bottle of gin standing upright. One would think it was such a trivial incident that it must be a coincidence. But it is not. It happens with great frequency. Let us look at a diagram for a moment (Figure 19).

The two horizontal lines represent two successive mental levels with the earth plane at the bottom. On this line some events in a sequence are represented by numbered divisions as on a ruler. They are separated since they are moving in time. On the higher horizontal line, the same sequence should be represented as a minute dot, but, entirely for convenience, we will separate and number each event in the same order as on the line below. There appears to be no moving time here; the events should be complete spheres surrounding the dot and without thickness or distance separating them. We cannot represent them in this way. We will be content with an expanded section of the sequence in a single plane. You find at once that on this second level, you have two marks for each event instead of the single one on the line below. The sequence can proceed backwards as well as forwards. Owing to the fact that the sequence has a rate on the Spiral of Rates, the second timeless origin of it will not be directly above the point of origin below. If your spiral coils outwards in a clockwise manner, the upper point of origin will be further out than the lower one. In a horizontal plane it will be about 80 inches, or two metres, higher up.

The events on the upper line are memories. If we now join the corresponding numbered points on the two lines, we find three possible kinds of memory: past, future and reversed; which type they will be depends on how far you have moved along the lower line. On the diagram the change from past to future memory occurs at 40. In any case you can only obtain a future memory when your mind has moved in sleep, or death, up to the higher level. That appears to be the explanation of all mediumistic foresight and of future dreams.

One other factor comes out of this. Owing to the expansion of the spiral, the points of origin of a given sequence on two levels can never be exactly above one another. Therefore the memory picture can never, in the parlance of colour painting, register exactly. A prophecy will never be completely right; although much of it may be, a remembered incident will

148

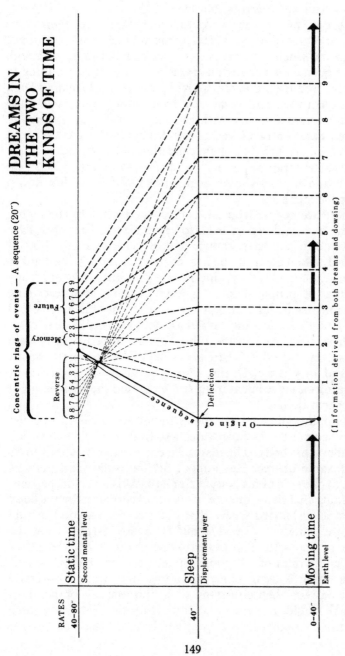

Figure 19. Although many people have a dislike for diagrams, I hope they will give this one some attention. It attempts to show why events may be appreciated in dreams, either in reversed order, or before they have taken place in earth time. There would be no spaces between the numbers on the top line.

always have some errors, however slight, in it.

I know this is very hard to understand and even more difficult to put into words. It took me hours of work to produce a diagram which gave me even moderate satisfaction; although I have been constructing diagrams for years. It is one thing to have to produce a diagram showing a section through a Dark Ages earthwork and what you have found in it, and quite another to have to deal with one explaining what appears to happen between two levels of mind. However, both are based on observed fact as far as I am concerned. I knew exactly where a particular scrap of pottery should be placed on a given plan and I know exactly how a given thought form fits into a particular picture.

There are people who can control their visits to the higher mental level and report back to some extent what they have experienced; we have known one of these, namely Mrs N whom I talked about in the first chapter. Although it is hard to believe the reports, they appear to be genuine. There are many accounts of people doing this kind of thing and describing what they have seen during their travels. They claim to be still joined to their sleeping bodies by an extensible silver cord, which is mentioned in the Bible, and some deliberately train themselves to do this. There are even greater numbers who get involved by chance. During illness, or under anaesthetics, or as a result of an accident, they suddenly find themselves out of their earth bodies.

The point which strikes me as important is that the person on his second level of consciousness finds himself to one side and above his body. The displacement frequently seems to be of the same degree. He is about 6½ feet above and perhaps 2 feet to one side of his body. I think that this is very important. Assuming that in a sequence of events experienced by the body the mind is located where that body is, on a second mental level the mind is located about 80 inches farther from the centre of the earth. This ought to give us the clue to the difference in the rates of vibration between the two mental levels.

One thing is clear: if my reasoning from what is observed fact is correct, then no person with a normal rate of vibration on earth would in ordinary circumstances be able to see people or events on higher levels. They would take place well outside the earth spectrum. Here is one facet of the block between the levels of existence. Those with mediumistic powers, who do get through the block, must somehow have their normal rate of vibration speeded up considerably. Thus our magician friend was only visible in our bedroom as a small light. This is frequently reported by Hindu and other advanced thinkers in India, who are said to leave their bodies and move across country as balls of light. It is possible that the phenomenon of foo-fighters, frequently noted during the Second World War by observers in aeroplanes and inexplicable to ordinary science, indicates that dead airmen from the next levels still took an interest in what was going on and followed the planes with their superconscious minds. We may imagine perhaps that they had not yet realised which mental level they were on.

I know this all sounds very difficult and possibly absurd. No one may believe that there are many separate levels of mind and that our earth mind is the lowest that we know about. Presumably the 'subconscious' is lower still and is only animal and to treat it as of vital importance instead of trying to smother it is a very great mistake. All advance in culture appears to be based on the very repressions which psychologists attempt to remove. There can be no civilisation without discipline to order the relationship of one man towards another. If you remove the so-called complexes, on which psychologists thrive, you destroy discipline and civilisation goes with it. For you cannot train a child to rational behaviour towards its fellows without restrictions. Remove the restrictions and you get an animal. Not only that, unless you can appreciate that your protection by your fellows in bulk can only be bought by certain duty to help and protect them, you are living in a world in which a carnivorous monster may at any time jump over the hedge and bite out your throat. The friendly exchange of duty between the members of a community keeps the monster in check.

Another difficulty is that there must be a personal code number and at present there is no clue as to how to find it. How widely would it differ from that of your next-door neighbour or an Australian aborigine? The whole question of heredity is an unsolved problem. You can breed a wild horse from the Steppes so that in time it acquires the extreme elegance and beauty of a Derby winner. But then you can reverse the process and in turn make its offspring revert to the scraggy objects named after Prevalski. All dogs and wolves apparently can breed together and produce fertile offspring and yet what could be apparently more different than a Great Dane and a Dachshund? What effect, if any, has selective breeding through the ages had on the mentality of man? Are all men blood relations or not? And this question is now becoming more complicated when people are asking whether humanity at one time had an infusion of foreign blood from another planet. If it did, of course all men are not brothers in anything but a remote sense. As men pry into the past, more and more evidence begins to collect in favour of this theory, which would have seemed quite fantastic at the beginning of the century. Although very much a child of the Edwardian period, and regarding that lost age as infinitely more civilised than the present, I do not view this strange idea as absurd. Neither do the canny scientists of Soviet Russia, who of all people appear to set the least store on heredity.

The reason why heredity comes into this story is a curious one. Some years ago when I had been working on the old gods of Britain, I published the results in a book (somewhat misguidedly called *Witches*, which was not really its subject). Among the pen friends which this book produced, were representatives of the old Witch religion. There are still some of these, who are quite distinct from the modern imitative covens. As far as I have learnt, the witch religion hardly differed from that of the gypsies before they became Christian. It was a relatively simple nature creed, but it made very great use of the psi factor. It generated power by mass excitement and anchored it in stones or trees. I have not been told how it was taken out again; but many people must have heard how the Hampshire witches sent a 'Cone of Power' against the Armada and in theory caused the storm which ruined the enterprise.

Now we come to the key point of this apparent digression. The witches (and probably the gypsies too) were in the habit of deliberately breeding people to increase their psychic powers. This is presumably why so many gypsies tell fortunes to this day. It is not their particular race or land of distant origin which gives them this faculty. It is simply our old friend selective breeding. Also, since this is obviously something which was tested by generations of trial and error, we must assume that the psi faculty can be bred in the human mind. It is not something mystic and wonderful outside it; but is just one of our senses, which science has neglected to study.

# Chapter 8

The Darwinian Theory of Evolution has been the most powerful of the forces behind the growth of materialism. From childhood it was always before my eyes. One might be taken to the church on Sunday, yet *The Origin of Species* was in the bookshelf all the week. Being greatly interested in living things, the theory of evolution cropped up in every book I studied on the subject. When I went up to Cambridge, as an undergraduate reading Natural Sciences, the Darwinian Theory was behind the whole teaching. One did not appreciate that it was still only a theory. It was taught as a fact. The geological evidence given in its support seemed convincing, because no other side was ever presented. There was no hint that, in many other countries, the theory had never been accepted at all. It was about thirty years before I even thought of questioning this dogma, which may be briefly summed up as the idea that all nature arrived at its present form because more efficient designs always ousted less satisfactory ones, by depriving them either of life or food supply. The survival of the fittest was Nature's great aim; although what Nature was, and how this aim was really achieved, remained a matter of faith.

Everybody must know the geological sequence of supposed evolution and there is no need to describe it here. But we should remember that the geological record only contains the remains of such animals as have happened to die in suitable places. It can never be even approximately complete, and evolutionary sequences, even though they may look very convincing in a textbook, have of necessity great gaps in them, which have to be filled in by supposition. Although the writer, or lecturer, may point to such cases as the change believed to have taken place in the gradual loss of the extra toes in the feet of ancient horses, it is still only an inference that this was in any real way related to the survival of the fittest. It is in the insect world that the whole theory seems weakest. Out of hundreds of possible life-cycles, which have been carefully studied and whose often incredible story is known, let us take one and see where it leads us.

At the time that the Coal Measures were being laid down, perhaps two hundred million years ago in what is known as the Carboniferous period, there were already dragonflies on the earth. As far as is known, there were not even reptiles living at that time and great amphibians were the most bulky beasts to be seen on land. Everyone nowadays knows the life-cycle of a dragonfly. Its child hatches out of an egg and becomes something, known as a 'nymph', living at the bottom of a pond. It is rather a repulsive-looking creature, grey-brown in colour, and appears not unlike a small dragon. Like the dragon too, it is carnivorous. It creeps about the bottom of the pond till it is full grown. Then it climbs up the stalk of a reed or some other aquatic plant into the daylight. Clinging to the stem, above the water, its body becomes dry. After a time the nymph appears to die. It splits open, and a perfect dragonfly, now known as an 'imago', emerges. When its wings are dry, it takes to the air, leaving its old cast-off body still clinging to the plant.

Now, let us look at this story in terms of Darwinian evolution. The race of dragonflies has survived on earth for about two hundred million years; nobody knows really how long it has survived, because, according to the evolutionary theory, dragonflies must have struggled against other contestants for a time and, being the fittest of this kind of insect, have held their place ever since. Well and good, but how did they manage it? We have a reasonable picture of what their Carboniferous environment was like. The Coal Measures were laid down in tropical swamps. There were some large amphibians, bigger versions of turtles, newts, frogs and such-like animals of somewhat peculiar forms. No doubt some of these ate some dragonfly nymphs and some were eaten by fish. But the nymph of a two-foot-long dragonfly was rather a formidable customer on its own account. Let us suppose, however, that life was so dangerous for the nymphs under water that they were pushed up the stalks of giant mare's-tails and such-like plants. Here, by some inexplicable miracle, they became provided with four most efficient wings and never returned to the swamps to breed, but only to lay eggs. Are we to suppose numerous nymphs clinging fearfully to plant stems and trying to think out how they could fly? One seems to hear the plops as the failures lost their hold and fell back again into the swamp, where they could not even breed. To me this idea seems just silly. So also is the idea that the chromosomes in the cells of the shoulders of the insects suddenly thought up the thing for themselves, just because wings were needed to fly. How could the idea of flying suddenly occur to a beast which had lived under water all its life? There only seems to be one possible answer to this kind of question. The life-cycle of the dragonfly, and the way the insect's body should develop, must have been thought out before they were dragonflies. The blueprints were already drawn and the insects were built to these plans.

As archaeologists, we have our evolutions too. We have numerous type series of development; of forms of pot perhaps, or of brooches, or pins, or of weapons, but we do not think that the objects made themselves into these forms of their own volition. We know perfectly well that minds thought out these shapes. We cannot see the minds, or rather the bodies, of the people who made these things in those particular shapes, but we infer that they were human minds, who had felt a need for these extensions of themselves.

All the great orders of nature, when they are discovered in the geological record as fossils, appear fully formed. The molluscs have shells like they have today. The crabs are crabs. The amphibians appear as amphibians and not things with a dozen legs. Reptiles are reptiles and mammals are mammals. It is probably the same tale with species also, if more specimens were available for study. The picture of life gradually crawling out of the sea, or primeval slime, to engage in millions of years of bloody war, until the species we see today were forced into their present shapes in the struggle, does not seem to have any foundation in fact. It is an explanation cooked up to fit a theory and not a theory based on the whole mass of observed fact.

156

Furthermore, this theory only seems to have firm believers in Britain, the United States and Russia. Such keen observers as the French naturalists have always regarded it with suspicion, because it does not work. The wonderful variety shown in the life-cycles of the invertebrates, insects, spiders and the rest, is totally impossible to explain by any theory of evolution of the Darwinian type.

Evolution, however, is an observed fact. There is clearly an orderly succession of forms of life, changing from the simple to the very complicated. But just as the bronze axe changed in shape through the centuries without any assistance from its 'struggle for existence', so surely we are at liberty to infer that our evolutionary successions in nature are the result of mental activity on the part of a mind or minds who have a necessity for producing the living objects. It was the mind of the man who wanted the axe to cut down trees, or to split his neighbour's head, which evolved its shape. And it was another mind which saw that it would cut better if the shape were changed a little. It seems to me, looking at the problem as objectively as possible, that it is far more probable that some external mind is responsible for living things, as we know them, than that they dragged themselves up into their present forms by trial and error.

All these life-cycles look like experiments with living things, carried out by minds which enjoyed doing them, much as the sculptor enjoys chipping out his figure from stone, or the mathematician enjoys solving his problem. There does not seem to be any place for chance development. Someone watching his experiment sees that the scheme for protective coloration, which he had worked out for certain conditions, is becoming dangerous to his particular specimen of the moment. He is the force which gives the chromosomes the push to change the coloration. It has been shown that man, by selective breeding, can change the shape of animals. It has also been shown that he can breed them back again to the original shapes. The characteristics, which are supposedly developed by the struggle for existence, are just the ones which appear to go back again and cannot be permanently maintained. When a new type of animal appears, it appears as the completed article. A dog's tail does not become any shorter because it is bitten off every generation.

157

I have often remarked in books and lectures that if a theory is on the right lines, it will continually gather to itself evidence in its support, just as a snowball gathers snow. Scraps of new knowledge come to join it from all kinds of unsuspected sources. If there is a flaw in a theory, however, obstacles are rising all the time in its path. This is clearly what is happening with Darwinism. The more people struggle to find out how it works, the further they seem from the solution. The obvious answer that the theory itself is wrong does not seem to occur to many thinkers. It has been so drilled into children as an accepted fact that few heretics dare to question it. It is not an accepted fact, but a working theory, and it no longer seems to work.

I have talked rather a lot about this matter of Darwinism, because we cannot take an objective view of the phenomena we are trying to investigate so long as we obscure the possibilities by dogmatic assertion that mankind is the result of so chancy a thing as 'the survival of the fittest'. If this is the truth, then you can at once rule out any likelihood of plans for an existence beyond this present life. There can be no possibility of communication with minds which are no longer in this world. All the great mass of reports of curious phenomena, which have been painstakingly collected and recorded by numerous observers, must be the products of the minds of people alive at the time they occurred.

Some philosophers and thinkers maintain that they cannot believe in a future life, because the brain disintegrates after death. But what happened to the dragonfly? Did it not undergo a kind of death and appear in a new element in an entirely different form? Could the nymph possibly have appreciated by observation that there was a flying insect inside it, when it was creeping about on the bottom of the pond? There are many thinkers who now hold that the brain is only a machine for censoring the sensations. This idea is certainly gaining strength at the expense of those who believe that brain and mind are one and the same. In spite of all the work done on the subject, it remains a matter of opinion and nothing else. In our study we must try to remain free from bias on either side. If it leads us to form conclusions from what we have observed, then we have achieved our purpose.

Let us look at the case of *Velella Spirans* or, in English, the

By-the-Wind-Sailor. This is a small, flat jelly-fish of greenish-blue colour with a purple-blue edging.

Jelly-fish are a most complicated and difficult study. What appears to be a single organism, a jelly-fish to the ordinary person, is considered to be, in reality, a colony of individual organisms known, quaintly enough, as 'persons'. The family to which the By-the-Wind-Sailor belongs is known as the *Siphonophora*. The simplest form of this is a kind of straight tube, with the individual persons of each kind branching out from it. At the end of this tube there is a kind of bubble-like bulge, full of gas, and known as a phenocyst. This acts as a float and keeps the whole colony at an even depth in the water. It was the development of this phenocyst, in itself not easily explained by any form of trial and error on the part of the jelly-fish, which ultimately formed the basis of the By-the-Wind-Sailor's sail.

Jelly-fish as a race live by netting their food out of the sea with their tentacles, which are often several feet long and highly poisonous as well. The best known of the *Siphonophora* on our shores is *Physalia physalia*, the Portuguese Man-of-War, whose phenocyst has become a kind of elongated and crested bladder. While most jelly-fish are at the mercy of the ocean currents for transport and can only move by opening and shutting their bowl-shaped cover, the Portuguese Man-of-War adds the chance of wind to blow it across the surface of the water. This is an important advantage to a catcher of fish, for it enables it to sweep a larger area of sea than can a non-wind-driven jelly-fish. But still it can only fish down wind. The By-the-Wind-Sailor goes considerably further and by sailing at an angle to the wind covers fresh areas of water all the time. The whole process is remarkably similar to that once performed by the trawlers of Brixham or Lowestoft, which sailed into the wind towing their trawl nets behind them. One can see that the apparatus for the evolution of *Velella* was already available in *Physalia* and that the drying-up and hardening of part of the bladder float could have produced *Velella's* sail at an angle to the longitudinal axis of the animal in such a way that the pressure of the wind and drag of the tentacles would send the colony at an angle to the direction of the wind. This is precisely the way in which a sailing vessel beats to windward.

This apparently trivial piece of information was enough to start me on a train of thought which has completely changed all my fundamental ideas about natural history and the world in which we live. Much of my time throughout the years has been spent in the study of ancient shipping and navigation. I have even written books on the subject: *Boats and Boatmen* and *Coastwise Craft*. To me, sailing into the wind, as opposed to running before it, was a great and difficult art which man did not learn until thousands of years after he became a sailor. If the Darwinian Theory of Evolution, on which we had all been brought up as if it were a religious belief, was correct, what possible combination of trial and error, and survival of the fittest, could possibly have evolved a fore-and-aft sail on a minute jelly-fish? The only possible answer that I could see was that some mind, of the same general type as the human mind, had deliberately designed the thing.

It is a great pity that the geological record can never be more than a shot-torn fragment and that the great holes in it have to be filled in by informed guesswork. It is the same of course with other subjects, such as history, anthropology and archaeology. Too many facts are lost for any of these subjects to be more than a précis based on inherent probability. Nothing can make any of them into exact sciences and the more they ape these the less convincing they become. Theology and philosophy have caught the disease with lamentable results. The reason I write this is because there is no geological evidence to show how mammals came from reptiles, if indeed they did, nor how birds turned their scales into feathers. There were real flying reptiles, but there is nothing to show that they were closely related to early forms of bird. As with the origin of all the great orders there is a complete blank in the record and each one appears to have sprung into being with no long evolution behind it. We cannot see a blennoid fish becoming an ancestral newt. We cannot see a winged lizard becoming a feathered bird with an entirely different wing structure and we cannot see a cold-blooded scaly lizard turning into a hairy mammal in however long period we give to the processes. Thousands and thousands of little mutations, we are told, did it slowly over hundreds of millions of years. Yet the fossils say nothing of this hypothesis.

Of course Darwinian evolutionists would say that the skeletons of birds and mammals are unlikely to be preserved in rocks as fossils. But there is an easy answer to that. I guarantee you would find far more skeletons of mice and blackbirds in the mud at the bottom of a pool in the garden than those of newts or frogs. As for lizards, you would never find one at all. Mice and other mammals are by far the most frequent victims in ponds. They are for ever falling into water and getting drowned; and the same is true of slow-running rivers. The dredgings from a river like the Cam are full of animal bones. I have seen the skeletons of two drowned humans found in one year in two different old fenland streams. One was of the earliest Bronze Age and the other perhaps earlier than Neolithic times. The first was in the peat and the other beneath it. No! If there had been a long succession of reptiles changing into mammals, it would have been found years ago. Birds might be rarer, for they are so light and float so long that the skeletons and bones are likely to drop to pieces and become widely scattered. But skeletons of mammals are as likely or more likely to be found than those of reptiles.

The earliest known mammals are found as fossils contemporary with the last phases of the great lizards. They are described as small and undifferentiated. This apparently means that no one knows what kind of animals they really were. However, they are assumed to be the ancestors of all mammals and so of man himself. This seems to be as wide an assumption as to say that the earliest known fossil plants, the giant clubmosses of the coal measures, are the ancestors of all the plants we know today. It is an assumption based on the Darwinian theory that every living thing evolved from an earlier type by trial and error. If this theory is wrong then there is no reason to believe that these first mammals are anything more than the first known experiments by some mind to produce warm-blooded creatures. They need not have been ancestral at all and when one sees the extraordinary developments in mammalian types in the succeeding geological ages it seems most improbable that the mutation idea is correct. It is hard to believe that a whale, a bat, an elephant and a gorilla are all derived from one parent stock. But it is perfectly easy to see that they could have been evolved by planning from one original

161

idea of mammalness. Deliberate experimenting by some external mind, who pushed the chromosomes about in the cells of embryos to fit plans already thought out, would explain everything.

Now the geological record, compiled from fossils collected over a long period of years by numerous enthusiasts, apparently tells us that the earliest land animals were amphibians, at home both on land and in the water, frogs, newts, toads, turtles and such-like beasts. We see no turtles here save for a few washed up on our west coasts, which have been carried across the Atlantic by south-west gales and the North Atlantic drift. But we all know frogs, newts and toads. The life history of the frog is taught to everybody and many children keep tadpoles and can watch the whole development for themselves. But although it seems reasonably certain that amphibians must have come from bony fishes in some way, there is no visual evidence for it in the rocks. In fact it has been frequently noticed that all the great families in nature seem to start already developed as birds, or mammals, or reptiles and so on. At the point in time at which they seem to have appeared there is a blank in the record. The blenny family does, however, give us a good clue as to what seems to have happened. The blennies seem to be explorers. They climb up a rock, or a tree root or shamble up a beach because they like it. From some ancestral forms of blenny then we might expect the colonisation of the land to have begun. At one stage of its embryo life the young frog or newt is very much like an embryo fish. In fact there is something about our shanny's head which makes us think of frogs and newts.

Very well then, we will take as a starting point that blennoid fish somehow evolved into amphibians and see what happens. It already seems improbable that their evolution was forced on them by a need to escape the ravenous attentions of their neighbours in the seas. They came ashore to please themselves. But a very great difficulty now appears. When the amphibians start to be found as fossils they are complete amphibians. They have four jointed legs with digits on them.

Everyone today is brought up on the theory that all characteristics are carried by the genes, and mutations can occur by a change in the order of the chromosomes. This theory is probably quite reliable as far as it goes. But does anyone seriously envisage a jointed leg with toes on it being slowly evolved in this manner? One can perhaps imagine that the effort of wriggling up the beach tended to produce a change in the shape of the fishes' front, the pectoral fins. But we are also told by Darwinian evolutionists that acquired characteristics cannot be transmitted to the offspring of the animals which acquire them. We will assume that this is wrong and that the blennoid fish slowly developed longer ones for their front fins, that some of the rays in the fins themselves jointed together and produced a second bony extension of the first and somehow digits evolved together with wrist bones to enable them to move about. Thus you have the framework of a leg. Of course all the muscles, nerves, blood vessels and so on have also to be modified and extended; but what of that? It is unfortunate that there are no fossils available to show this process taking place, but it may have happened. Actually the development of the tadpole shows what must really have taken place. The hind legs develop first and then the front legs grow. But a fish is not built in such a way that this could happen in adult life. All land vertebrates from frog to man and including birds have a strong bony structure attached to the back-bone on which the hinder pair of legs or, in the case of birds, the only pair of legs hinge. But with almost all fish there is no lateral pair of fins except in front of the body. So, although there is something in the nature of a cartilagenous arch which might conceivably have mutated into a pelvic girdle, there are no paired fins which could have developed into hind legs. Since the hind legs are of much greater importance than front ones, for they have to carry most of an animal's weight, it seems evident that the change from fish to amphibian cannot have taken place by mutations in the structure of adults. Here we have a race of fish which is well on the way to becoming amphibian in habits, but it seems quite impossible that they could have become amphibian in structure. It seems far more reasonable to suppose that the idea of growing legs was thought out in detail and then added to the embryo state.

So far in this study we have found little to support the Darwinian Theory of Evolution. The complexity of the design of the sailing jellyfish, *Velella*, seems quite beyond the possi-

163

bility of any chance development. When we find a family of fish which appears to be well on the way to leaving the water for the land, we see that, far from being driven by fiercer rivals to do so, they do it simply because they enjoy sitting in the sun. The most powerful fish in northern waters turns out to be a semi-vegetarian living on plankton, while two of the most important food-fishes owe their great numbers to the multitude of their eggs. Competition is far fiercer in the water than on land, yet many primitive forms survive without difficulty for millions of years. It seems probable then that the great variety of form, and above all the beauty of colour, of fishes has nothing to do with competition and must be ascribed to an entirely different cause.

Now I have never been afraid of being a heretic. Whenever I have found archaeological theory being quoted as law, I have suspected and often attacked it. Darwinism was never meant to be more than a working hypothesis. It was seized upon however with such fervour by its supporters, in particular by Huxley and Spencer, and raised so much ill-directed opposition from the Church that it became a kind of religion: no faith in Darwinian evolution, then no job for the young biologist. It became a tyranny, a kind of holy belief which could not be questioned. I may not remember Kipling's comment on this kind of attitude correctly, but I think it went like this:

'Whatsoever, for any cause,
    Seeketh to take or give
Power above or beyond the laws,
    Suffer it not to live!
Holy State, or Holy King—
    Or Holy People's Will—
Have no truck with the senseless thing.
    Order the guns and kill!'

And this should have been done to the Darwinian theory, for it has caused immense harm throughout the world for too long a time.

That does not mean that I do not believe in evolution as such. Of course I do. But I no longer believe in the Darwinian explanation of it. I do not think this has ever been proved, or is

164

likely to be proved, for it is only half the story and a half-truth is generally a falsehood. I think Darwin deserves much credit, shared of course with A.R. Wallace, for the theory they produced on the evidence they had at the time. But all the same, readers must remember that Darwin was warned by his Cambridge professor, Adam Sedgwick, that if he persisted in publishing his theory it would wreck the world and utterly debase mankind. The older man knew what he was talking about. The theory, as narrowed and enforced by Spencer and Huxley, has very nearly wrecked the world. Without it Marxism would never have got the hold that it has, and Freud would not have formulated his somewhat degrading theories. For it set a premium on sex and greed. The 'survival of the fittest' meant that anyone who thought he was a specimen of the fittest, one of the *Herrenvolk*, could stamp on the faces of everybody else. It also meant that, since the development of the world was governed by chance and there was nothing else to account for it, you had to use your short life to the best of your own advantage, and to tramp over anyone who stood in your path.

Of course Darwin himself never meant this. He had a bright idea and all the available facts at the time seemed to support it. Nevertheless, if there was anything in the prophecy of the coming of Antichrist, he fulfilled it. The theory took God right out of the picture. Mankind in future reverted to the animal side of his nature and became 'red in tooth and claw' — at least a large part did. We have been paying for our too easy acceptance of the theory ever since.

When carrying out our experiments it became clear that there is a universal range of rates peculiar to each and every thought form. The rates fell between the figures of 0 and 40 inches, and I also noticed that groups of important ideas all fell at the quarter points, as I have said before. This was so remarkable that I found it hard to believe. Here was most dramatic evidence of the existence of a master plan behind the rates. It could not possibly have happened by chance. Furthermore, had I not been working in inches and had been using the fashionable scale of centimetres, it is most unlikely that I would ever have noticed the symmetry. But the inch is a natural measurement derived from the human thumb, which the centimetre is not.

What I was looking at was a perfectly natural plan derived from a perfectly natural set of measurements, and the evidence shown by the rates implies a creative mind working in much the same way that the human mind works. Anyone who can use a pendulum can find all this out for himself and see that I am telling the truth. But if all the facts support this inference, a matter in which I feel I am really scarcely qualified to judge, then it is quite clear that some mind beyond any possibility of chance has always been at work creating and thinking out new forms. I say mind, but looking as widely as possible over the range of living forms and at the remarkable life cycles which have been discovered amongst them, I seem to see ample evidence of the operation of not one mind, but many. It has all the appearance of delegated authority. When one considers for instance, the life story of such parasites as the well-known liver fluke, which begins the cycle as a small snail on damp meadow grass, is eaten by sheep and finally changes into a sole-shaped organism feeding on the sheep's liver, or that of ichneumon wasps, which lay their eggs on caterpillars to hatch out and eat the caterpillars alive, we seem to get a glimpse of an entirely different type of mentality at work from the one which designs the innocuous beauty of a brilliant butterfly. At the risk of upsetting conventional religious beliefs, which I have no wish to do, I think the evidence of this earth, and of the universe as a whole, all points to a hierarchy of creators working under one, far greater mind. I do not think, either, that the stage of mental development attained by what we might call the subcontractors is so very much higher than the one reached by mankind itself. Whereas the mentality of the master mind is infinite, that of the creator of the liver fluke has the appearance of being strictly limited, and itself one of a series of inventors to whom the mechanics of evolution has been entrusted. It is the manner in which this evolutionary process may have been carried out which we have to investigate next.

It is usual for those who think about the great variety-show of nature to visualise it as an orderly succession of development starting with the formless amoeba and ending up with man. A family tree is drawn up which shows where each great branch, known as a phylum, left the parent stem and spread out on its own evolving course. This looks tidy and convincing, even though like many another family tree it has many gaps and guesses in it. It used to be, and still is, widely believed, that if you reduce living tissue to its smallest components you would eventually discover what life is and so be able to produce living organisms. But even if this should in the end prove true and the germ of life can be found, there is still another factor. You cannot make that germ of life develop without adding thought to it. Life must always be a compound of its chemical constituents and mind itself. And you cannot take mind to pieces and examine it under a microscope. When man conducts mass experiments in breeding small organisms and observes changes happening to them after so many generations, he is not really observing changes in natural genetics, but these changes plus the effect of his own mind on the organism. I hope to show that this must be the case. You cannot do anything in this world without adding part of your own mind to what you do. It is probably man's own restless and unhappy mind which is causing the observed variations in the bacteria and viruses from which he suffers. This is why he only succeeds in mastering one disease for a new variety to appear. The medical world recognises this when it speaks of a psychosomatic illness.

The study of thought is of fundamental importance. With it you seem to be able to create. It is the force with which Mind operates. Enlarge your thinking and you extend your mind. Do not do so, or rely on the products of other people's thinking, and you are more useless than a slug creeping on the surface of the earth.

For evolution appears to be a command from the Creator of the Universe, though it differs very much from the evolution of the Darwin and Huxley variety. Although I have taken little interest in the theory of reincarnation, yet it seems very probable that those who have not bothered to develop their minds will have to return to earth again after death and do the whole business again.

It may be of interest to describe one of my attempts to investigate the old gods. There was a god of the sea, Manannan, to whom the Celts of Britain paid homage. Very little is recorded about him, yet his name remains in Clackmannan in Scotland, which means Manannan's stone. There are also well-known hobby-horse rituals performed on May Day down the coast of Devon and Cornwall by sea fishermen and it is assumed that the hobby-horses may well be the white horses of the sea, who also belonged to Poseidon. Therefore one might suspect that Poseidon and Manannan are two names for the one god. This happens to most ancient gods. Isis was said to have a thousand names.

Yet who really thinks there was such an entity as Poseidon? I can't say that it seems possible today to visualise anyone of the sort. But, if for hundreds of years men concentrated their thoughts on a figure of this kind and wished fervently for its help, what would happen? Each one probably detached something of his mind into the creation of this non-existent figure. Poseidon became a mass of detached thoughts and there was a Poseidon. I think that he would not be what we would call alive in the earthly sense. But he would be a cloud of force, which some might be able to tap. We surely must not look on the old gods as never having existed. They existed as long as men believed in their existence. The old witches still believe that they can see them if they go through the correct ritual.

As we have seen, a single individual can produce a ghost or a ghoul by his thought or memory projected into an electro-magnetic field. Many people together in a similar way can project a mass thought or memory and it becomes known as a god or demon. Both types really belong to the second mental level on which time does not appear to operate and so to earth-living minds they may appear in past or future time. Without some other interference they would never end at all. The gods are immortal.

# Chapter 9

Although much of what has been written so far is not strictly orthodox, the present chapter is far worse and deals with matters which are fit really only for the television plays called 'Dr Who'.

My wife had nearly finished typing this book when a friend, Group Captain Guy Knocker, sent me a copy of Erich von Däniken's *Chariots of the Gods?* His book was so similar to this part of mine in many ways that I felt tempted to destroy my version. However, I saw that there were points of difference and that this was an interesting example of the often observed phenomenon of a particular idea occurring to people in different parts of the world at the same time, just as if it had been put into their heads from outside. The best known case, of course, is that of Darwin and Wallace who shared the Theory of Evolution in 1859.

As it happened I had been interested in the problem of who were 'the sons of God' for many years and had sought enlightenment from archaeologists, anthropologists and theologians at Cambridge and elsewhere without getting the slightest satisfaction. Nobody knew the answer. If von Däniken's ideas and mine have any sense in them, nobody could have known the answer before the present generation, for travel to other planets was unthinkable. Since this has now changed, it is obviously time that people did begin to think about these matters which clearly affect the whole meaning of life on earth. Is there more than one species of Man and is he found on many different planets?

I could not be expected to know the answer, of course, but it is worth throwing a stone into the pool to see what then moves in it.

My wife, who is my great helper and best critic as well as carrying the burden of typing it all, seems to think I am not crazy in formulating these ideas and so I will throw the stone and hope for the best.

When I was still at Cambridge and digging for the museum and the Antiquarian Society, I happened, as I have said, to find a giant figure, or rather three giant figures, cut in the turf of the chalk hill at Wandlebury, some three miles to the south of the town. About half the students of British archaeology realised what they were: the more vociferous half were unable to understand. I thought that it was not worth the trouble to be involved in lengthy arguments with them and left the decision to future generations. I had no wish to be 'the grandest tiger in the Jungle', as Little Sambo would have put it. However, this find started me off on a quest for information about the ancient gods of Britain which involved me in many adventures of research which I had never thought to explore. I published the results in a couple of popular books, *Gogmagog* and *Witches,* as well as in technical reports and thought that I had finished with the subject; but it has been with me in one way and another for more than a dozen years. What were gods? And why apparently had the bulk of mankind always believed that there were such things?

Of course there are many thoughtful answers from those who have made a real study of it all and it is very rash of me to offer any new ideas. But I do not think that there has been anything which seems completely satisfactory. Totemism, anthropomorphism, ancestor worship and the rest sound very convincing, but before we go any further, let me quote three verses from the sixth chapter of Genesis and see whether anything we have heard of really provides an answer:

> And it came to pass, when men began to multiply on the face of the earth, and daughters were born unto them, that the sons of God saw the daughters of men that they were fair; and they took them wives all which they chose (verses 1 and 2).

Then follows verse 3 which seems to have no connection with the first two and after that verse 4 takes up the story again:

> There were giants in the earth in those days; and also after that, when the sons of God came in unto the daughters of men, and they bare children to them, the same became mighty men which were of old, men of renown.

Now how does this piece of legend fit in with any known 'ism'? It is not totemism, anthropomorphism or anything of that kind. It is a definite statement of fact that a race known as the sons of God intermarried with another known as the daughters of men. But who were the sons of God? This problem has puzzled me for years and I have met no one who can supply the answer.

There is the same kind of thing in Greek mythology where one race is apparently actually described as Gods. They have unions with mortal women and produce heroes. One finds it, too, in the northern lands. Many of our early Anglo-Saxon kings claimed to be descended from Woden, that same Odin of the Norsemen, who was the equivalent of the Greek Zeus, the chief of the gods. Let us forget such terms as polytheism and see whether there is any other explanation which might fit this seemingly impossible situation. After all there are many people who believe that every word in the Bible is true and to them the sons of God must mean, not only that God had children, but that He also had a wife.

When I first thought about this matter, it seemed obvious that the sons of God must have been some conquering race who thought a lot of themselves and to whom it was at first unthinkable that they should actually intermarry with the people they conquered. The whole caste system of India was apparently based on such a situation. The race, formerly known as the Aryans and now generally spoken of as Indo-Europeans, thought it sinful to mix their blood with that of the people they had vanquished. But they had gods of their own, not one. If they had been or believed themselves to be of divine descent, they would have surely been called the 'children of the gods'. Aryan appears to mean 'noble' and nothing more.

This problem is not entirely foreign to us in England. Very large numbers of people are known to have descended from Edward III. Edward III was descended in blood from Alfred. Alfred claimed descent from Woden. Are all these people then entitled to put 'son of God' after their name? Of course it sounds ridiculous when said like that but, funny or not, it is interesting to wonder whether they might be. Who was Woden anyway? Was he just the wandering chieftain of a barbarous war band, or was he something else?

So much difficulty lies in the meaning of words. A god to ancient Romans could be simply an outstanding man and he could be deified in his lifetime. We all know the unpleasant results of this process when Herod was hailed as a god by the populace! The practice of calling Roman emperors gods is also well known. It may appear strange to those who hold that the term only refers to the creator of the universe, but as a matter of historical fact it needs to be considered.

It is even more strange to find that the term 'devil' is simply a distortion of a word meaning 'god'. The gods of one religious belief became the devils of another. Lucifer, the light bearer, a god to many races (including the Celts, who called him Lugh), was also the wicked angel who was thrown out of heaven. Perhaps it is even more peculiar to learn that the original holder of of the Greek title was the planet Venus and so female. Lucifer, Satan, the Devil, the dragon and the serpent all came to mean the spirit of evil, not only in the Christian world but in many others also, which brings us to a second curious puzzle: what was the war in heaven?

Unless the meaning is very obscure, I far prefer the language of the old James I Bible to that of the modern 'told to the children' versions and I think that there is nothing obscure in the following quotations which all bear on the same subject. The first is from Revelation, chapter 12, verses 7 to 9 and is the most complete statement of what was evidently, at the time of Nero, a very ancient legend:

> And there was war in heaven: Michael and his angels fought against the dragon; and the dragon fought and his angels, and prevailed not; neither was their place found any more in heaven. And the great dragon was

cast out, that old serpent, called the Devil, and Satan, which deceiveth the whole world: he was cast out into the earth, and his angels were cast out with him.

Also in St Luke, chapter 10, verse 18, Jesus himself is reported as quoting: 'I beheld Satan as lightning fall from heaven.' These are not unique survivals in old Hebrew writings, for something similar is preserved by the Hindus, while the serpent or dragon is even found in old Norse mythology. There was a story spread widely in the ancient world that there had been a war in heaven and the vanquished side had been driven to live on earth.

Of course it is possible to reject anything of this sort as pure imagination by men long ago seeking for an explanation of the reason for the conflict between good and evil. In almost every ancient religion of which we have record there is this story of conflict between the powers of light and darkness. The ancient Greeks did not have it, but then their gods were quite frankly 'not respectable' in a Christian sense; neither were those of the Romans, Saxons, Norsemen or Celts. These had all the vices as well as many of the virtues of mankind. They were simply men and women with greatly enlarged powers.

If we take the view that all legends of this kind are no more than fiction, there is no point in going on with this study; but as the years go by, it becomes increasingly clear that many, if not all, have some foundation in fact. They may be greatly embroidered and appear as fairy stories, but there is something in them based on memories of events which really happened. They are not the same as myths, which are the counterparts of religious ritual; although these themselves often contain genuine pieces of tradition. The long labours of Sir James Frazer which resulted in that ponderous series of books known as *The Golden Bough* brought this home to many readers. Tradition itself tells that he was locked up in his study for many hours a day by his ferocious French wife to compel him to write his daily quota. Certainly he seemed to wear a haunted look.

I am going to take it for granted that there was some truth at the back of the two scraps of legend which I have quoted and see whether we can find anything to suggest an explanation. It is a kind of exercise in detection, but it is not fiction. The guesses may be wrong, yet there is something to be investigated.

Our questions then are: who were the sons of God? and what was the war in heaven?

If anybody reads the early chapters of Genesis with care, it becomes clear that some editor has linked together at least two traditional accounts of the Creation with remarkably little skill. The Adam and Eve story is the kind of thing you might find in the religious beliefs of many an African tribe today and we need not bother with it yet. However the other, which in itself looks like a blend of more than one tale, has a lot of legend in it. At the very start of this we meet another puzzle in Chapter 1, verse 26: 'And God said, Let us make man in our image, after our likeness.' Who did God say this to? We have always been led to understand that there was only one God and that He was absolute. He created everything from millions of nebulae to bacteria. Yet in the chief religious book of the early Hebrews He is pictured as talking to others of like form. Were they perhaps the sons of God? One can hardly assume that He was talking to Himself. It is even more remarkable when we find a similar kind of story preserved on the other side of the Atlantic. There several descendants of God are reported as having more than one trial at making man like themselves. There were also failures of the same kind as is described in Genesis. This is some world-wide traditional story and not confined to the Hebrews. It seems most unlikely that it is more than some ancient theory, but at the same time we must observe that it had once a very wide distribution. How was it spread from one continent to another before the days of efficient ships?

Curiously enough this question is not confined to traditions. When I used to study archaeological problems in the Cambridge Museum of Archaeology and Ethnology, I happened to notice a similarity between some groups of ancient objects found on the two continents. Types of stone axes and little female figurines were strangely alike on both sides of the Atlantic. But, oddly enough, the two areas in which they had been found were not those closest together in distance. In fact they were the eastern shores of the Mediterranean and the islands of the Caribbean. At the time I took this similarity to be entirely accidental. In any case they were not large or important things with intricate patterns or anything of that sort. Still the resemblance could be observed and had it been noticed in, say, Norway and Denmark, would have been taken without demur as an indication of a former close connection between the two countries.

Of course many people have noted that pyramids were built both in ancient Central America and in Egypt and I well remember the violence of the academic quarrel when it was suggested that certain American carvings represented elephants. Perhaps they did. I was not impressed one way or the other, but I was greatly entertained by the rudeness of the old professors to their opponents. They are less outspoken today than they were at the end of the Kaiser's War.

All this was part of the great controversy which was known as 'diffusion versus independent invention'. One school of thought held that once something was invented the idea spread from one centre round the world — it was diffused. The other side believed that mankind frequently invented the same thing in different places. As an example of the kind of problem which could be raised, there is the comparatively recent case of the Jericho skulls. During the excavations of prehistoric Jericho, a collection of several human skulls was found. These had had clay faces modelled on the bones and cowrie shells set in the eye sockets. Precisely the same procedure was followed in New Guinea till quite lately. We had several modern examples in the Cambridge Museum. Both peoples were living in a Stone Age civilisation, but separated in time by several thousand years. Had the people of New Guinea invented this curious custom on their own, or was it one which spread across land and sea and had endured for a vast period of time? It is such a curious custom that one would think that the answer in this case is diffusion. This would have caused great excitement two generations ago, but scarcely raised a ripple on the pool of anthropological thought today. Both archaeology and anthropology have become so specialised that few men or women remain who are capable of letting their minds range widely about the world.

To balance the scales between diffusion and independent invention, I had better mention another case. About fifteen years ago extensive settlements and burials of an early Eskimo community were found and excavated not far from Point

175

Barrow in Alaska. At the time they were thought to be the earliest Eskimo remains to have been discovered. When the published report reached me I was greatly astonished. It was evident that, although these Arctic hunters were making the most delicate and beautiful flint implements, even finer and more competent than those of the famous 'laurel leaves' from the French palaeolithic cave of Solutré, yet they clearly showed by their carvings in ivory that they had once been well acquainted with the use of metal. There were long carved chains of interlocking rings. There were swivels obviously copied from iron ones and so on. Finally there were a very few tiny tools, one of which still had a minute iron blade in it. These men, although they had once been efficient users of metal tools, had been forced to become high artists in working flint which is always thought of as being a far more primitive condition. Their progress had not been evolution but devolution. They had, for some unknown reason, been compelled to adopt a more primitive way of life and their flint work was so similar to that of some of the Upper Palaeolithic perhaps 10,000 years earlier, that anyone might have been excused for thinking that the two cultures must have been closely related. This can surely have only been a case of independent invention.

Therefore it is quite unsafe to make comparisons between pyramids in Egypt and America with a view to saying that they had a common source. A pyramid after all is surely no more than a respectably constructed heap of stones: a burial cairn perhaps, modernised by a more civilised community.

However, our Eskimos draw attention to another feature of the ancient world. Driven out from some unknown homeland over Bering Strait into a new continent, thrust into an arctic climate and eventually forced to adapt their square wooden houses to small stone hovels more suited to the cold, they had lost at the same time a vital source of supply. Iron was no longer obtainable. They must have looked back with sorrow to an age of iron where everything was much happier and easier. This is what we gather was the outlook of the ancient world on our side of the western ocean: they looked back to an 'age of gold' and not forward to one in the future. This seems very remarkable when we know how much thought their brilliant men expended on trying to explain the mysteries of the universe.

However, it is a well known trait of humanity to think that everything in the past was better than it is today. The old men in sailing ships always looked back to the ship before their last one as the finest vessel that there ever was. They cursed the one they had just left as an unhandy hard-working bitch. But the one before that was an able beauty.

Archaeology on the other hand appears to tell of a progress, interrupted at times of course, from barbarous stone age to rocket propulsion and journeys to the planets. Why then the ancient belief in a past golden age? Was there ever such a period? You would have thought that men in an age when bronze tools were plentiful would have thought that the conditions had advanced enormously from those of their grandfathers. When iron became common, surely this was another great step forward. But suppose for a moment that there were such people on earth as the sons of God. Would they not presumably once have been as far ahead of the men of the iron age as those were ahead of the cave men of the palaeolithic? Their remote ancestors borne by the daughters of men might well have looked back to the golden age of their ancestors. So many legends, too, affirm that such and such a god taught mankind such and such an art. Hu the Mighty, for instance, so the Welsh Barddas say, taught men agriculture. Man did not evolve it himself by painfully scratching with a pointed stick in the ground: a god taught it to him. It is not so easy to say this story is just a piece of traditional imagination when all over the world you find primitive tales of gods teaching men essential techniques. There is a puzzle here which is not just a bee in my bonnet.

The question of who the 'Sons of God' might have been is bound up somehow with the evidence for an extraordinary spread of people all up the western seaboard of Europe who put up very great numbers of large upright stones for some apparently inexplicable reason. Single ones are perhaps not of very great interest, for they might mark the site where someone had been killed, or be a boundary between two different communities. But when you find great rings and lines of stones set up in Brittany, Cornwall, Wiltshire, Ireland, the Outer Hebrides and the Orkneys, it surely means something of vast importance to the people who put them up. No one has the least idea why great rows of stones were set striding over Dartmoor, or why a huge ring was erected at Stennis in Orkney. Only one thing is obvious and that is that a race of seamen must have done it for an important purpose. Why do seamen put up marks? As far as I know it is only for one purpose and that is to show themselves or other seafarers how to get to some place in safety. But many of these indicators are far inland and could not be seen from the sea at all. Although the suggestion may seem fantastic, could it possibly be that they were meant to be seen from the air?

No, I am not crazy, but, although I have had no personal experience of the matter, I cannot fail to be impressed by the bulk of testimony that unidentified flying vehicles are frequently observed in our skies. Could it be that, in the Bronze Age and before, they were also numerous and needed direction points?

Let us go back to the ancient Greek gods. Till the second half of this century, it would have been quite absurd to suggest that there might have been some truth in the flying chariots which the gods possessed and the thunderbolts which Zeus threw. Furthermore it would have been ridiculous to think that these gods might have come from an unknown part of the universe and sometimes begotten children on women of the earth. It is no longer absurd — clumsy though our efforts may appear to be, man is already starting on his first tentative exploration of other planets and is there any reason to be sure that he is the first race to do so? Obviously the answer is 'no'. We have really very little idea of what may go on in outer space and it is an impertinence to think that man on Earth is the most advanced of all creation.

The Greek gods passed with great rapidity from their home on Mount Olympus to anywhere they wanted to go and if they were said to go in flying chariots, this only described the fastest things that man had by that time invented. It was all rather fantastic and even a little comical, but why did men believe anything of the sort unless sometime, somewhere, something of a vague resemblance to this picture had once existed? It was not only the product of Greek imagination, for there were Hindu stories, too, of godlike personages who actually had remarkable flying machines and destructive weapons. Nobody knew how they worked, of course, and it was all long ago. So

178

was the chariot of fire, which took Elijah up into the heavens. I do not believe all this, of course, for there is very little to go on; but I do think that there is enough to make us wonder whether there is a possibility that for a short period long ago there may have been visitors to this earth from another and that they were so relatively advanced in technology as to be completely bewildering to the earth men of those days. If there were visitors of this kind, it is more than likely that they would need landing signs here and there. Supposing that they were beginning to investigate an unexplored world, which was completely unmapped and they were putting down a few parties of explorers, it would be necessary to have indications where these parties had been dropped. What would be more natural than to enlist native help to set up such marks?

It is hard for us today to visualise the Britain of, for instance, five thousand years ago. The vast extent of natural woodland is unknown today, except in tropical vegetation. Brambles and fallen trees made paths through it extremely difficult and it covered the bulk of the country. Only on some downlands was passage relatively easy and that was not free from large patches of juniper trees, thorn bushes, gorse and bramble. The wide vistas of rolling grassland did not exist. One can assume that exploration parties would be dropped at the edges of all this and traces of them would be found, if at all, in the kind of situations where we do find these stone set rings and alignments today. A stone ring would be noticeable from the air, just because such things do not often happen in nature. Neither would straight lines be frequent.

But there may have been another reason for setting up the stones, even if its object were the same. For untold generations it has been believed, especially by the devotees of the old witch religion, that by means of exciting people to execute wild circular dances, power could be generated and stored in stones and trees. Actually this appears to be scientific fact. It has been demonstrated by Mr P. Callahan in America that moths generate bio-electricity by the heat caused by the movements of their wings and they use this to locate their mates or food supply. I have described how I detected the same thing with beetles in an earlier part of this book. This is observed fact and no longer something on the fringe of knowledge. Now if you have a large number of people dancing wildly round in a ring, you obviously generate a great deal of this bio-electricity, living electricity. If you carry out this performance in rings formed of stones with gaps between them, you have a form of dynamo. It has been shown that the electro-magnetic fields of stones, trees and water will absorb bio-electricity from outside and this is the probable reason why some people see ghosts in situations which were favourable to such impressions being preserved. I have elsewhere suggested the names of oread fields for those of stones, dryad fields for those of trees and naiad fields for those of streams in accordance with the Greek belief that nymphs with these names were to be found in such places.

We now apparently see why my wife and I experienced electric shocks when trying to date the stones of the circle of the Merry Maidens in Cornwall. The bio-electronic force had been stored at one time by the exertion of dancers in that circle and it had never been taken out again. The circle is still complete. But why did anybody wish to store up electronic power in such places? What possible use could it be put to?

Well, experiments with the pendulum have shown that the electronic fields about an object are double cones of limitless height and depth. It has also been shown that a pendulum length of the same radius as the base of the double cone will register contact with that cone. If, then, you had an apparatus in a flying machine set to the right wave-length, you could pick up the rays from the stored energy in the stones and home on it like the moth to its mate. These rings of stones could have been used both as visible and invisible navigational beacons.

This suggestion sounds absurd to those who have got no further than believing that the stones were set up by shaggy and uncultured savages whose only aids to life were stone tools and soft, badly baked pottery. But what if there were two completely different races of people involved, the sons of God and the daughters of men?

Of course, I may well be talking complete rubbish, but before the reader dismisses it as such, perhaps he will tell me why the stones were set up at all. In the whole of western Europe, it used to be done and in the same area the excited ring dances were once commonplace. No one can give a reason for either. When explorers get up tributaries of the Amazon, they find the naked women of unknown tribes dancing in excited rings in forest glades. It is no answer to say that primitive man does this as a primitive religious rite and you did it in a sacred circle of stones or trees to make it more religious. Or children do it naturally and so it is a natural form of worship. But do any children do it unless they are first taught by some elder who has herself been taught as a child? What were the dances of Baal which so upset the Hebrew prophets? The Baalim were little stone jujus of the gods and the people danced before them to put power into the stones. The One God, Yahweh, was not supposed to like it. It was not only the Hebrew prophets who had this trouble. If you read the Koran of the Muslims, you find that Mahomet had the same difficulty with numerous godlings. We may think perhaps that these Baalim represented the sons of God, but with the passage of time nobody really remembered what that meant.

As a purely hypothetical exercise then, let us put up a probably absurd problem. Was there a long time ago, perhaps five thousand or more years it might have been, a series of exploratory visits to this world from another? Did they have considerable contact with the people then living on earth, including some degree of intermarriage? Did the explorers persuade the natives to help them in setting up direction beacons and similar constructions in return for being taught how to work metals, practise agriculture and even build primitive towns? Then, for some unknown reason, did it all come to an end, leaving some degree of hybrid population behind it? Were the visitors known as the sons of God, because they had a belief in a single deity?

I think it is impossible to imagine a large immigration of people from elsewhere. Had there been anything of the sort and had settlements been formed of foreigners, it seems impossible for no trace of them to have come to light. So much digging and construction work has been done that some totally unknown culture of objects must have emerged somewhere for the acute bewilderment of archaeologists. This has not happened. There are stories published of a very few unknown things being found in rocks, but until I see quite a numerous collection of such things I shall not believe it. Archaeological study is really quite advanced and I think we can say with confidence that no such foreign culture has come to light. You may say that Atlantis,

Mu and even Tartessos have not yet been found and I say we have no vestige anywhere of any Atlantian culture, which must have existed, other than on the drowned lands, if there had been one. The Atlantis at present claimed at the eastern end of the Mediterranean cannot be right, because Atlantis was outside the Pillars of Hercules, that is west of Gibraltar. If it existed at all, one would have thought that the shoals off Cape Trafalgar might mark its grave. Yet the only unexpected things dredged from the bottom of nearby Cadiz harbour are Irish bronzes, and Irish goldwork has been found as far away as Palestine while Greek and Egyptian ornaments have been found in Bronze Age graves in Britain. People got about the world all right in those far off days, so where are the traces of the Atlantians who are said to have been so advanced that they had flying machines?

Perhaps, however, Atlantis was just another explorers' base and quite small. If so, there might be very little to find except the equivalent of the empty bully beef tins of the explorers of my day. At least we buried these out of a sense of decency, now lacking in the bulk of our population, even in the wastes of Jan Mayen or Baffin Land.

This investigation becomes more and more complicated as it goes on. Nothing seems to have an obvious answer and yet all sorts of books are written and hundreds of lectures given about this very period, none of which gives us much hint of the astonishing things which have taken place in a raw, new world some five thousand years ago.

The sea journey today from Kyle of Lochalsh opposite Skye on the Scottish mainland to Stornoway on Lewis in the Outer Hebrides is more than twice the distance from Dover to Calais and, even in summer, the passage is often cold, wet and stormy. Of course it is not so far from Duntulm in the north of Skye, out north past the Shiant Isles, but it is still twenty-five miles. Yet somewhere, perhaps five thousand years ago, men crossed in some numbers. About fourteen miles west of Stornoway, near the shores of Loch Roag, stands one of the most remarkable stone monuments in western Europe. And it is not the only one on that strange and desolate strip of country. Up to about a hundred years ago only the tops of the stones showed above a deep blanket of peat, which covered all that area. Now for several miles the peat has been removed and burnt. Beneath is the land surface on which the stones were set up and the land surface is under cultivation once again as it probably was before the wet period of the Later Bronze Age.

The standing stones of Callanish are in their way quite as remarkable as those of Stonehenge, for they form a strange pattern. In the middle is a single pillar fifteen feet high with a small and, probably later, rifled megalithic tomb at its foot. The central pillar forms the hub of a circle of stones enclosing an area thirty-seven feet across, of about the size of a tennis court. From this radiate one double and three single lines of uprights. They nearly form a cross, but do not quite do so. It is a strange and rather uncanny place to see in the usual pouring rain as it stands on a low hill. The double avenue heads almost true north for nearly a hundred yards.

Loch Roag is divided into two by the island of Bernara, which fits into it rather like a biscuit stuck in a dog's mouth. On the shore of Bernara facing Callanish are two more standing stones, looking as if they once marked a path across to the island where now is sea. It was probably dry land when the stones were put up, for fresh water Bronze Age peats can be seen round the shore today for several feet below high tide mark.

Archaeologists as a whole pay little attention to Callanish. It does not appear strange to them that such a remarkable construction should be found in such a remote setting. If it had been in Kent or Gloucestershire it would be thronged, but in the Outer Islands nobody cares. Yet it is the very situation of the thing which is so strange. It stands far out on the rim of the western ocean and there seems to be no possibility that there can ever have been a large population out there. Why should there be? The land must at the best of times have always been very poor. The Ring of Stennis in Orkney is not so strange, for the Orkneys are not so bleak as this stretch of the Long Island.

Not long ago it was suggested that Callanish was raised as a kind of substation of Stonehenge and both were intended as observatories to plot lunar eclipses. Even if this idea were correct, it implies a great organisation far away who could journey to the distant north and either bring their labour with them or collect enough local men to do the work. I do not feel that it makes sense. Neither do I see how any great religious

183

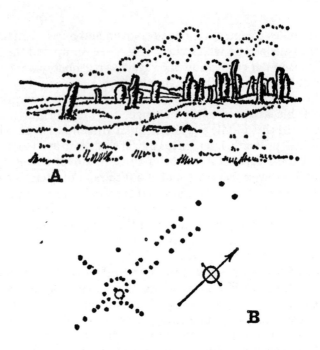

Figure 20. A. Rough sketch of Callanish avenues and circle from the south-east. Central pillar 15 feet high, mound of burial cairn to its right. B. Rough plan of the monument. Overall length about 123 yards.

idea could have been called into play. Why put it there? There must have been more populous areas elsewhere, where such things could have been needed.

However, suppose that some survey party had been dropped out there to look for minerals or any other purpose, it might have been necessary to construct a landing mark of identifiable shape so that supplies could be dropped, or the explorers could be picked up when their time was up. Callanish in Lewis and Stennis in Orkney, could they not have been the identification signals set up by two exploration parties to draw attention to themselves so that there would be no doubt where their bases were situated? All this would be hundreds of years before another station, the bluestone ring, was transported to Stonehenge.

If this possibly absurd suggestion has any foundation in fact, was it all in vain? Were none of these stations ever collected again because something happened to their home planet? Did these pioneers work their way back to more developed lands and there, by their superior technical knowledge, become for a time sons of God? Did they naturally become kings and rulers and try to keep their stock reasonably distinct for thousands of years, until philosophers formulated the idea that all men were equal? Probably we will never know the answer, but it is possible to ask the question now; first because men are beginning to make exploratory expeditions to other worlds themselves and second because a very great quantity of information is being published suggesting that unknown flying machines may be coming from outside to examine our own planet. As I said before, I have had no experience of this, yet I find the mass of observed facts needs an explanation.

There seems to be a considerable difference between the monuments on the outlying islands and peninsulas and others far inland. They may represent successive stages in some form of exploratory development. If I am right in identifying Tipperary as the original site of the Stonehenge bluestones, its situation is not unlike that of Stonehenge, being convenient to river systems and old trackway routes along both of which native labour could be called in to help. Another famous circle, Avebury, could have been the original central point in the south of Britain before Stonehenge was thought of. If we are trying to plot the possible plan of exploration, then Avebury would come high on the list. But Avebury was less convenient by water though better situated for movements by land.

Of course the most dramatic of all these constructions in the west, for the later Stonehenge is in a different category, is Carnac on Quiberon Bay in Brittany. Here the remains of eleven long avenues of standing stones still survive, with parts of a great stone circle largely ruined by recent houses. The stone avenues apparently once extended for several miles and over a thousand stones still remain in place. If there was a central base where power was generated to operate bio-electronic beacons, this would have been the place. Although much further south, it stands in a somewhat similar position to Callanish, with a drowned land surface beneath the sea in front of it.

The purpose of these great stone avenues is completely unknown. There are many burial mounds associated with them, as there are around Stonehenge; but that does not say that the rows had anything to do with burial. If there was any religious purpose in their construction, surely it implies a population much more of the order of that today than one of scattered and primitive farmers? One would have thought that the whole population of Brittany in those days would not have provided a fitting congregation.

We will leave Carnac for the moment and return to Britain. I have already mentioned the stone rows on Dartmoor. Of course these are in no way comparable to the massed avenues at Carnac, but they are reasonably impressive and there are quite a number of them dotted about the moor. I have taken the approximate bearings of eight of them and projected these lines to see what happens. It was obvious at once that the one at Black Tor when projected cuts another row at Warren House, in an area seamed and scarred with very ancient tin workings. It may be a coincidence, but these two lines could have given you a cross-bearing on rich deposits of tin, long before maps are supposed to have existed. In any case how did anybody know that there was tin in Britain without long and elaborate prospecting? I have never liked theories based on ideas of projected lines, but it is curious nevertheless. If there is anything at all in the beacon idea, this gives it some confirmation.

The two rows mentioned are not the only suggestive ones. That at Sharp Tor when produced runs very close to Avebury itself. Those at Fernworthy, Chagford and Higher White Tor hit the great monolith on the summit of Exmoor near The Chains. None of this is quite exact according to modern measurements, but if you were making observations in an unknown and unmapped land, they would be remarkably good. It may all be nonsense, or it may not. But if it is nonsense something will turn up to show that it is.

It has been hinted that Carnac might be the most important place in the whole system. If so, and if there is anything in the idea at all, one at least of the stone rows on Dartmoor should give an approximate bearing on Carnac. Actually three do, the double row on Headland Warren and the single ones at Dartmeet and Butterdon.

I do not even suggest that this idea of bio-electronic beacons is the right answer. All I am trying to demonstrate here is that there is something here which could possibly fit into a picture of ancient exploration which we know nothing about. If there is anything in this clue, it is not related to ordinary exploration by sea and land, but concerns something carried by air transport. This would have seemed utter rubbish a generation ago, but is it quite so absurd today?

The problem of the stone circles and alignments is really one proper to the old world although others are known, particularly in Peru. The new world has others of its own. For instance, what are we to make of the remarkable animal mounds found in considerable numbers to the south and west of the Great Lakes? The Indians have no idea who made them and there seems to be little archaeological evidence for their date. The largest of these appears to be the great Serpent Mound of Adams County, Ohio. The mound is five feet high on a thirty foot base and if straightened out would be more than a thousand feet, say three hundred metres, long. The work necessary to produce a mound of this size is great and what possible purpose was it intended to serve? Seen from the ground it is nothing but a bank. Only from above is its serpentine form obvious. It is the same with the tortoise, alligator, eagle, lizard, elk, bear, otter, wolf and frog mounds, while some apparently represent human beings.

When once the possibility of the stone circles and alignments of the old world having been used as beacons for aerial navigation has entered one's mind, the same possibility can be appreciated with regard to the animal mounds of the United States. However, in their case the beacons would only be visual ones, unless there was some method of charging them with bio-electronic force. This is not so impossible as most people would think today.

Now I will bring in a new puzzle, even if I seem to be involving the reader in the imagination of space travel. As before, I do not know the answer, but it is evident to me that an answer could be found and ought to be sought, even if the seeker may be greeted with ridicule by those who have not the imagination to look for it. Of course I refer to the huge and growing mass of statements, often by highly competent eye-witnesses, that strange flying objects are frequently seen in the sky. These are known widely now as UFOs, unidentified flying objects.

I have no personal experience of this kind. Or, to be more

accurate, the only experience I have ever had was not of a kind to inspire belief in visitors from another planet or anything of that nature. I had better report it because it is an example of how difficult this kind of observation can be. It was in the summer of 1931 and I had been down to visit my sons at school near Fareham on the Solent. I was driving back, alone in the car, to spend a night or two with my mother at Bracknell before returning to Cambridge. When nearing Alton I ran into a very heavy rainstorm. It was so heavy I turned my lights on and dropped into low gear. I doubt whether the car was moving at ten miles an hour.

On approaching Alton, I rounded a bend and was looking down a lane on my left side. There were bushes and then a wall on its far side. Above the middle of the lane, apparently about twelve feet up, was a great shining disc or globe, which appeared far bigger than the moon as we see it from the earth. Not knowing exactly where the thing was as there was no visible background, I estimated its size as roughly three feet across. It was much the same colour as the moon seen on a clear night and it was slowly descending towards the road. The edges of the object were not distinct, but in any case the rain was too heavy for them to appear so. Of course it did not take me many seconds to pass the end of the lane, but at its apparent rate of descent it might have hit the ground almost directly after I had passed. Of course I ought to have stopped the car, got out and gone to see whether there was any sign of it. There might have been a mark on the road or even a hole in it. But there was no bang. It was very wet and I had no coat handy. I drove thoughtfully on. I did not know what I had seen.

On reaching my mother's house, my story was greeted with obvious disbelief. So was it at Cambridge, except for one person who said it was ball-lightning. So it may have been, but what is that? I do not think that this was one of the things called UFOs, or flying saucers, but to this day no one has given me a plausible explanation. My own idea was that it was an incandescent ball of gas. As far as I could judge, its circumference was a perfect circle. It was not a tilted disc or anything of that kind.

That is my sole personal experience of unknown objects in the sky. But I have had some practice which may perhaps help me in considering the reported experiences of other people. In the summer of 1937, I helped physicists studying cosmic rays to let up and plot the course of fairly large balloons on the west coast of Greenland. Thus I have a very good idea of what such things look like at varying heights. For instance I know that once you lose the image of a weather balloon in the field of your theodolite at as low a height as five thousand feet, it is most difficult to pick up the minute dot in the sky again. The objects which people see must be very large indeed.

John Lorne Campbell, who is a well-known scholar and author, is also laird of Canna in the small isles off the west of Scotland. Some years ago he showed me on a projector a colour cinema film of an object, which appeared high in the sky above the opposite isle of Sanday. People had said that this was a weather balloon. The object was clearly at a considerable height as could be judged by the height of the cliffs beneath it. It was a shining disc, but not a perfect circle. Whatever the thing was, I do not think that it can have been smaller than a tennis court and probably much larger. It had remained there almost stationary for a long time.

What, too, was I to think of a visit from a well-known Honiton merchant who came here to tell me that he had watched through a small telescope the evolutions of objects like wheels in the sky? He obviously believed he had seen them and had seen them also changing formation and performing various exercises.

Now people may exaggerate and they may mistake what they think they see. I have seen photographs in the papers, which look as if they had been the shades of Tilley lamps and I have read accounts which were obviously distortions of the real facts. However there is a large residuum, which clearly needs an explanation. People as a whole report truly what they have seen to the best of their ability.

A recent announcement on the BBC news makes it obvious that something needs investigation. As far as I can now remember the radio said that the American Air Force was closing down a department formed to investigate reports on UFOs. They had examined thousands of reports of sightings and there were only about seven hundred which they could not explain. Good heavens, could any official department expect to get away with that? Seven hundred unexplained cases of what might be visitors from another planet, and it was not worth the trouble and expense of trying to find out what they were! Suppose you had many reports that there were thousands of spies in your country and of these only seven hundred could not be shown to be innocent, what would you think of a government which gave up vetting them? If correctly reported, this must surely be one of the most naïve announcements in history! I don't know whether UFOs exist or not; but I do think that it is most important to find out whether they do.

Before talking more about these UFOs, however, let me return for a moment to the report of wheels in the sky. There may be nothing more in it than coincidence. Someone, being unable to describe it in any other manner, may call a revolving object a wheel; but it is at least curious that symbols described by archaeologists as 'sun discs' are by no means rarely found carved on stones of the Megalithic and Early Bronze Ages in western Europe. Sometimes they are simply a ring; again they may be a ring with a dot in the centre and, more curiously, a ring with a cross carved on it. A sequence of these carvings, not infrequently found together with symbols of ships, is published from Brittany to Ireland and from there to the celebrated Swedish rock engravings. A case has been made out for the existence of a complete sequence of ship and sun disc symbols from Scandinavia to ancient Egypt. Frequently they are so crudely executed that without a knowledge of more perfect examples it would be impossible to interpret the pictures. But with a sequence available there can be little doubt what was intended by the carvers. In the most celebrated burial cairn of New Grange on the Boyne in Ireland there is one of these symbols in the central chamber. No one would probably have been able to identify it without a knowledge of the Swedish and Breton engravings; but with this knowledge the intention is clear. Are these discs meant to represent the sun at all; or was the idea to picture the vehicles in which the gods were transported through the heavens?

For many years I have just taken it for granted that when the older generation of archaeologists talked of these things as 'sun discs', they knew what they were talking about. Now, as with so many other current dogmas, I am not so sure that they did. Even if the ancient Egyptian symbol did come to represent the

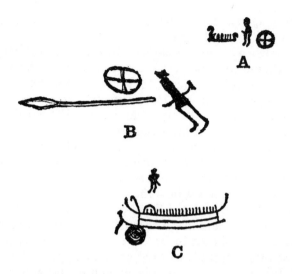

Figure 21. Wheels in the sky? So-called sun discs from Scandinavian Bronze Age rock engravings. A. Giant, ship and wheel, Bohuslan, Sweden. B. Giant, spear and wheel, Stjørdal, Norway. C. Giant, ship and wheel, Bohuslan. Similar but rougher engravings have been found elsewhere in Western Europe, including Ireland.

Sun God, Ra, and the boat in which he daily crossed the heavens, is this what was originally intended? Was not Ra himself one of the sons of God, venerated in later years as the great God himself? Of course it would be much less trouble to leave it all unquestioned; to go on as if nothing had happened and nobody had ever reported seeing wheels in the sky, or photographed objects up there which could not be explained in terms of present day knowledge. But, if we have any real curiosity in our make-up, we cannot just shrug it all off.

What we can say at this stage is that at the approximate time when men all over the old world were apparently beginning to venerate a multitude of aerial gods, they were also suggesting that they moved about the heavens in boats and things with or like wheels. Through the ages these gods took on varying characteristics, but this was doubtless due to frequent repetition and downright invention by the priestly castes, whose job it was to keep the beliefs in being. All this too was imposed

191

apparently upon a set of earlier beliefs in which men had a tribal totem in the form of some animal. The combination of the totem animals with gods in human form who flew about in the heavens produced some very curious creatures indeed.

Although I am not qualified to do so and have no real personal experience of the matter at all, I must try to make some estimate of how the problem of the UFOs strikes me as an ordinary member of the populace.

I look on it all with a completely open mind. I neither believe nor disbelieve. My object in writing this book is just this, to stimulate people to think, observe and experiment for themselves and not just to swallow the sayings of the authorities of the time as if these were the Word of God. However I do have one article of faith and that is that a witness should be believed until he can be shown to be either lying or mistaken. The answer so often returned to a report on the supposed sightings of an UFO, that it was the planet Venus, has added to the general popular disbelief in the announcements of specialists. Next to the sun and moon Venus has always been the most well-known object in the night sky. One of the first questions asked by children when shown the darkened heavens is: 'What is that bright star?' When, in addition, the supposed specialists have on occasion claimed this well-known object to have been the cause of a report and it has been shown that the planet was not above the horizon at the time, one's doubts of the specialists' qualifications rise considerably. In fact the frequent mention of Venus and the recent statement from America that there are about seven hundred reports which they have not been able to explain, convinces me that there is a case to answer. Either there is something to hide, or the authorities are completely stupid. One remembers Bernard Shaw putting into the mouth of a foreign politician: 'For God's sake don't frighten the British.' Now it should be changed to the 'Americans'. For obviously if there are people capable of flying here frequently in large machines from outer space, they would also be advanced enough to flatten America, Russia, China and the whole caboodle had they wished to do so.

The reports on the size of these objects vary very much, but all agree that they are often much larger than the present day aeroplane and that they travel at much greater speed. They can also change their course at right angles to the line of flight which no earthly plane can attempt to do.

Accounts of the lighting of these machines vary considerably. They may appear as silvery discs in daylight or glow with different colours at night. They may also, when seen fairly close at hand, appear to have a ring of windows or ports which emit bright light.

There are a fair number of reports that these machines have been observed to land and also that humanoid figures have been seen to emerge from them. It is doubtful whether any of these reports can be taken at their face value. However it seems possible that some of them may be true. I rather discount the accounts that observers have talked to persons emerging from these things and messages on the soles of shoes seem most improbable. If any conversations have taken place, which I doubt, they have not been recorded in such a way as to carry conviction. If visitors from elsewhere wished to make contact with people on earth, it does not seem probable that they would do so in American deserts or waste places in Scotland. Since they apparently can operate the machines at far greater speed than any earthly aeroplane, it would be reasonably safe for them to land openly on some civil airfield. But they have been chased, so the reports go, and apparently attacked, with dire results to the attacker.

There seems to be little doubt that these things have been picked up on radar screens and that warplanes have been sent up in pursuit; but whether this has only happened in America is not disclosed.

The term 'flying saucer' is not so inaccurate as anyone might suspect. A fair number of photographs appear to show large objects in the sky, not unlike a saucer with a rim facing downwards, but on what should be the base of the saucer there appears to be a small tower and something like a short mast. Seen from below these objects appear as discs and so we come to the description of 'wheels in the sky'.

There are many reports of these things flying in formation and in quite considerable numbers. By that I mean you might observe eight or ten at a time.

There are also reports of giant cylindrical mother ships on which the saucers home and into which they return. As far as

I know there are no reports of such things from Britain, although there are several from France. More than one saucer is also not common in this country.

Of course all this rigmarole seems very improbable to many people and quite incomprehensible until this century. But students of the subject have noted that it is nothing new and that there are accounts at various stages of history, which could well be taken to refer to the same type of object. Pride in the achievements of modern aeronautics and conceit in the intelligence of the people on earth make it hard for most to look at all this objectively. For so long a time has humanity been taught that it is the highest product of nature that it is difficult for it now to believe that some other organism somewhere else might be more advanced. But this is not improbable at all. In fact it is more probable than not.

There are a few other significant points. For instance, it is not uncommon for it to be reported that the passing over of a saucer stops the magneto of a car, which in itself suggests some very powerful electronic device in operation. Then some observers, including policemen in South Wales, have apparently observed a succession of saucers diving into the sea. They were well scolded for their pains! Other policemen on night patrol in Devon have chased apparent UFOs in fast cars and been told that they were observing planes refuelling in the air. I am sure they did not believe this explanation. Policemen have to be good observers.

There are accounts, too, of filaments of unknown substance falling from these machines and known as 'angel's tears'. No one appears to have been able to collect and examine any samples. However 'angel's tears' was the name given by German children to the fine silvery ribbons dropped by our planes during the war to deflect the German radar. I have seen plenty of these 'angel's tears', but do not know of what metal they were composed.

This is a very brief summary of what appears to be known about a very curious subject. There are a host of books available from which the reader can attempt to form his own ideas. However, I think that it must be a very dull-witted person who does not want to know the answer. Is a very large proportion of humanity suffering from delusions or are we really having visitors from outer space? If the second is the right answer, what are they coming for?

The Russians are a hard-headed and incredulous breed, but years ago they let it out that they believed they had found evidence that there had been visitors from outer space. Of course they have also announced that some of their scientists had chased what we should call a 'Loch Ness Monster' in a motor boat. This is another subject which is anathema to our orthodox zoologists. Neither account may be true. We have no means of checking them. But here is a curious point: if either the Russians or the Americans had any doubt that the things were coming from elsewhere, one would surely have accused the other of infringing their air space. Both must have been having the same kind of visitors, or hallucinations, and they know it. It is interesting too that both countries are working hard to find out the facts of extra-sensory perception or bio-electronics. They both hope to be able to talk by telepathy to people in rockets on the further side of planets which cannot be reached by radar. In our investigation then we appear to be chasing something which is cloaked in layer upon layer of official secrecy.

I will now return to our other question: what was the war in heaven? I do not think that there would have been any possibility of guessing what the war in heaven might have been before the landing of the first man on the moon and photographs taken of the surface of Mars. The moon has little or no atmosphere and is covered with dust composed of tiny globules of fused glass, which must be melted dust. There are craters of all sizes all over it and these look like the relatively tiny craters of the Hitler War. Could this possibly be the explanation? Was the moon bombarded for a long time by something resembling rockets with atomic warheads; was the atmosphere burnt off in the blasts and the dust converted into globules of glass by the heat of the explosions? Did the same thing happen to Mars? Today this is a wild guess and presumably nobody will give it a second thought. Still, if there was a war in heaven, an all-out struggle between the planets, have we been looking at the traces of it ever since we focussed a telescope on the moon and looked with some awe at the craters?

I said before that this investigation was likely to get like a science fiction novel and this is what is happening. We may not be getting satisfactory evidence for flying saucers at an early time, but may we perhaps be getting suggestions that vehicles, resembling more efficient rocket capsules, may have been circling Earth a long time ago and looking for places to land? Is it not possible that the war in heaven may have been a fight between two planets as to which of them should colonise the Earth?

Let us, for our amusement, and not with any sense of conviction, try to draw a picture. A very long time ago, somewhere about 2500 BC perhaps, there were two planets in the solar system rather more advanced technologically than Earth is today. One was Mars, the other perhaps Venus. They communicated with each other yet suffered from the human failing of jealousy.

Mars, let us suppose, set up bases inside the crust of the moon, and began to dispatch rockets carrying parties of explorers and prospectors to earth. It was during this period of exploration that the primitive Neolithic natives of the earth were persuaded to set up rings of stones and timber circles to act as guiding beacons for the use of incoming spacecraft. All round western Europe from Sardinia to Scandinavia teams were at work and beacons were set up. Perhaps farther east other ways of directing air traffic were devised.

For a relatively short time this reasonably happy state of affairs continued and then the jealousy of the other planet flared up into open war. Probably it also claimed Earth as its private possession.

The first campaign in the war centred on the Martian moon bases, then there was a slogging match between the two planets themselves. As a result of this, Mars was knocked out and the other planet so badly disabled that it has as yet been unable to take advantage of its victory.

But the interest of all this is in what happened to the exploring parties marooned on Earth by the destruction of the bases on the moon. There was little they could do and after a very short time the Martians had to go native. In the hope, however, that relief expeditions would eventually be sent to fetch them home, they persuaded the real natives to keep up their dances at the stone circles and so on as a religious rite pleasing to the

Great Ones in the sky, who had sent them down to live among them and bring them marvellous benefits.

This is a fairy story. I have made it up. But it is curious how it might be true. So much that happened in later history seems to add to the possibility. Let us see what might have happened to the Martians. Remembering that I have been on three Arctic expeditions myself, it is possible that I might have some idea how it all might develop. We will continue our fairy story with some groups of isolated men and perhaps women too, dotted about on the surface of an undeveloped and foreign planet with little hope of ever returning home again; being shipwrecked on a desert island would be far less drastic.

These stranded astronauts would all be specialists in some way or other. If we may judge from modern trends in education, they might be deplorably lacking in simple general knowledge; but some of them must surely have known something about growing things in gardens. This was to be vital in their predicament and may well explain why such and such a god is responsible in tradition for teaching a particular people agriculture. Botanists among them would recognise what plants might possibly provide them with grain and would institute an immediate search in the particular part of the world in which they had been stranded. A little was probably known by the natives already. Much the same thing was likely to happen in the case of metals. There would be men among them skilled in the identification of metallic ores; but there was no fuel to provide great heat for smelting. Metal for tools was an urgent necessity and copper was available in many localities. Thus such and such a god became the Smith of the Gods, by teaching the natives how to make simple cupellation hearths. It is interesting to remember in this connection that the earliest metal tools were made of pure copper and only later was tin added to it to make the more satisfactory bronze.

The earliest copper axes and knives found by archaeologists remind me of my childhood's efforts and are the kind of things which might have been produced by men who knew that copper could be melted from its ores and made into tools, but did not know the technique and had to build it up from their own imagination. It is hard to see otherwise how metalworking could have been invented by chance. It is perhaps easier to think that some unknown 'God' appeared from the sky and taught men how to do it. Easier perhaps, but not very much easier, for you are only pushing it further back on to another world in another age.

There was little else they could do to better their situation. All the mechanical civilisation in which they had been brought up vanished with the failure of their fuel supplies. It was useless to try to build a boat, as many men have done on the loss of their ship, to take them home again, for their home was far away across the heavens and only a relief expedition could take them back. But to the natives, to whom they had miraculously appeared from the sky, they were still wonderful. For a while they may well have retained some ammunition for firearms of some kind and from this the stories of the power of the gods to strike a man dead in an instant could well have arisen. So too could the idea of Zeus' thunderbolts have originated in some kind of hand grenade.

As time went on in their isolation from normal life, 'the sons of God saw the daughters of men that they were fair; and they took them wives of all which they chose'. Isn't this exactly what was bound to happen? In our story too, we must assume that this took place not at the base of one lost expedition, but at several. The exploration parties were often cut off from one another by hundreds or thousands of miles of sea or impassable forest. The world they had come to was young, with none of the roads, towns or vehicles of civilisation. Of necessity they must have taken to the sea, in the hope of joining up with others of their kind.

Thus, we may think, there slowly arose on Earth little tribes of hybrids with a greater knowledge than others in the world at the time. Unlike the rest, they knew how to provide a subsistence from agriculture, they knew how to make metal tools and they learnt how to use the sea. But the leaders in each group proudly claimed descent from their forefathers, who had come from the sky. Although this blood was slowly diluted by admixture from the natives; yet when possible they intermarried with those of their own kind and, throughout the old world at any rate, they became the ruling caste. How much was handed down by word of mouth of the remembered lore of the lost planet is anybody's guess. Scraps of the knowledge of how to handle bio-electronic power apparently spread to every corner of the globe and large sections of more detailed information remained in such doctrines as that of the Kahuna people in the Pacific.

The most colourful traditional picture of all this fairy tale is undoubtedly that which survives from ancient Greece. Here the myths and legends are just the kind of thing which one might have expected to be found circulating hundreds of years after the astonishing and little-understood happenings; but, even in the old Celtic tradition, there seem to be traces of similar ideas. There we find cauldrons which revive dead men, magic spears, inexhaustible sources of food and suchlike things which, although clearly imaginary in their context, might yet be reflections of older events of a more concrete nature. Right down to the Viking age, men still wore coats in battle on which swords would not bite and carried unbeatable weapons.

Somehow it all seems too much for the imagination of the early Semitic, Indian and Greek peoples. We know the kind of thing which is imagined by the so-called primitive folk: 'You must not swim in the sea, or a little worm will swim up inside you and you will have a baby.' Of course you would not get anything quite so simple from people who watched and hunted wild beasts for their food, or kept them in domesticity for the same purpose. Yet even the hunters on the hill, however much they watch the soaring of the great birds of prey, would surely not have imagined easily gods who flew about the heavens and resembled them so closely; while the agriculturalists hardly bothered with the sky at all, except to watch for the signs of coming wind or rain.

But if anything remotely like our fairy story should ever have happened, it appears to have been a mixed blessing. Did we not guess that the strangers came from Mars and was not Mars the planet of war? Why was it thought to be so, unless there was some vague tradition at the back of the idea? With the coming of metal, not only were improved tools for peaceful uses made available, but the weapons of war were rendered far more efficient. 'I beheld Satan as lightning fallen from heaven.' War between group and group and tribe and tribe became endemic. The greed which had wrecked the original planets seemed to have come down to earth.

However, to return to the spread of the remnants of bio-electric knowledge, let us look at some of the traditions still handed on. The islanders of Easter Island believe that the great stone statues there were set up by the 'mana', that is the extrasensory power of the king, who was especially trained to develop it. This takes us at once to the world wide belief that such power was available and could be used. If such power can be utilised, surely that is how Stonehenge and other monuments must have been moved and erected? Merlin is said to have done it by marvellous power. Is this very different, except in degree, to the almost universal stone-throwing trick of the poltergeist, which is frequently reported from all over the old world and the new? A poltergeist is apparently the involuntary mental movement of solid objects by what is now known as telekinesis. If the mind of a somewhat mentally retarded girl can somehow produce numerous wet pebbles from the bed of a stream and throw them about in a house, what could have been done by a mind specially trained to use this power?

What is known about telekinesis, if we must use this depressing technical term? It is probably much more common than most people suppose and frequently passes unnoticed. It may even take place at times in every family and simply be unrecognised as such, for the bulk of modern town-dwelling humanity is deplorably unobservant. How many people have not had the experience of a letter vanishing completely? Of course they usually put this down to carelessness on somebody's part, or forgetfulness, or something of that kind. But very often there is no reason to suppose that this is the right answer. Yet it is usually so small a matter that it is passed over as an accident. It is only when poltergeist activity becomes really violent that anybody takes any notice of it and even then they often try to explain it by trickery. It was not so in earlier times. Everything out of the ordinary was carefully noticed.

But are we talking nonsense? Is there any such thing as mana? I must say that I existed for quite a long time with a complete disbelief in such a force; now I am not quite so sure. I rather wonder whether civilised man has not just forgotten how to use it through being so pleased with his other attainments. Even today people still say 'thought is power', although I doubt if many of them know what they mean by this remark.

Now it is possible to demonstrate that there is something in this theory of mana. We have, as I have described earlier, done repeatable experiments with pebbles picked off the beach at Seaton and tested them with a pendulum. If the pebbles are picked up with a pair of tongs and then tested one by one, they only react to their chemical composition. But if I take one out and throw it against a wall, then it will respond to the 24 inch male rate. If my wife does the same, the answer is 29 inches for the female. This can be repeated as long as you can be bothered to do it. It is a scientific test, in that it is repeatable, and it shows that some unknown property of the man or woman passes from him or her to the stone. This makes the existence of mana a little less absurd.

The thing which surprised me most was that mana is extremely long lasting. I found the dates for the sling stones from the camps to be all around 320 BC. Was it then mana which gave the effect of an electric shock when my wife and I tested the stones of the Merry Maidens stone circle in Cornwall? It seems that it must have been. If so mana is apparently a bio-electronic force and it should be possible to learn a lot about it.

These experiments with pebbles differ from poltergeist phenomena in one important matter. The poltergeist operator does it involuntarily and probably has no idea that he or she is doing it. Our experiments were deliberate. We were trying to see whether we could put anything into the electromagnetic fields of the stones which could be detected. Call the anything mana if you like; whatever name is given to it, it appears to exist.

Now, if by using trivial objects such as pebbles off the beach you can show that it is possible to alter their electro-magnetic fields by making use of them, what could be learnt if you really got down to years of study of the why and wherefore of it all? Suppose many men through long periods studied it as closely as modern physics has been studied, might not the results be quite astonishing? It seems to me that scraps of evidence all over the world appear to indicate that this has once been done. But was it ever done here? Is it not possible that what now survives is but a fragment of all that could be remembered of what was taught to the local people by our hypothetical explorers? Were the local people not encouraged to build up the power of the stone circles and other beacon marks by dancing, and had not some explanation been given to them of why it was necessary for them to do so? Of course this is just a guess, but where did so-called primitive peoples such as the Kahunas of the Pacific get their learning? There is no anthropological suggestion that Pacific Islanders ever sat down to think out metaphysical ideas for themselves. The teachings of the Kahunas seem to have been derived from a far higher level of civilisation than anything ever observed by Europeans when they first made their way into the Pacific. Their control of fire, the forces of nature, of disease and so on and their beliefs in the different levels of man's existence seem to argue a long period of deep reflection and study behind them. The higher self, for instance, is surely something which is only beginning to be glimpsed today by people working on extra-sensory perception; while the lower self seems to have been just touched on by modern students of the subconscious.

Your higher self, said the Kahunas, if you could get in touch with it, could do anything for you; but you had to be able to contact it. It was not God and you were part of it. In fact it was very like the group soul, whose existence was apparently reported by Myers and others, after their deaths, to the research workers of a generation ago and to the spiritualists of today. It is remarkable that something of the kind can be deduced from a study of the pendulum.

# Chapter 10

The ordinary belief of those who have convinced ideas about flying saucers is that these machines originate on Venus. The Russians of course reported that their probe showed that the atmosphere of Venus was not suitable for life, but this may not deserve complete credence, as the rocket passed a very long way from the planet. However, there is another school of thought with a far more original idea. This school believes that the visitors do not belong to our time at all; but are people living in the future who will have invented machines which are capable of coming back down the ages to see what was going on at a given time. We will now see whether we can conceive any possibility that this might be true. However we must note that, in the event of its being correct, there is clearly no possibility that people in flying saucers could ever have been thought of as the sons of God or have fathered children on the daughters of men. They could only have been something resembling ghosts to the people in whose ages they appeared, for they would be on a different level of vibration, with no bodily functions comparable to the people they went to investigate. At least this is how the situation would appear to me with my very limited knowledge.

However, if we remember what the pendulum has told us of future time and the second level of existence or vibration, there is much to be said in favour of this explanation of the appearance of flying saucers. Interest in the past is very widespread today and appears to be growing. It would be completely fascinating to be able to go back and see exactly what really went on in bygone ages. Should the construction of such machines become possible, they might well become subject to commercialism. You could hire a seat in a saucer to watch the building of a pyramid or the battle of Marathon. They would be of the greatest value in the study of geology and for estimating the probable changes in climate or sea level. In fact they would be of considerable importance in many ways. The way that saucers are reported as remaining stationary in the sky for hours at a time is what you would expect if a party was examining a particular place at a particular period of time. The casual way in which only some people see them while others do not suggests that they may not be visible to anybody who does not have a high vibrational rate himself. In fact they are future ghosts if this explanation is correct.

We need not boggle at the word ghost. A ghost is something out of its normal earthly time sequence. All recorded television pictures are ghosts. They appear absolutely real on your television screen, but they are not there at all. Neither would this hypothetical type of unknown flying object be real in the sense that your breakfast is real. It would be something completely upsetting to what is called our 'space time continuum'. But many upsetting things are always happening nowadays, so why not this?

This moving between two levels of existence, however, does not seem to demand any vehicle of transport. Our lady magician, who claimed to visit us in the night, also stated that she often talked with people living on the higher level. I asked her one day to see whether she could find out from her friends what flying saucers were. A few days later she returned with the answer: 'They told me that they were made by the back-room boys. I asked them why and they said it was the kind of thing the back-room boys liked to do.' I have no idea what degree of reliance to put on this statement. But if, by any chance, the saucers were the mechanical toys of experimenters on another level, it would explain why only certain people see them. There is no reason to suppose that men's mentality would change after reaching the next level. Since everything else, but time, appears to be there, people with a mechanical bent might well experiment in many ways, and only those with a certain degree of psychic ability on this earth level would be able to see the results.

In one way this theory ought to be a considerable encouragement to the numerous people who work themselves into a fret through expectation of the destruction of humanity in an atomic war. If people are coming back from the future to look at us, there can have been no universal destruction before their time. Still, once again this is not necessarily correct. The visitors need not be coming from the earth plane future. They may be people living on the second plane itself and be what is in earth terms described as dead. Of course if you have a rigid belief that life is confined to one short phase on earth, there is no point in thinking about this possibility at all. But this is only a dogma and really the antithesis of any scientific outlook. You do not know the answer and your belief is on a par with that of the moon being made of blue cheese. It is known that the composition of the moon is rock and not cheese, while such evidence as there is appears to point to the conclusion that life continues to infinity. If it does, and people continue to live on a higher vibrational level on the next whorl and even on others above that, then presumably they might at times use the intelligences they had brought with them to study the past of the level which they had left. They are not in the time sequence and not in the earth body, but it might be easier for them to lower their vibrations and even get out of their machines than people from the earth level itself. Have they ever done this? If they did, could they have had real personal contact with the earth humans they met on their trips?

I have asked a lot of difficult questions already in this book, but this one is more likely to land me in a pickle than most. All through history there have been occasional great teachers, often now spoken of by the Hindu term, 'avatar', whose births seem to have been inexplicable and teachings far higher than those of the surrounding populace. Did these avatars come down from higher levels of deliberate purpose to try to help people living on a lower level of vibration? There appear to have been female avatars as well as male; although they are not often mentioned nowadays. Aradia, the avatar of the religion now known as witchcraft, was supposedly born of the goddess, Diana, and taught her disciples both how to handle the bio-electronic power and the freedom of the individual, in a manner strongly reminiscent of the great male teachers. The only candidate that I know of from America was Quetzalcoatl, also a character of mysterious origin. It is interesting, too, that, though he did not apparently claim that rank, Jesus did not deny that he was a son of God. He seemed rather to imply that all or many men were this, although they did not know it. At the same time he insisted that he was the son of Man. Presumably here once again we are up against the old difficulty of the real meaning of words.

The paternity of all the avatars is mysterious. This of course may be an idea of the priestly caste to add glamour to the founder of their particular religion. Even Buddha, although claimed by the orthodox to have come from a respectable princely family, is said to have been fathered by an elephant. By this one supposes that the elephant-headed god, Ganesa, is implied. However to go into the maze of Indian mythology would be more trouble than it is worth. It is more incomprehensible to the western mind than that of ancient Greece or Rome. The point to remember about three of the avatars at any rate is that they were able to instruct their followers not only with a general code of behaviour but how to control the power of living electricity, which is apparently what ESP is. The Buddhists took this teaching to much greater lengths than anybody in the west. The Christians largely either failed to grasp it or forgot it. The witches knew a lot about it and even bred people deliberately to increase their so-called psychic powers.

The importance of this in our particular inquiry lies in the fact that anyone living on a level of what we might perhaps call 'higher potential' would have to lower his voltage in some way before being able to cope with earthly surroundings at all. He would also have to register. That means that somehow he had to make allowances for the distortion due to the position of things on the two, or perhaps more, different whorls on the spiral. It is here then I can see a possible error happening nearly two thousand years ago. In the Biblical story of the terrible future calamity in which the sun would be 'turned into darkness and the moon into blood', had there been a mistake in which ring in the sequence on the timeless level had been taken? Was Jesus really talking about something which had already happened? If it has been recorded correctly, Jesus evidently thought that it would happen in the lifetime of some of his companions.

Some of them may well have still been living at the time of Titus' siege of Jerusalem in AD 70, but, although this was a revolting siege according to Josephus, it was nothing to compare with the events which Jesus apparently foresaw.

I am well aware that many far more clever men than myself must have spent many hours thinking about this discrepancy and my suggestion may be offending a lot of people. Yet one must tell the truth as far as one can see it. In this particular matter there was an error, either in foretelling the future or in the recording of what was said. The great trouble, which looks like the description of an atomic war, had either happened long before or was not going to happen for perhaps two thousand years. At least this theory appears to be the explanation of all the conflicting statements in the Gospels.

It surely explains too all the difficulties, heresies, schisms and the like which follow all attempts to make a coherent picture out of an imaginary interpretation. If the avatar were omnipotent, then surely everyone would believe in him at once and the whole world would become a good and kindly place. Instead of that, rival variations of beliefs pursued one another through the ages with fire and sword. Jesus realised this and said it would happen: 'I came not to send peace on earth but with a sword.'

To return to the problem of UFOs then, we are left with two possibilities. They may be either contemporary visitors from some unknown planet or they may be the work of people, spoken of today as dead, living in a timeless zone above that of our own earth. The first supposition would have seemed utterly impossible before the days of H. G. Wells, but is today quite a commonplace idea. It may be difficult to guess what planet they might be coming from but no longer utterly improbable. Even with our primitive modern rockets, it is possible to see that the problems of long space travel might be overcome by any fortunate, or perhaps unfortunate, discovery in a comparatively few years.

The second idea would still seem fantastic to very many people who are still wedded to the concept of only one stage of living and that confined to the surface of a single earth. An earth with onion skins of different levels of existence cannot easily be grasped by people with a materialistic or rationalistic upbringing. Yet this idea would not seem particularly strange to advanced Buddhist or Hindu thinkers. The Buddhists with their 'wheel of life' are very near it but have not apparently as yet seen that the wheel is a double spiral. In fact, as Jesus so so rightly said, you have to 'become again as little children' and reorientate all your ideas from the start. This, thanks largely to the inventiveness of television script writers, children of today appear to be quite ready to do. It means little to them that people should jump about in time and space. I have quite a number of letters from teenagers who obviously have a good idea of the possibilities, although they tell me that their views are ridiculed by their elders.

There are pointers to the occurrence of the second type of happening in the Bible itself, but since the witnesses who observed the incidents clearly did not understand what appears to have been taking place, the orthodox interpretation is not particularly convincing nowadays. You can appreciate that much of the reporting in the Bible is true without believing a word of the dogma, which has been built up upon it through the ages. That is one of the difficulties today. Because of the incredibility of the dogma, people tend to throw away the baby with the bath water.

The two incidents which we must look at both concern ascents into heaven. The first is that of Elijah and is simply a traditional story somewhat dramatised by whoever wrote it down. The second is the Ascension itself and apparently a far more accurate account. But there is a great similarity between the two stories. Not only that, but also they are very much like the dematerialisations which are reported as being performed by Hindu and Buddhist sages to this day.

The Ascension is by far the most important and is entirely distinct from the vexed question of what really happened at the Crucifixion. At the Ascension a living man actually vanished in the sight of a large number of people. It is very hard to dismiss this as an account of a conjuring trick because it made such a great impression on those who saw it that it has not been forgotten for nearly two thousand years. Conjuring tricks are a commonplace in the Eastern world and had it been one no such impression would have survived. The incident carried complete conviction.

I may seem unduly credulous here, but one must remember that very little history is in any way exact. As recently as the great battle of Jutland, when I was still at school, there was only one case of exact reporting. A boy seaman in a destroyer was made to write in the log the time and the exact bearing of every incident which took place. As a reward for this devotion to duty, the boy was taken ashore afterwards and given the best meal his heart desired at the expense of the destroyer's first lieutenant. The lieutenant himself, the only man in the whole British fleet who realised the importance of a record, received no commendation at all, although he eventually retired from the Navy as a captain.

Having said this much, let us see what the Gospels appear to relate. I have taken the two following accounts from J. B. Phillips' recent translations of the Gospels, but they are little different from the wording of the James I version:

> Then He led them outside as far as Bethany, where He blessed them with uplifted hands. While He was in the act of blessing them He was parted from them and was carried up to Heaven. (St Luke)
> When He had said these words He was lifted up before their eyes till a cloud hid Him from their sight.
> (St John)

It is clear, I think, that the witnesses did not understand what had happened and the words 'carried up to Heaven' and 'a cloud hid Him from their sight' were added to the straight-forward report in explanation of an apparently impossible event. However, if we remember the numerous reports of 'out of the body' experiences and the evidence of the spiral, it is possible to see what had happened. Jesus, a master of bio-electronic power, had simply accelerated his vibrations and moved up on to the next whorl of the spiral. There, as we have already observed, he would be invisible to the watchers. There are numerous modern Hindu accounts of this feat being per-formed by their learned men and also of their subsequent return. The whole Ascension story in the Gospels is claimed as the promise of human survival of death and, as far as one can judge, indeed it is, but hardly of the type of survival which is generally imagined. This is in itself a glorified picture of what was believed to be the most happy situation two thousand years ago. The harps and songs and all the rest of it are a reflection of that bygone age, when a feast was the height of enjoyment.

The Elijah story may well have once been similar. In fact some Hindu experts believe Jesus to have been a reincarnation, not of Elijah but of his disciple Elisha, who was promised a double portion of Elijah's spirit if he could see him carried into heaven. The point about Elijah's aerial exploit is that it has been quoted in various works as evidence for the former existence of flying saucers. What actually does the Bible say?

> Elijah said unto Elisha, Ask what I shall do for thee, before I be taken away from thee. And Elisha said, I pray thee, let a double portion of thy spirit be upon me.
> And he said, Thou hast asked a hard thing: nevertheless, if thou see me when I am taken from thee, it shall be so unto thee; but if not, it shall not be so.
> And it came to pass, as they still went on, and talked, that, behold, there appeared a chariot of fire, and horses of fire, and parted them both asunder; and Elijah went up by a whirlwind into heaven.
> And Elisha saw it, and he cried, My father, my father, the chariot of Israel and the horsemen thereof. And he saw him no more. (Authorised Version. 2 Kings, 2, verses 9–11)

This dramatic story had probably been handed down by word of mouth for a long time before it was put into writing. The vehicle, if there was one, was indescribable and so spoken of as a chariot. A chariot had to have horses and they were added, quite reasonably. But nobody emerged from the chariot; although Elijah apparently knew it was coming. When it came he vanished in a whirlwind.

One can see how this story fits in well with modern accounts of flying saucers; but we are left with a doubt whether anything more than a dust-devil, or willy-waw, was ever seen. Elijah, an accomplished practitioner of ESP (or shall we call it magic?) simply vanished. How he went nobody, probably not even Elisha, ever knew. I don't know how it strikes others, but I personally suspect that Elisha had to say he had seen the chariot to explain his subsequent magic powers. One wonders too whether the scribe who wrote this story down was familiar with the Greek beliefs in which gods flew about the heavens in chariots drawn by horses.

Whatever may have been the truth of Elijah's disappearance, a feeling remains that it may have been very like the Ascension. Unfortunately there was only a single witness and there is quite a possibility either that he may have been biased in his subsequent account, or that the author of the second book of Kings was somewhat carried away by the drama of the incident. On the whole it does not seem possible to use this story as an argument in favour of the former existence of flying saucers.

When we turn to the problem of how anyone could possibly pass from one level of vibration to one of a perhaps four times faster rate, we are humbugged by a lack of general knowledge. It is a problem well ahead of science at its present stage. We do know that a living scientist today is not the solid object he appears to be, but is really almost entirely empty space, a series of holes joined together by French knitting. In fact he may only be there at all because somebody else thinks of him. In any case you could have dozens of different scientists fitted into the holes in the first one.

People used to think that they knew all about matter; but today they do at least realise that they hardly know anything at all. Matter may be energy, still what is that? Energy may be vibrations. What are they? All that is really known is that if you do certain things, certain results will follow and the range of action in which the foreseeable results are known is very limited. It has not even begun to dawn on the scientific world that, by changing the rate of vibration, you might land bang in another scientific world much more advanced than your own.

As I said at the beginning, I am only putting up questions to most of which there is no known answer. I do not believe in the answers I have put forward, except to a very limited degree.

For instance I do think that I have got the right method by which the bluestones were transported to Stonehenge. But I hope that it will provoke enough interest for others to try to solve some of the problems which are too difficult for me to answer.

In any case this is all imagination and we do not really know what unidentified flying objects may be: ghosts, hallucinations, time machines or honest to God visitors from another planet. Whatever they may be, they offer us an interesting subject for talk and speculation and the answer may come sooner than anyone expects.

I shall finish now. Many people will think it is all rubbish. Others will see some sense in it, even if I have produced no hard and fast theory. At least I hope I have given a few something to turn over in their minds, to see whether they can produce anything more satisfactory than I have been able to do.

# Index

213

214

stone circles and rows, 177, 180, 182-7, 196-7
Stonehenge, 183-6, 200, 212
stoneware pottery, 37-8, 45; Fig.6, 40
sulphur rate, 101, 104, 107
sun disc carvings, 190-2; Fig. 21, 191

Tartessos, 182
telekinesis, 200
telepathy, 20, 30-1, 125-6
tests, double blind, 80-1; Fig. 10, 81
'thought' rate, 91-6, 101
time, 137 ff
time displacement, 22, 116-117, 138, 148, 149; Fig.19, 149
time rate, 100
trees, 73
truffles, 60-3
truth, 98

'Uncle', 47-8
unidentified flying objects (UFOs), 187 ff

van Someren, E. H. S., 64
*Velella spirans*, 158-60, 163
Venus, 172, 192-9, 203
Volunteers, Argyleshire, 133-134
von Däniken, E., 169

Wandlebury, 86-92, 170; Fig. 11, 87; Fig.12, 89
'war in heaven', 172-4, 195 ff
warning rates, 97, 101
water divining, *see* dowsing
Wells, H. G., 207
west, 98-101
witches, 66, 76, 152, 205
Woden, 171, 172
W. S. B., 14-17

yellow rate, 101

216